Flying Cloud

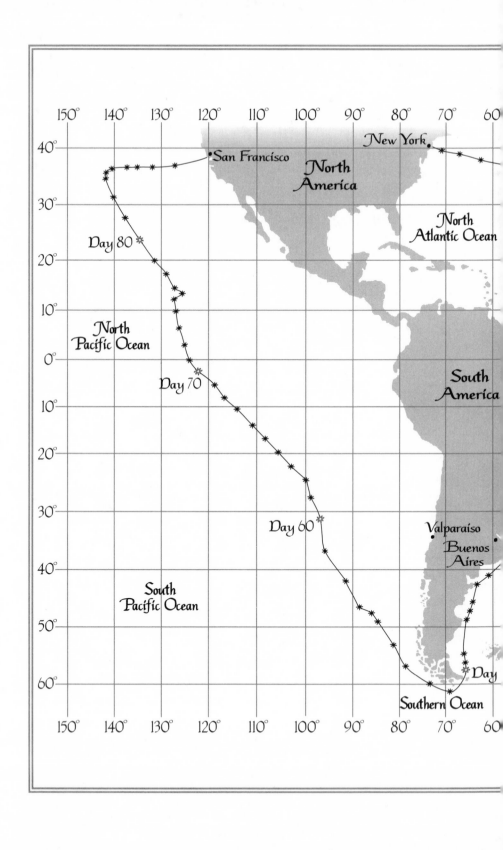

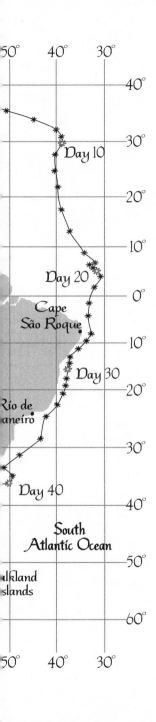

The 1851 Voyage of Flying Cloud

From
Manhattan, NY
To
San Francisco, CA

June 2nd – August 31st

*Flying Cloud's noon positions

Miles

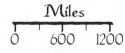

0   600   1200

ILLUSTRATION BY MARGARET WESTERGAARD

Flying Cloud

The True Story of
America's Most Famous Clipper Ship
and the Woman Who Guided Her

David W. Shaw

William Morrow

An Imprint of HarperCollins*Publishers*

HarperCollins books may be purchased for educational, business, or sales promotional use. For information please write: Special Markets Department, HarperCollins Publishers Inc., 10 East 53rd Street, New York, N.Y. 10022.

FIRST EDITION

Designed by Debbie Glasserman

Printed on acid-free paper

Library of Congress Cataloging-in-Publication Data has been applied for.

ISBN 0-688-16793-4

00 01 02 03 04 RRD 10 9 8 7 6 5 4 3 2 1

For my uncle,
David Enggren,
who took me sailing as a boy and
inspired my deep love and respect
for the sea

Sing and heave, and heave and sing,
To me hoodah! To my hoodah!
Heave and make the handspikes spring,
To me hoodah, hoodah, day!

And it's blow, my boys, blow,
For Californi-o!
For there's plenty of gold,
So I've been told,
On the banks of the Sacramento!

—*from "The Banks of the Sacramento,"*
a popular capstan chantey sung while
weighing anchor during the gold rush

Contents

Illustrations

Author's Note

As a sailor myself, I admired Eleanor Creesy for her skill in navigating *Flying Cloud* on her record-breaking voyages from New York to San Francisco. I wanted to know more about what Eleanor faced during that eventful maiden voyage in 1851, what she saw and did as the weeks passed and the vessel sailed on toward Cape Horn. My curiosity led to the writing of this book.

The most important step in understanding Eleanor involved plotting *Flying Cloud*'s daily progress on nautical charts based on the information contained in the ship's log. The original handwritten log of *Flying Cloud*'s first voyage from New York to San Francisco is in the Peabody Essex Museum in Salem, Massachusetts. Another frequently cited copy appears in Carl C. Cutler's *Greyhounds of the Sea*. The log entries provide the date, the ship's position, the course steered, distance made good, wind directions and approximate velocities broken down into the three parts of a sea day, and remarks concerning important events that transpired over a twenty-four-hour period.

Using this information, I plotted *Flying Cloud*'s daily runs. I noted the course steered in blue pencil versus the course actually made good in black pencil. It was not enough just to mark the ship's daily latitude and longitude as asterisks on the chart. I had to know if Eleanor's intended course actually corresponded to her true course. Currents, wind, and waves can move a vessel off the intended track. By plotting the course steered in addition to the course made good, I discovered discrepancies that led me to a more refined understanding of what Eleanor faced at various points throughout the voyage. The illustration of the ship's course through the doldrums and the influence of an easterly current on the ship's track is a good example of this. (See page 114.)

The log provided all I needed to plot the direction of the winds *Flying Cloud* encountered relative to her course through the water. I drew arrows on the chart to show the wind directions during each part of a nautical day, enabling me to see clearly the angle of the wind in relation to the sails. This was important because certain wind directions are more favorable on a given track than others. *Flying Cloud* sailed the fastest when the wind blew over the left or right side of the stern. Conversely, if Eleanor's course put the wind over either side of the bow, *Flying Cloud* sailed more slowly. The plots on the chart revealed all the good and bad days from an efficiency and speed standpoint better than words could paint the picture.

The log included terse comments from the captain, many of which proved invaluable when it came down to reconstructing the voyage. In particular, references to the mutinous acts of two of the crew and insubordination of the first officer opened up a glimpse of the tensions aboard the ship. Other more routine entries indicated what sails were set and what sails were not, steps taken in heavy weather, accidents, and other details of vital necessity in my effort to write about the voyage in a realistic manner.

Of key importance as well was the ship's position in relation to landmasses, trade wind belts, and ocean currents. All of these factors were foremost in Eleanor's mind every day of the journey, and they were in mine as well, as I found myself transported back in time to the deck of the ship, figuratively looking over her shoulder as she went about her duties.

A study of Lieutenant Matthew Fontaine Maury's sailing directions added further insight into Eleanor's duties as navigator. She had his book, *Explanations and Sailing Directions to Accompany the Wind and Current Charts*, aboard during the voyage, in addition to his charts. Studying a volume of Maury's sailing directions at Princeton University helped me understand Eleanor's ability to absorb highly complex subject matter, as did my study of the basics of celestial navigation.

Technical knowledge, however valuable it may have been, amounted to just part of the overall foundation upon which I built the narrative. I needed to know as much as I could about Eleanor and her husband, Josiah Perkins Creesy. In some short accounts of *Flying Cloud*, Eleanor Creesy is said to have been kind, sensitive, and fond of socializing. She is said to have acted as the ship's nurse, to have been benevolent to the crew, and to have helped plan the provisioning for the voyages.

My own research bears this out. According to the Samuel Roads Papers in the archive of the Marblehead Historical Society in Marblehead, Massachusetts, a crewman who served aboard *Flying Cloud* in a later voyage stated that they were well fed and ate fresh meat twice a week, which was quite unusual on most merchant ships of the day. This is direct evidence that Eleanor saw to it that the men under her husband's command received better than usual treatment, at least in terms of their meals. Also among the primary sources related to *Flying Cloud* at the Marblehead Historical Society is a letter written by a passenger aboard the vessel during the maiden voyage, Sarah Bowman. She stated that Eleanor was kind, sensitive, social, and fond of art and poetry. Bowman also described her: "Such glorious eyes I never saw, large liquid and hazel, soft as a gazelle's and always beaming with kindness on someone." The letter also related that Eleanor "treasured a blade of grass" during the long voyages far from anything green and that on her trips to China she was unafraid of storms.

References in a diary by one of the passengers aboard *Flying Cloud* during the maiden voyage were also helpful. The diary of Israel Whitney Lyon, I. W. Lyon Papers, at Mills College Library in Oakland, California, indicated that he spent time reading poetry to Eleanor. He noted twice during the voyage that his two sisters, who were traveling with him, were ill, and that another passenger, a Mrs. Gorham, drank poison by mistake. As the ship's nurse, Eleanor took care of the passengers. Eleanor's duties extended well beyond those associated with navigation.

Birth, marriage, death, and other records from the Marblehead Historical Society provided additional insights into both Eleanor and Josiah Creesy. Records from Arthur Cheever Cressy, of the Creesy family, also assisted me in gaining insights into Josiah's background and family history.

Many of the published sources I consulted in my research referred to Eleanor as "Nellie" and to Josiah as "Perk." I found no primary documents to account for these nicknames. The Creesy letters, archived at Mystic Seaport in Mystic, Connecticut, contained a collection of correspondence by Josiah Perkins Creesy and members of his family. In all of these letters Eleanor was referred to as Ellen and Josiah was referred to as Perkins. I have therefore referred to them in the same way in the narrative. (The following letters were used in the text: a letter by Josiah P. Creesy to his brother William, dated March 28, 1851, and an excerpt from a letter by Emily Lord, William's wife, dated April 13, 1851 [VFM 1559, Manuscripts Collection, G. W. Blunt White Library, Mystic Seaport Museum, Inc.].)

The Creesy letters proved invaluable. Before he took command of *Flying Cloud* in April 1851, Captain Creesy was captain of *Oneida,* a ship engaged in the China tea trade. The letters confirmed that when *Oneida* arrived in port in April, Perkins's brother, William, took over command, and that Perkins was unsure what commission he might receive next. This was new information. No published account addressed the fact that other captains were considered as possible commanders of *Flying Cloud.* The letters showed that Ellen went back to Marblehead to see her family on March 20 and that she returned to New York City a week later. They also related how Ellen was with Perkins when he finally received command of *Flying Cloud* and took the ship under tow from Boston to her berth on the East River in lower Manhattan.

In addition, the letters revealed Perkins's tendency to be a perfectionist and to find fault with his men. He noted that he felt the first officer of *Oneida* was incompetent. Aboard *Flying Cloud* he showed the same tendencies, and near the end of the voyage he dismissed his first officer.

The Samuel Roads Papers established beyond a doubt that Creesy was not opposed to kicking and slapping a man, nor keeping all sail set in squalls. These papers also showed he prevented the officers under his command from reducing sail when they wished to do so in heavy weather. However, they exposed a more cautious side of Perkins as well. At times, when he deemed it necessary, he reduced sail before nightfall when rounding Cape Horn. He was a complex man, with a wide range to his personality that Ellen must have had to deal with through subtle though assertive handling when it came to navigational decisions aboard the ship.

Other primary sources included the S. Griffitts Morgan collection, Baker Library, at Harvard Business School, volume 21. This collection included business information related to *Flying Cloud*, provision and freight lists, bills of lading, correspondence, and other useful material. Contemporary newspapers were also helpful, particularly the detailed description of *Flying Cloud* by Duncan McLean that appeared in the *Boston Daily Atlas*, April 25, 1851.

Primary and contemporary sources were the foundation of knowledge I needed to reconstruct *Flying Cloud*'s maiden voyage and bring out Ellen's important part in its success. However, there was much more work to do. I had to have a firm grasp of the gold rush, the political and economic issues important in the United States in 1851, what the cities of Boston, New York, and San Francisco were like, current fashions, the sailor's lot in life, and much more. I spent well over a year reading everything I could find to help me achieve my objectives. The bibliography contains more than fifty books, all of which played an important part in my research.

The synthesis of all this data provided me with enough material to flesh out Ellen and Perkins as people. The log, the Bowman letter, the Whitney diary, the Samuel Roads Papers, the Creesy letters, and published short accounts of *Flying Cloud*'s voyages rounded out my research and enabled me to gain a good understanding of what went on during the voyage from those who were on it, as well as what weather they experienced and what life aboard a clipper ship was really like.

The commands Perkins shouted through his speaking trumpet when working the ship came right from Richard Henry Dana's *The Seaman's Friend*. I also consulted the United States Coast Guard's manual for its ship *Eagle*, a square-rigger used to train cadets. I took great care to maintain accuracy in all aspects of the book, including those related to the way square-rigged ships were sailed. However, the story is for the general reader. I therefore have tried to keep the technical language to a minimum, and there is a glossary of nautical terms in the back of the book for easy reference should the need arise.

Dialogue is sparse throughout the book. When I do use it the lines reflect what would naturally be said in a given circumstance or are based on information contained in primary sources. None of the scenes are make-believe. They are all drawn directly from primary sources and reflect what was occurring at any given time during the voyage.

Acknowledgments

The enthusiastic support of people close to me who believed in the merit of a book about *Flying Cloud* counted for much in making the book a reality. No author can ever succeed alone. I was lucky enough to have plenty of good people behind my effort. My wife, Elizabeth, as always, patiently lived through the process with me and offered words of encouragement when they were needed. My agent, Jill Grinberg, and my editor at William Morrow, Zachary Schisgal, gave me their unstinting encouragement from the very start of my work, and for that I will be forever grateful.

Others lent their support and their expertise with regard to clipper ships. My thanks go to Captain Charles M. Quinlan, president of the Shining Sea Foundation in East Boston, a nonprofit organization dedicated to the construction of a new American clipper ship equaling the dimensions of *Flying Cloud*. William L. Crothers, author of *The American-Built Clipper Ship* and a leading expert on these ships, deserves my gratitude as well. Both men spent hours answering questions about obscure matters such as fids and tyes and other details I needed to understand as I went about interpreting the log of *Flying Cloud*'s maiden voyage. They also read the manuscript and provided helpful insights and advice.

Many thanks to Harold Foster, an old friend of mine well versed in celestial navigation. He spent hours walking me through what today is fast becoming a lost art. With the advent of satellite global positioning systems that can pinpoint a boat's position at any location on earth, fewer mariners need to know how to navigate using the sun, moon, planets, and stars. Harold helped me cut down to the most basic details of celestial navigation, enabling me to reveal for readers a glimpse of the complexities without going into the often difficult mathematics.

My research on *Flying Cloud* did not occur in a vacuum. Many authors have written about the clipper ships, and most of them mention the voyages of *Flying Cloud*. To these individuals, both living and dead, I must give credit. I cannot mention all of them, but I feel compelled to cite a few here. First and foremost, I must thank two contemporaries of Josiah Perkins Creesy, Jr., captain of *Flying Cloud*, and his wife, Eleanor, the ship's navigator. Richard Henry Dana, Jr., wrote a highly technical work on how square-rigged ships were sailed, *The Seaman's Friend*. An old copy occupied my desk throughout the writing process and provided a reference when questions arose. Lieutenant Matthew Fontaine Maury, of the United States Navy's National Observatory, changed the way ships crossed the oceans with the many editions of his book, *Explanations and Sailing Directions to Accompany the Wind and Current Charts*. His work guided me as I interpreted what Eleanor Creesy faced as she navigated *Flying Cloud*.

Margaret Lyon and Flora Elizabeth Reynolds in 1992 published a thin, scholarly volume entitled *The Flying Cloud and Her First Passengers*. This book brought to light for the first time a diary of one of the passengers, Whitney Lyon, of whom Margaret Lyon is a descendant. This and other information provided me with insights into the people aboard the ship during the maiden voyage.

I owe thanks to archivists at the Baker Library, Harvard Business School, Harvard University, Mystic Seaport, Mystic, Connecticut, and the Marblehead Historical Society in Marblehead, Massachusetts, for allowing me to publish valuable primary source material from their collections. I also wish to thank Arthur Cheever Cressy for providing me with records in his possession that assisted me in learning more about Josiah Perkins Creesy's background and family history. Many thanks to Margaret Westergaard for her computer graphics work on the charts and diagrams.

In addition, the following museums deserve thanks for granting me permission to include images from their collections in the book: the Mariners' Museum, Newport News, Virginia; the Boston Athenaeum, Boston, Massachusetts; the Massachusetts Historical Society, Boston, Massachusetts; the Peabody Essex Museum, Salem, Massachusetts; the Hart Nautical Collection, MIT Museum, Massachusetts Institute of Technology, Cambridge, Massachusetts; the Museum of the City of New York, New York; and the San Francisco Maritime National Historical Park, San Francisco, California.

Introduction

Flying Cloud is America's most famous clipper ship, a tall ship built to speed goods from New York to San Francisco during the California gold rush. Back in the early 1850s, however, speed was a relative term. The typical merchant ship sailed about as fast as a person might walk in a hurry. At such slow speeds, a voyage to California averaged two hundred days. Of course, the Panama Canal did not then exist, which meant ships bound for San Francisco sailed down the Atlantic Ocean to the tip of South America, around Cape Horn, and up the Pacific Ocean to reach the Golden Gate, a voyage of sixteen thousand miles. The journey was long and dangerous, and it claimed the lives of many sailors.

But even in the 1850s, technology was speeding things up. The clipper ships were a new type of vessel capable of sustained speeds in excess of twelve knots, about the pace of an easy bicycle ride. The clippers were a giant leap forward in American shipping. In 1851, on her maiden voyage, *Flying Cloud* stunned the world when she sailed through the Golden Gate after a passage of only eighty-nine days, twenty-one hours. She set a world record and grabbed headlines throughout the United States and Europe.

Flying Cloud broke her own record in 1854 with a passage from New York to San Francisco of eighty-nine days, eight hours. No sailing vessel of the wooden clipper ship period and none of the iron windjammers that followed ever bested *Flying Cloud*. The record she set in 1854 stood until 1989, when a modern yacht called *Thursday's Child* sailed from New York to San Francisco in eighty days, nineteen hours. In subsequent years, yachts have sailed the course in as little as fifty-seven days.

Flying Cloud's swift passages remain a well-known part of American maritime history. However, one of the most interesting aspects of the story has never been fully explored. Few people know that *Flying Cloud's* navigator was the captain's wife, a fascinating woman way ahead of her time. As navigator, Eleanor Creesy set the courses and established the ship's position every day. She guided *Flying Cloud* through the vast network of ocean winds and currents and around dangerous shoals. She used the latest scientific data and navigation techniques that many others ignored. Aboard a racing vessel—and the clipper ships were racers—the navigator is as important as the skipper in determining whether a boat crosses the finish line first. Eleanor's role in *Flying Cloud's* story was important, and yet it has remained nearly forgotten for 150 years.

There were some clipper ship captains who took their wives with them on the long voyages. For the most part, though, the wives remained in passive roles typical of the day. Women, especially married women, had few rights in the eyes of the government. Women were not permitted to vote until 1920, after passage of the Nineteenth Amendment, which it took almost fifty years to push through a highly resistant Congress. A woman had no right to property, no right to any wages she might earn, no right to her children in the unlikely event a divorce was granted, and no right to work or to a comprehensive education. At the time *Flying Cloud* sailed from New York in 1851, only one liberal arts college in the country, Oberlin, in Ohio, admitted female students.

There were instances, however, when a captain's wife took a more active role aboard the ship, usually during emergencies. One of the better-known cases involved the clipper ship *Neptune's Car*. In 1856, as the vessel reached the region of Cape Horn, the captain became too ill to navigate. His first officer was confined to quarters because of insubordination. The second officer lacked the knowledge to guide the ship. The captain's wife, Mary Ann Patten, who was pregnant at the time, used what she had learned from her husband about navigation to bring the ship around Cape Horn and more than six thousand miles up the Pacific Ocean to San Francisco.

During the days of the windjammers that followed the clipper ships, having the captain's wife aboard was quite common. Like Mary Ann Patten, some of these wives filled the shoes of their husbands when necessary, or served actively as the ship's nurse. But few, if any, of the captains' wives took on roles that made them the equal to their husbands; their husbands did not allow it. A woman's place aboard a ship was not much different from what it was at home on land. She was expected to provide companionship for her husband, to wash and iron his clothes, and to see that he was well fed.

Eleanor Creesy differed greatly from the other wives. She married her husband, Josiah Perkins Creesy, in 1841 and served as navigator on the ships under his command throughout his career. She bore all of the responsibilities that came with the job. She was not out there dabbling with a sextant. Far from it. Her insights and talents as a navigator contributed much to the ultimate success *Flying Cloud,* and her husband, enjoyed after the record-setting voyage of 1851. Her accomplishments showed that even in the male-dominated arena of the merchant marine, a lady with wit and courage could leave a lasting mark on history and outdo all but the best men who picked up a sextant. That she owed her opportunity to her husband's willingness to count her as an equal detracts nothing from her accomplishments. Rather, it reveals that the Creesys together made a remarkable couple.

Flying Cloud's record-breaking maiden voyage was extraordinary. She maintained speeds during the passage that nearly reached the limit of theoretical probability. In fact, the clipper missed a near-perfect run from New York to San Francisco by only four days. A leading authority on the clipper ship routes at the time *Flying Cloud* sailed was Lieutenant Matthew Fontaine Maury of the

United States Navy's National Observatory. Maury addressed the issue of just how fast a clipper ship might complete the California route in his book *Explanations and Sailing Directions to Accompany the Wind and Current Charts.* He wrote: "It is, therefore, we may infer, within the range of probability that the passage by ships, at their present rate of speed, may be made in 85 days from the Eastern States to California, but it is scarcely probable, for it is barely within the range of possibility, that it will ever be made in less time."

For a ship to sail from New York to San Francisco in only eighty-five days—in other words, to reach top theoretical speed—would require a perfect combination of winds and currents in the best sailing months of the year for the duration of the passage. The odds of this happening in reality were extreme. The difficulties of the voyage made it unlikely that a clipper might even approach a run of eighty-five days.

Flying Cloud did not sail at the best time of year for maximum speed. The clipper left New York Harbor at the start of summer in the Northern Hemisphere. However, when she arrived off the desolate coast of Cape Horn, she sailed deep in the darkness of the southern winter. This was the worst time of year for an east-to-west passage against the prevailing westerly winds. As *Flying Cloud* sailed north across the Pacific Ocean, winds were less favorable for a quick run from the equator to San Francisco than later in the year. She battled storms, and on two occasions she was partially dismasted. There were also problems with mutinous crewmen and insubordinate officers.

In light of the poor odds for such an outstanding voyage and the adversity Eleanor and Josiah Creesy encountered on the way to California, it is little wonder that people still remember *Flying Cloud* 150 years later. Here, then, is the true story of America's most famous clipper ship and the woman who guided her.

Flying Cloud

Chapter 1

The surf broke steadily on the east side of Sandy Hook, carrying sinewy lines of foam and bits of kelp up the hard-packed beach toward the high-water mark. The breakers established a natural rhythm far older than the barrier of outstretched sand crooked four miles northwestward into the bay off the Highlands of Navesink. A moderate southerly wind whispered through the tall dry grass on the dunes and jostled the branches of the short, scrubby stands of cedar and holly along the spine of the peninsula, clearly visible from the heights above.

Seen from the summit of the Highlands at the approaches to New York Harbor, the vast reaches of Raritan Bay stretched out to the north to embrace the edge of Staten Island and Long Island's southern shore. The sails of coastal schooners, bluff-bowed merchantmen, and lean, narrow packets splashed patterns of white against the water. Oceangoing steamers and diminutive local ferries darted among the sailing vessels working down toward Sandy Hook or running free with the wind astern toward the Verrazano Narrows.

Atop a semaphore tower commanding an unlimited view of the sea, an observer scanned the horizon for the first appearance of sails nudged above the expanse of deep blue ocean to the east. The color of the sea struck him as distinct, its crisp clarity juxtaposed against the sky. The mid-March sun did little to dispel the cold, nor did the occasional puff of warmth from the wind as it passed over the farmlands of Monmouth County and crested the purple hills of the Highlands. The observer lifted the spyglass once more in a habit second nature to him after thousands of repetitions over hundreds of days, most of them routine and some of them dull.

Still, there were worse positions at the factories and railroads, on the docks and on the farms, than spending days, weeks, months, and years spotting the fortunes on the wind bound for the piers along the East River. As soon as he identified an inbound ship, he worked his enormous signal flags to convey news of the new arrival to the semaphore station on Staten Island, and his colleague there relayed the signal to the observers on the Battery. Once the information was received, it was run to the owner or agent in lower Manhattan, who started making arrangements to off-load the cargo well before the vessel nosed through the slot of the Narrows. Ships were off-loaded and loaded as quickly as possible. Fortunes accumulated with vessels at sea, holds packed tight with valuable commodities bound for a hungry market, not when they were moored to a wharf. Each arrival was anxiously awaited, and the ships that made fast passages became the toast of the town.

The docks of New York City teemed with transatlantic liners, ships in the East India and China trade, and, most recently, new clippers built for the California run. Every captain worth his commission drove his ship hard, and every fast passage set the stage for a faster one to follow. It was not uncommon in early 1851 to see several swift sailers race into port together, a sight that made the most lubberly dandy wax poetic. From his vantage point in the tower the observer witnessed the romantic side of the harbor's works, and even after long, cold watches the special moments retained their ability to entrance.

Earlier that day the observer watched as the brand-new clipper ship *Alert* slowed momentarily, her main topsail backed to act as a brake, and discharged the pilot. *Alert* was 152 feet in length with lofty spars and acres of canvas spread out on massive yards and slender booms. She was the first clipper built in Maine, which wisely followed shipyards in key shipbuilding centers from Portsmouth to Baltimore already aggressively in the clipper business. At 764 tons, *Alert* was not overly large, but her owners thought it probable her maiden passage to San Francisco might earn profits enough to fully recoup the construction costs. It was not an unrealistic hope. The pilot safely back to his schooner, *Alert* braced her yards around to catch the wind and made her way south-southeast out to sea, headed for the Golden Gate.

In 1849, the year the gold rush started in earnest, only a few dozen clipper ships existed, and most of them were engaged in the East India and China trade. The slow, full-bodied merchant ships built to haul bulky cargoes and even the finer built, much sleeker packets designed more for speed averaged two hundred days from New York to San Francisco that year. The following year, more clippers took up the gold rush route, and while most ships required well over a hundred days to make the passage, several set records, each of which was soon broken.

Sea Witch, an early clipper ship, under command of Robert Waterman, made the voyage in ninety-seven days in 1850, and *Surprise,* which set sail on December 13, 1850, was at that very moment three days out of San Francisco and about to raise the bar for the record another notch. When word reached New York that *Surprise* had beaten *Sea Witch*'s time, arriving in port after a passage of ninety-six days, fifteen hours, the race for speed further intensified in the shipping business and fueled demand for ships of even greater swiftness and size. Major shipbuilders, primarily in New York and Boston, tooled up for what many perceived would be America's biggest shipping boom. Since the new year, nine clippers, including *Alert,* had left New York Harbor bound for San Francisco.

On the horizon, a patch of white caught the observer's practiced eye. It could have been a cloud or a trick of the light. He trained his spyglass on the speck, steadied his hand, and squinted. The skysails of a merchant ship gradually took shape, and as time passed each succeeding tier of sails lower down also materialized, as if the earth were forcing the vessel straight up from the ocean depths, until finally the black hull appeared. Her sails were set to catch the wind as it blew briskly over the left side of the stern, a fast point of sail. The observer noted that the studdingsails were set, extra sails for maximum speed suspended well beyond the yards on stout booms.

The commander is a driver, he thought, and smiled at the grand sight of the ship as she lifted and fell with the waves, kicking up fans of white that contrasted nicely against her hull. High atop the main topgallant pole mast at the truck, the very tip of the tallest spar over one hundred feet above the deck, the swallowtail house flag of Grinnell, Minturn & Company of New York at last became visible. Soon thereafter, flown from the mizzen truck, a series of signal flags revealing her individual number gradually came into view. The observer checked his book to match the numerical code of the signal flags to the name of the ship.

"*Oneida,*" he mumbled as he dipped his pen into the inkwell. He blotted it, entered the ship's name in the logbook, and went about the business of signaling the day's newest arrival to her owners in New York. Bound in from Shanghai and Woosung, the holds packed with exotic teas with names like Lumking, Mofoong, Hyson, and Bohea, *Oneida* was among the first of the China fleet in with the new crops. Market prices stood high, at just about their highest point of the year. The ship would receive a warm welcome from all with a financial interest in her.

Miles away on the gently rolling poop deck of *Oneida*, Eleanor Creesy pulled her best overcoat close to ward off the cold wind at her back, looking forward to her first night ashore in more than three months. The officers and crew were also dressed for the city, though the latter had donned newly mended denim trousers, flannel shirts, and wool pea jackets instead of suits and topcoats. The old ship they had made to look new, topsides painted, all rigging tarred and taut, the deck and deckhouses cleaned, even the anchor chain scraped for good measure. It was a ritual Eleanor had lived countless times, the making ready for port, the boarding of the pilot, the maneuvering in a tight anchorage or alongside a wharf, the crew singing out a chantey. There was an odd comfort in the ways of the sea, a stable rhythm of work and rest different from any on land.

Eleanor was of average height for a woman of her day, about five feet tall, and she had dark brown hair most often pulled up in a bun, fine brows, and a delicate nose. Her ten years at sea with her husband, Josiah Perkins Creesy, Jr., had left her face permanently tanned. At age thirty-six, the ravages of the sun and weather had etched laugh lines on her cheeks and fine wrinkles on her forehead and around her large, hazel eyes. Her manner of walking was not that of a dainty lady, but had in it the distinct roll of a sailor's gait, and she was as surefooted as any man on a pitching deck. She had spent more time afloat than on land since she married and went to sea with her husband. With the wind whipping her hair loose from her combs, her body braced against the motion of the ship while she lifted the heavy sextant to take an observation of the sun or other celestial body, there was a wild beauty to her.

Eleanor lifted her spyglass and trained it on the red hull of Sandy Hook Lightship riding to her anchor just under seven miles off the lighthouse on Sandy Hook, her twin masts with the globelike lights affixed at the heads rolling to the swell. Not far away the black nun buoy number one and red nun buoy number two marked the entrance to the outermost approaches of Gedney Channel, a narrow cut across the shallows of Sandy Hook bar favored by the largest ships inbound to and outbound from New York Harbor. As *Oneida*'s navigator, seeing the lightship after a round-trip voyage of thirty thousand miles meant more to Ellen, as she was known, than the comfort anyone feels upon seeing a familiar landmark after a long absence from home. It was to her one of many floating and fixed navigational aids scattered about the harbor. Taken collectively they represented signposts whose interpretation relative to the position of the ship meant the difference between safety and danger. Though the beauty of a lighthouse or a lightship did not escape her, their practical merits far outweighed their aesthetic appeal.

The cold brass tube of the spyglass began to make Ellen's hands tingle beneath her gloves, but she did not lower it just yet. Off

Oneida's bow she saw one of the dozens of pilot schooners that served the harbor. These schooners often sailed far offshore with a number of pilots ready to step aboard inbound ships and, upon reaching Sandy Hook, guide the captains through the shoals. In return for the service, the captains paid a fee based on the length and draft of the ship. Many incoming ships picked up a pilot well before land was sighted, but others did not. It was a big ocean, and a vessel bound for New York might well remain unseen until close to Sandy Hook.

The approaching schooner sailed close-hauled, with the sails trimmed in tight to take her as close as possible toward the true direction of the wind. She tilted over on her side, natural enough when sailing close-hauled in a good breeze. Heeled hard on the wind with billowing clouds of spray flying over the bow, the schooner drew close to Oneida.

"She's coming on fast, Perkins," Ellen said, and glanced over at her husband standing beside the helmsman. He was a stocky, muscular man, with a bold forehead, bushy brows that accented his eyes, and a well-trimmed beard flecked with gray. His face struck her as one reflecting strength, both of character and body. His voice boomed through the speaking trumpet or caressed her in quiet times alone in their private cabin. His hands were calloused and toughened from the sea, but they still touched her with tenderness. Though he was surrounded with crew at the mizzen mast ready to man the sails, from his demeanor he could have been standing alone, hands clasped behind his back, keenly observant but detached as well, an expression of inscrutable origin masking his thoughts. He merely nodded in her direction.

"Lay aloft and furl fore and main courses," he shouted to the chief officer positioned on the forecastle deck.

"Furl fore and main courses, aye!" the mate shouted in reply.

The mate bellowed a rapid succession of orders, and instantly the men rushed to take in the lowest sails on the fore and mainmasts. The studdingsails were already taken in, the supporting booms retracted and secured on the yards ready for port. The crew eased the lines that held the lower edge of the sails and simultaneously hauled on others to pull the canvas up to the yards. The movement emptied the sails of wind, but they were not yet fully tamed. The sails thundered in the breeze as dozens of men left the deck, scurried up the ratlines, and fanned out along the yards, their feet balanced on footropes, their bellies to the spar. They hove the sails up and made a smooth skin of them, knowing the Old Man would tolerate no dead men, the odd bunching of canvas that looked as though a corpse had somehow found its way into the furl. They secured the sails with gaskets plaited from tough, thin hemp lines.

With the studdingsails and courses in, *Oneida*'s progress through the water slowed. Perkins ordered the ship brought around to face about sixty degrees from the true direction of the wind. The breeze blew against the front of the main topsail and pushed it back against the mast. The force of air blowing against the canvas further slowed the vessel. The pilot schooner dispatched its yawl, a swift rowboat. Moments later the pilot climbed the rope ladder slung over the side of the ship and stepped aboard to assume command. Over the next nineteen miles to New York City, across the bar and up the busy channel to the anchorage off the Battery, *Oneida* sailed, her passage marked in hours of anticipation among all aboard.

The moment the pilot came aboard upon making the approaches to a port signified the end of a long voyage for Ellen, more so than even the splash and rattle of chain as the anchor plunged to the bottom of the harbor. Making the landfall meant the end of her daily navigational duties for the duration that Perkins was on the beach. She found the art of fixing one's position every day exceedingly engaging and immensely satisfying, and she often missed it after too long a stay ashore.

The desire to know one's position stands as one of the most basic and natural components of human nature. Whether it is in a physical sense or on a more emotional level, a deep-seated unease results from the notion of being lost and a well-appreciated feeling of comfort and security results from being in control, aware, and able to move forward with knowledge and forethought into the unknown. Finding her way with a sextant and nautical books and tables provided an uplifting freedom, a chance for her to meet the challenges of the sea with wit instead of brawn.

Ellen suddenly felt a longing for home, a longing that surfaced intermittently on the lengthy voyages. She kept it hidden deep inside her at sea, even alone in the darkness of her husband's cabin, where occasional tears went unnoticed more often than not, with his attention wholly given over to the ship. There were days at sea when, for a moment, she dearly missed the comfort of a warm fire, a soft chair, the steady swing of the clock's pendulum as they sat together reading, playing chess, or simply staring into the flames. In those moments her senses called up the smell of cut grass and the roses so common in their hometown of Marblehead, a little town on the coast east of Boston. But at sea it did not suit to dwell on the land. Such thoughts only made the darker moments all the more inky.

Oneida was her home, in many respects more than any place on land. For five years the small cabin aft had been her retreat, a private world where she read or worked through her calculations in fixing *Oneida*'s daily position. Down the China Sea, through the Sunda Straits off Java, across the Indian Ocean and past Africa's Cape of Good Hope, up the Atlantic Ocean to home, the last leg of the voyage took them over fifteen thousand miles through light, baffling winds that seemed intent upon blowing from the direction they wished to go. Ellen tracked the ship's position and set the courses for the fastest possible passage, and was not always successful in finding the best route. The routes to China were less refined than the Atlantic routes in terms of avoiding the calms, storms, and contrary winds and currents.

Built in 1841, the year she and Perkins were married, *Oneida* was a swift sailer for that time, and large at 793 tons and 150 feet in length. On five occasions under Perkins's command she had made the passage home from Anjer on the coast of Java in less than ninety days. Those were respectable passages, but not anywhere near the clipper ship *Sea Witch*'s record of seventy-four days set in 1849, a fact Perkins frequently noted aloud. Every passage home from China became a race against *Sea Witch*, and Perkins drove the ship and crew hard. Yet, without a superior vessel such as *Sea Witch*, no hope existed of setting a new record. A captain's seamanship and his willingness to drive on with as much sail set as possible regardless of the weather accounted for only half the speed equation. The other half lay in the ship's length, her hull design, and her ability to spread vast amounts of canvas aloft.

Ellen was keenly aware of Perkins's desire for a bigger, faster ship. She knew that his ambitions had outgrown *Oneida*. The clippers coming out of the shipyards for the California trade had captured his imagination, and they had similarly engaged hers. The future aboard *Oneida* remained entirely predictable. But aboard a bigger, faster ship, it expanded into a range of limitless possibility.

Once *Oneida* reached the upper harbor, the crew dashed about furling sail in Bristol fashion as Perkins shouted orders to the mate on the forecastle deck, directing the balletlike choreography of men linked to the ship's every maneuver over a network of ropes, spars, and canvas. Running with the wind astern, *Oneida* slowed as the crew took in the royals, flying jib, and the topgallants on all masts until only her topsails, jib, and spanker remained set.

The port anchor, her working bower, hung ready to lower on the cathead, a heavy wooden timber protruding from the bow. With a hard strike of a maul to free the pin securing the anchor, the mate could release it in an instant. Lengths of chain heaved from the locker below lay faked out on deck in front and aft of the windlass to ensure it ran free when the order to lower boomed from the poop deck.

Seeing he still had too much headway on, Perkins ordered the helmsman to round up. The helmsman turned the wheel. The ship began to point straight into the wind while men at the braces pulled the main topsail yard around to allow the breeze to push into the sail from the front. At the same time, the mizzen and fore topsails kept drawing forward. The ship lost headway.

"Pinch her close, helmsman. Closer. Closer," Perkins said. The seaman at the helm inched the wheel one spoke at a time to bring the ship's bow dead to windward, and all sails went aback. *Oneida* slowly moved backward, making sternway.

"Ready forward?"

"Ready forward, aye, sir," the mate replied.

"Let go port anchor!"

With a tremendous splash, the anchor plunged into the shallow water off Governors Island. The anchor chain rattled through the hawsehole in the bow and pounded against the iron-reinforced rim of the opening, sending sparks flying. The mate ordered the men at the windlass to ease chain until he let out enough to ride safely. The sternway *Oneida* had on backed the anchor into the mud, and the ship eased to a stop. As the men up in the rigging and perched on the yards on all three masts worked in unison to bring in the last of the sails, the vessel came to rest.

To the north the trees at the Battery created a green foreground to the upper stories of the squat brick buildings along the piers of the shipping district. The spire of Trinity Church poked skyward in the distance. Forests of masts, many adorned with the house flag of the owner's shipping company, rose above all else on the river's edge. Vessels of all manner cruised in every direction from the docks of Jersey City and Brooklyn to those farther up the Hudson River. A passenger steamer bound for Albany hissed and hooted its horn, spewing columns of black smoke and cleaving a path of clear water through small craft that easily darted out of the way.

"Well, darling," Perkins said, smiling slightly at his wife, "we're back in the thick of it again."

Ellen leaned against the taffrail and gazed at the city, thinking about the comfort of the coming evening at the Astor House, and her family in Marblehead. "Yes, we are, Perkins. Indeed we are."

Chapter 2

Returning to shore after a long voyage always required adjustments to all aspects of life, even at the most basic level. The very land appeared to move underfoot in mimic of the ocean swells. The illusion continued for a few days while the body adjusted to walking on solid ground, and it was particularly noticeable when leaning over to pick something up. The steady rhythm of the watches, augmented by the ringing of the ship's bell through a watch from one strike to eight, imparted a regularity to the day and night. Ashore this regularity vanished and everything progressed in apparent chaos and always at a fast pace.

The world dropped away as the ship traveled from one trade wind belt to the next, down the span of entire continents month after month. The only news came in old, tattered newspapers from major ports passed from ship to ship on the rare days when two vessels hove close enough to speak. The ship was its own community, and in the larger world around it, it appeared minute. The greater community of countries and states, industries and workers, the tide of humanity shaping the nature of the world, continued to press on in pursuit of its larger collective destiny. When going ashore, Ellen realized just how left out and left behind being at sea for months had made her.

Shortly before *Oneida* departed for China the previous year, President Zachary Taylor had died and Millard Fillmore had taken over the presidency. Fillmore immediately found himself in the middle of a great controversy, partly the making of his rather bellicose predecessor, the resolution of which became known as the Compromise of 1850. It temporarily ended a debate among the loosely bound sections of the Union, the North, Midwest, and the South, that had threatened to send the young nation into a civil war. While there was a deep sense of nationalism among the American people, there was also a strong identification with one's specific locale, be it the cotton fields of the South or the wheat farms in the Midwest. States saw themselves as autonomous in most areas of government, and the North, South, and Midwest saw themselves as collective bodies of states bonded together by virtue of their shared region. This led to a tendency to view national issues through the lens of a highly regional perspective, and that bred conflict. The views of the North differed greatly from those of the South, particularly with respect to slavery.

At the time, Congress still had not entirely put to rest a controversy over the issue of slavery in the new territories ceded to the United States after the Mexican-American War ended in 1848. The war added lands covering the future states of California, Nevada, Utah, and Arizona and parts of Colorado, Wyoming, and New Mexico. Texas had already been annexed, and the vexing question of control of the Oregon Territory had been decided with Great Britain; the lands below the forty-ninth parallel, it was agreed, belonged to the United States.

While *Oneida* was at sea, the debate in Washington had grown over what to do about slavery in the vast new territories. The South had begun to see itself as distinct from the other parts of the Union, as a separate culture superior to that of the North. The North felt equally lofty. The Southern states hoped to expand the scope of slavery where possible, and the North and much of the Midwest, though condoning the institution's existence in the South, opposed its expansion. Southern threats of secession, or disunionism, roared out in volleys during meetings of Congress. There was open talk of war between the states, and many politicians feared it might lead to bloodshed if the issues were not quickly resolved.

Ultimately, in late 1850, while the tea fleet descended on the ports of Canton, Amoy, Foochow, Ninghsien, and Shanghai, the North and the South worked out a deal. The all-important California was admitted to the Union as a free state in September, but slavery was not excluded from the New Mexico or Utah territories. It was an uneasy truce, one that simmered and smoldered, with occasional flare-ups until the Union finally tore apart a decade later in a war that cost the lives of more than 600,000 Americans. The tensions between the South and the rest of the nation remained because the underlying cause of the problems was not sufficiently addressed.

Against this backdrop of quarrels among the states and the rapid expansion of the nation's territory—roughly one million square miles added from Oregon to Texas—the gold rush continued to unfold in its full glory. Already nearly 100,000 men had taken to the goldfields of California. In 1849, gold nuggets had been found lying among the rocks and silt of river valleys, in veins soft, visible, and easily mined with no more than a jackknife. The news of this incredible find ignited the United States, spurring the westward migration that had been taking place. It drew immigrants from Australia, Russia, France, Germany, Mexico, Chile, Peru, and Great Britain. California became a rich mix of diverse cultural backgrounds. Although the miners were not above jumping a claim, there was very little crime based solely on hate due to those differences.

San Francisco, less than a decade before a sleepy hamlet called Yerba Buena, now approached a population of well over twenty-thousand residents, enough to qualify the territory for statehood. The city dwellers lived mostly in tents and shacks built from wood and canvas scavenged from the ships rotting in the harbor, desolate hulks abandoned for gold. The haphazard homes often caught fire and large sections of the city burned. No sooner had the embers cooled than the inhabitants rebuilt. The city almost instantly assumed its former character, like a hardy seedling unwilling to die in the harsh red sand hills surrounding the bay.

The rapid changes occurring in the United States, many of them prompted by the huge westward migration, opened up lucrative business opportunities for those in a position to take advantage of them. Grinnell, Minturn & Company, acting on its recognition of California as a prime arena for profit-making, had implemented changes while *Oneida* was away. Chief among them of concern to Ellen was the promotion of Perkins's brother, William, to the command of *Oneida*. The partners of the company said another, better command awaited Perkins, a promise that could be taken at face value, but not relied on absolutely. The times did not merit blind trust. Captains, at least the smartest of them, were keen businessmen able to carve out a piece of the prize for their own pockets. But they were dependent on the shipowners and the whims of the market for goods. A captain who performed poorly was always expendable. In fact, he was considered a liability to be disposed of as quickly as possible.

Perkins welcomed the company's decision, because it meant William would progress in life to a higher level both personally and socially. That was something Perkins could not find fault with, in spite of the uncertainty of his own future. As the eldest of three brothers, Perkins was the one the others looked up to, especially after their father's death from consumption seven years earlier. Perkins would have had four brothers, but one of them had died before reaching one year of age in 1822. He also had five sisters who were living, two of them his senior. Like his infant brother, two of his sisters died young, one shortly after birth, the other at age two. The family endured the loss of three children, not unusual in those times, and the loss of the father, leaving the mother alone in the world. The losses reinforced a loyalty to family that was as firm as the granite of New Hampshire, where the Cressy parents had first lived after their marriage in 1809.

Perkins's father, Josiah Perkins Creesy, a wealthy architect and builder in the lumber business, had also owned a number of schooners he dispatched to the rich fishing grounds on the Grand Banks, off Newfoundland. He and his wife, Mary Wooldridge, had moved the family early on from the woods and mountains of New Hampshire, leaving Francistown, and he established himself in Marblehead as a leading citizen of the small, coastal village. He was a Freemason, and he instilled in his sons and daughters a strong belief in family and the virtues of honesty and honor. The Freemasons, an ancient fraternal order, were a very strong presence in American life in the early 1800s, though in recent times they had come into disrepute. Nevertheless, the Creesy family remained faithful to the ideals of the Freemasons, and family values were a vital component.

William had proved himself an able seaman and officer aboard *Horatio,* another Grinnell, Minturn vessel, and other ships. The brothers enjoyed a close relationship, which they cultivated when Perkins came home between voyages. Both of them were wedded to the sea, whereas their other siblings were not, and Perkins wished William the best life had to offer and supported him in any way he could. As it was William's first commission as captain, there was a celebration in order, as soon as he could get down to New York from Francistown with his wife, Emily. Both men perceived the change as a step up, an opportunity for each of them to further excel in the merchant marine.

The market possibilities in the California trade had not been lost on Grinnell, Minturn & Company's directors, and they were moving quickly to position the firm to best advantage. Surely there was room for both the Creesy men to show their worth to the rich owners of the company. The impetus behind the changes stemmed from the grossly inflated prices for the most basic commodities in burgeoning San Francisco. Eggs sold for one to three dollars apiece, as did a single candle. A barrel of salt pork went for $210, and a barrel of flour that cost five dollars in the East cost ten times that amount. Prices soared even higher at the diggings. Most of the lumber used in the early days to build San Francisco came off the abandoned ships or was imported from the East all the way around Cape Horn aboard slow-moving, large-bodied timber ships. A single board foot of pine sold for a dollar, assuming any was available.

The days when a lone prospector could stroll out into the hinterland and stake a claim to a rich gold deposit had ended. Claims yielding one ounce of gold a day were considered good, and at fifteen dollars an ounce such a claim promised comfort but not the great wealth most gold-seekers envisioned. Many became discouraged and took up farming in the Central Valley or opened shops in the city. Savvy merchants in the East were aware that the market was changing, and that it might not offer such handsome profits indefinitely, hence there was a great rush to get in with both feet and grab as much return as possible before it all went bust.

There were increasingly more common instances when the market became flooded with a specific product and the price dropped below an acceptable margin. In one case, scores of ships arrived in the harbor laden with heavy iron stoves, so many that they became impossible to sell. Frustrated store owners heaved the stoves out on the street. However, the peaks far outnumbered the dips in profit. No other market offered a quicker road to wealth, though the European trade dwarfed California's in tonnage. Many shippers on both sides of the Atlantic earned handsome sums shuttling goods and people between Europe and the United States, and many, such as Grinnell, Minturn & Company, owned ships serving the transatlantic, East India and China, and California markets.

One of Grinnell, Minturn & Company's main objectives in late 1850 and early 1851 was to gain a substantial foothold in California. Consequently, the company purchased a brand-new clipper, *Sea Serpent,* and sent her off to San Francisco on January 11, 1851. At 1,402 tons and 196 feet, *Sea Serpent* was one of the largest clippers to come down the ways of George Raynes's Portsmouth shipyard, and she was one of the largest in the fleet as well.

The firm planned to buy another clipper for the California line, and they were not enthusiastic about waiting the average of three months it took to build a new vessel. Their scouts had identified a prime specimen of a clipper up in East Boston at Donald McKay's yard. His first clipper, *Stag Hound,* had attracted notice in the shipping world and he was considered among the best shipbuilders in America. His latest creation, the largest of all vessels in the clipper fleet, was nearing completion. Grinnell, Minturn & Company contacted the current owner, Enoch Train and Company, out of Boston, which had named the ship *Flying Cloud.* Moses H. Grinnell, the head of the New York office, offered to buy her. Enoch Train and Company named its price, and Grinnell met it.

As the bigger story played out in the well-appointed Fletcher Street offices of Grinnell, Minturn & Company, all Ellen and Perkins could do was wait for a ship, something neither of them found easy. Ellen was anxious to see her thirteen-year-old sister, Matilda Abby. Ellen regarded Abby, born late in their mother's life, with both sisterly and maternal affection. That was natural enough, since Ellen was twenty-four years older than Abby. Ellen was also anxious to see her parents, John and Elenor, who were getting on in years, and other relatives and friends in Marblehead. Despite the uncertainty, it was more than likely she and her husband would soon be at sea again for another long voyage away from home. She was not tied so much to the land, but to her people she felt an abiding connection.

Ellen made her way to the Bronx to catch a six-o'clock overnight steamer on March 20, bound through the East River and up Long Island Sound for Stonington, Connecticut. Upon the steamer's arrival the following morning, she rode the railroad to Boston, then transferred to the Eastern Railroad direct to Marblehead. Traveling alone, the train speeding down the tracks, wood cinders flying upward and back from the locomotive's stack, she had time to herself, to think, rest, and just stare out the window at the farms and hamlets along the way.

Ellen's visit to Marblehead meant she would not be celebrating Perkins's thirty-seventh birthday with him on the 23rd, but he seldom put much stock in things such as birthdays and anniversaries. If practical business called, the rest of life waited until there was time enough to enjoy a special moment. From as early an age as fourteen, Perkins had lived his life on the sea. Such a hard existence had taught him the value of seeing his duty done first before engaging in any celebration. It seemed best for her to go. Besides, William was to come down to New York from Francistown with Emily, and together the four of them would catch up on lost time before William set sail aboard *Oneida*.

As Ellen walked down through Marblehead toward the harbor, deep and well protected behind a great neck, past the clapboard homes tucked up close on narrow streets, she reflected on her life with Perkins, her family, her future. At age thirty-six she had no children, nor was it likely she would, not at her time of life. Like most women she had felt the desire, and the realization she was getting older. But the sea was not kind, not a place to bring a child, though she knew of many women who had done it—given birth in the captain's cabin with no midwife or surgeon to help if something went wrong. Yet, the sea was by choice the essence of her world, and while it could not replace the rewards of motherhood it nevertheless filled her life.

Gazing out at the fishing boats, coastal schooners, and small sloops anchored in the harbor, Ellen pulled her coat close to reduce the chill. The late March weather did hold some promise of the warmth and fragrance of April. The air, though damp with the ocean's cold touch, seemed a bit warmer than it had even a few weeks past while *Oneida* sailed homeward to New York. The sun each day moved a little farther north at noon, indicating the approach of the summer solstice in June and the rich explosion of verdancy that would precede it.

Ellen was aware of the slow changes that occurred as spring gave way to summer, summer to fall, and autumn to winter. As a woman of the sea, she was bound to possess a greater sensitivity to nature than many of her female counterparts ashore. Her role aboard ship demanded such knowledge. The motion of the stars, moon, planets, and sun, the workings of the tides, ocean currents, and winds—these natural cycles of the earth appeared both marvelous and simple once the trouble had been taken to understand them. The workings of man's enterprises, his quirks and foibles, prejudices and greed—these easily flummoxed Ellen. At sea, life boiled down to simplicity. On land, the complexities of business, politics, ambition, and power eclipsed any hope for absolute clarity of what action to take next. On March 15, the day they made port, all had appeared hopeful for the future. But now it was not certain when Perkins would receive his next commission, or on what ship. It was all a product of the times, crazy with business, bigger and bigger ships, and more and more profits.

Ellen had left Perkins at the Astor House, one of the finest hotels in New York, with gaslights, bells to ring for room service, and a wonderful restaurant. They both loved the Astor House and considered it their city residence. The best hotels in New York charged a dollar a day for a luxury suite. It was an expense the Creesys could easily afford. While Ellen enjoyed visiting her family and friends, Perkins kept hard at work for Grinnell, Minturn & Company dealing with the off-loading of *Oneida,* as well as preparing her new captain for his post. On March 28, he wrote to William in New Hampshire to bring him up to date on personal and business matters.

> Astor House, New York, March 28
> My dear brother,
> I am exceedingly grieved to think I should have caused you one moment of unhappiness by my omission to write you at an earlier time than the date of the letter which you must have in your possession, and which gives the reason for my neglect.
> I fear it will be impossible for me to visit you in Francistown as I cannot leave before the ship is discharged and so soon as she is discharged it will be necessary for you to be here as I wish to give you all the information I can respecting the ship. Mr. Hathaway [part owner of *Oneida*] asked me yesterday when you would be here. I told him I did not know. I should be very glad if you were here and should have written you to that effect, but did not wish to put you to any unnecessary expense. I should get everything in readiness to start when called for, as that will be very soon.
> Our tea sales come off on the second of April, and we discharge on the third, delivering the cargo from the ship. If I could trust to my mate in delivering the cargo I should have seen you

both [Creesy was referring to Emily] ere this. Ellen left here a week ago yesterday and I expect her back again Sunday or Tuesday morning. I have not been to Marblehead myself as yet, and think it would be doubtful whether I can go before I get you off. With regard to the ship I mentioned building for Grinnell, Minturn & Company, Mr. Hathaway tells me they do not give much encouragement for my going in her, as for myself, I do not think they would.

I am in no hurry to go away, still I do not think I shall be long idle.

When you come to New York, COME TO THE ASTOR HOUSE, as this is the only house worth living at in the city. If you would like to come on I should be very glad indeed to have you leave on receipt of this, taking Emily with you. Then we shall have a better opportunity of enjoying ourselves while here, and for a longer time. Should you come and wish to return again before sailing that can be arranged very well. But I do not wish to have you go to any unnecessary expense at my account. You must exercise your own good judgment and count the cost.

Now my dear brother, I must conclude with love to Emily and yourself with kind regards to Mr. Lord [Emily's father] and family and all others of our relatives that you may see. Mean time believe your much

Affectionate Brother,

Josiah P. Creesy

PS If you do not come on—on receipt of this, please write. Yours, JPC.

Chapter 3

With the arrival of dawn at Donald McKay's shipyard came the daily influx of men as they trickled down to the foot of Border Street in East Boston for the day's work. The bang of hammers and mauls, the hiss of the steam derrick used to lift heavy timbers, the rhythmic bite of saws, and the chip of the adze would soon fill the cool spring air with the cacophony of the shipbuilder. The sound of horses, snorting as they dragged long logs weighing tons, would mingle with the shouts of the workers and the jangle of chains. But in the first moments of the day the cry of a lone seagull easily carried far. The yard stirred slowly awake while the pale blue rim of the horizon to the east brightened with the rising sun.

Throughout the shipyard lay piles of timber, most of it squared and ready for conversion into keelsons, stems, sternposts, bowsprits, and bitts, beams, knees, bulwarks, and decks. In a yard the size of Donald McKay's, the huge stockpiles of oak, pine, and rock maple often looked jumbled into a thicket, one known well to the workers. The rush to complete the orders for the new clippers made each day a ritual of controlled chaos. Most every man working on the ships appreciated the magnitude of the building and worked all the harder at turning trees into vessels of unparalleled swiftness.

Every piece of a ship was selected from wood that naturally matched the desired shape. The reason was simple enough. The strength of wood lies with the grain. A gentle curve of a tree trunk was shaped into a transom, the rounded part of a clipper ship's stern. A long, straight trunk was ideal for use as a mast. Another part of the same tree might form a right angle as a branch grew outward. The junction where the branch met the trunk was shaped into a knee, a heavy piece of wood resembling an L. Knees supported and held major structural components in place, such as the ship's decks. There were men at the yard whose sole job involved timber tracking, knowing the various types and shapes on hand, the costs of the raw material, and the gaps in the inventory as the stocks were depleted.

Demand for quality wood employed armies of lumberers. Since the 1820s, timber had constituted the major export in many coastal towns, and landowners had measured their wealth in terms of trees. No other place on earth was cutting lumber at a pace similar to that in New England. The timber piles in McKay's yard were the refined remains of trees cut in the cold of a previous winter when the sap settled low in the trunk and thus permeated less of the wood, which meant it better resisted rot. Teams of a hundred oxen dragged the trees on sledges across the snow or on special wheels as much as eighteen feet tall over the rough floor of the forest to the edge of a river. When the spring thaw came and the water ran wild, the lumberers sent thousands of logs seaward down the rivers from Maine, New Hampshire, Vermont, Massachusetts, and Connecticut. The many years of harvesting thinned the forests of the old growth, especially the coveted white pine ideal for masts. The industry flourished just the same. The end of what lumberers called "the long stuff" still hovered beyond the immediate.

On the ways of the shipyard, the nearly completed hull of *Flying Cloud* loomed up at the water's edge. The ship's black sides above the bright copper sheathing below the waterline glistened with dew, the surface as smooth as glass. Only a close inspection of the ship's sides revealed the intricate curves of her plank seams and the thousands of round impressions beneath the paint where the locust treenails penetrated the wood.

Straight-grained, dense, and very strong, the treenails functioned as massive nails; many measured more than a yard in length. Kept dry in a snug storage shed until shaped, driven, and wedged into place, the locust swelled in the moisture of the marine environment and created a virtually unbreakable bond between the plank and the thick ribs that supported it. Throughout the ship these fastenings, along with iron and copper spikes, held the vast assemblage of frames, beams, and knees together. More than one million board feet of oak and fifty tons of copper fittings went into *Flying Cloud*'s form.

Just three months earlier the ship had been nothing more than an idea based on McKay's carved half model. The shape of the ship and her multitude of fittings were drawn in chalk in the shipyard's nerve center, the mold loft, where a template for each part of the vessel was fabricated according to McKay's specifications. Using the templates, the men in the yard duplicated precisely the thousands of pieces that went into building the ship.

McKay designed *Flying Cloud* to weigh 1,782 tons. After the months of work, her graceful lines stretched 235 feet from the knightheads at the bow to the taffrail at the stern, and 225 feet on deck. She was McKay's largest clipper at that moment, and she represented the best in his thinking on what might make a fine merchant vessel. He had no reason for great expectations regarding his latest creation, though. Her lines were not that much different from those of other clippers already sailing the sea or under construction in Boston and New York. How she would perform was completely unknown. She was, however, the best he could build, and there were hopes for her future, that she might show a good potential for speed and have a crack at *Surprise*'s record. The partners at Grinnell, Minturn & Company shared these hopes. But then any builder or owner wanted the best outcome. In New York, other builders and owners were striving for the best and were building clippers that would outdo *Flying Cloud* in scale and power, most notably a ship called *Challenge*.

Looking down the length of the ship from the bow, the narrowness of her forty-one-foot width in proportion to her length gave her a sleek and sharp appearance. Her lines stood as evidence of an ability to reach high speeds. The long fine concave bow with a sharp entry at the cutwater and a long waterline with an easy run for the sea on its way aft to the stern exemplified the practical design of a clipper ship. Under a press of canvas set on high masts, the bows of these ships lifted as they surfed the waves, and a white boil of eddies reached far beyond the stern.

Men climbed the plankways up the side of the ship and set to work caulking the weather deck, the longest portion of the clipper. The caulkers worked together, everything perfectly timed in assembly-line fashion, each man repeating the same task. McKay's pride in efficiency made his yard one of the smoothest-running operations on the coast. His use of the steam derrick and steam saw to replace the old-fashioned two-man pit saws added to the speed with which his men converted wood into sailing vessels.

One caulker stooped low and forced tar-coated threads of hemp deep into the groove of the plank seam. Another followed with a horsing iron to press the caulk, or oakum, into place. Once the iron was in position, a mallet man hit it to drive the oakum deep and firm up the seal. Another worker poured hot tar into the seam to complete the job. The strikes of the mallet kept steady time, a beat that directed the pace of the crew.

Belowdecks the craftsmen continued their work on the three cabins aft for passengers and officers. Satinwood, rosewood, and mahogany scraps lay strewn about on the floors among the corkscrew leavings of wood after boring, wood shavings, and sawdust, the ubiquitous dust. On windy days, clouds of it rose above the yard and layered a beige film on the water near the ways. Panels of satinwood set in mahogany frames edged with rosewood, intricate wainscoting, enameled pilasters, giltwork—these and other final touches of beauty were still in the making.

Flying Cloud had come a long way since the start of construction, when the men laid her rock maple keel out on the blocks. The workers hoisted the giant white oak frames and braced each one into place, giving the clipper the skeletal appearance of a whale. The steady work continued as the planking proceeded and the decks were laid. Every step forward through the end of March transformed her into her now nearly completed form.

For McKay, *Flying Cloud* represented the culmination of all his work thus far over a quarter century. He had come down to New York on a coastal schooner from his home in Shelburne, Nova Scotia, in 1826 and found work at one of the best shipyards on the East River, that of builder Isaac Webb. His apprenticeship with Webb taught him the basics of shipbuilding, and with that knowledge McKay began his quick ascent. At age thirty-four he had his own shipyard, with the backing of Enoch Train. In September 1845, he launched his first packet built at the East Boston yard. An uninterrupted line of ships followed in the years after—packets, barks, traders, and clippers, first *Stag Hound,* now *Flying Cloud,* and many more with no foreseeable end in sight.

McKay consistently worked toward a blend of perfection and art in his designs, function and form, practical yet beautiful. In *Flying Cloud* he had achieved it. He stretched the limits of naval architecture and experimented with ever higher masts. He constantly fine-tuned the clipper hull. Shipbuilding was an ongoing process. There was always something new to try. Each ship coming down the ways was one of a kind, based on a half model carved to represent what the vessel would look like when it was completed.

In designing the half model for *Flying Cloud,* McKay slowly shaped the wood into a form that typified the new, innovative clipper hull. There were many intricacies that went into the development of her lines, and many of them depended not on technical know-how, though that was certainly important, but on the designer's flair for art. Seen from above, the ship's bow came to a sharp point, and the sides of the ship ran aft in graceful curves that terminated in an aesthetically pleasing elliptical stern. Seen in profile, her bow arched outward from the bowsprit with ample flare toward the rails. After the curve of her small transom, the rudder presented a vertical line.

A more traditional ship looked much different from a clipper.

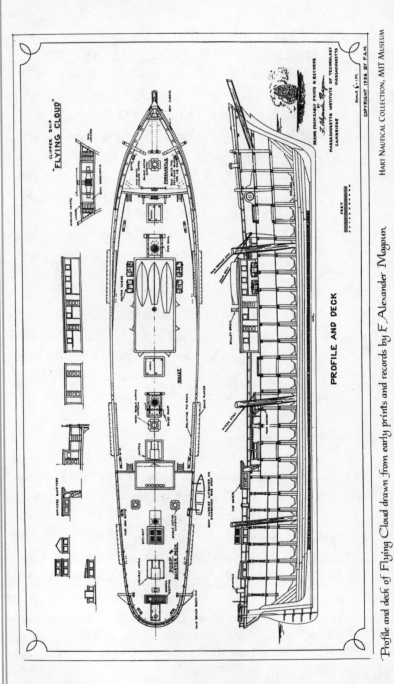

Profile and deck of *Flying Cloud* drawn from early prints and records by *F. Alexander Magoun*.

Seen from above, the bow formed an obtuse rather than an acute triangle. The ship continued to widen aft of the bow until at its greatest width, still forward of the beam, the sides gradually tapered toward the stern. The overall appearance resembled the profile of a fish, and the resemblance was not a coincidence. Early shipwrights built vessels with a "cod's head and a mackerel tail" because they assumed the natural form of a fish represented the best shape for a hull. It was not unusual for a designer to find inspiration in the natural world. Lighthouses were copied from trees. Like a tree, they had a wide base that narrowed progressively toward the top.

The problem with the cod's-head-and-mackerel-tail design was that it forced the ship to push the water aside. The hull was wide, or beamy, as the sailors called it. The wide beam and the rounded shape of the hull created space for a large hold. But it also created drag that slowed the vessel. On average, these ships sailed at roughly six to eight knots. A clipper ship could sustain speeds of more than twelve knots, and often better.

The clipper ship was not perfect, however. These ships lacked buoyancy at the bow and stern, and they were thought dangerous by traditionalists because of the possibility of driving the bow under in a gale. Over time, the lack of buoyancy caused the bow and stern to sag lower than the center of the ship, a condition known as hogging. The clipper was also tender, meaning she leaned way over on her side when the wind blew hard. The traditional ship was more stable.

The owners of the clipper ships overlooked the shortcomings, at least for a while. Speed overruled all other considerations. Shipowners sacrificed cargo-carrying ability for it. They willingly bore the costs of the fifty-to-sixty-man crews needed to sail a clipper ship, as well as the expensive repairs necessary at the completion of a voyage. The profits justified the expense. There were even some along the waterfront who predicted that the clippers would maintain their supremacy over the steamers. Relatively slow, always hungry for coal, and prone to breakdowns and explosions, the steamers did not appear to pose much of a threat to the clippers. A few clearheaded, forward-thinking merchants saw the future in steam, but they were in the minority.

The owners of the shipping lines were equally willing to pay enormous sums of money for a clipper ship. *Flying Cloud* was evidence of just how much. The Boston-based Enoch Train and Company paid Donald McKay $50,000 to build *Flying Cloud*. The company then sold her to Grinnell, Minturn & Company in New York for $90,000. Based on historical consumer price indexes from the American Antiquarian Society, in 1999 dollars the sum Enoch Train paid for the ship amounted to the equivalent of $900,000 and the sum Grinnell, Minturn paid for it to $1.6 million.

From the modern perspective, paying $1.6 million for a clipper ship sounds like a bargain. Luxury sailing and motor yachts sell for much more than that. However, the United States dollar in 1851 had much more buying power than it does today. A pound of coffee cost seven cents, a pound of rice four. A one-pound tin of roast beef or ham cost ten cents. A man could buy a fine suit in New York for just twelve dollars. A workman paid ninety-eight cents for a pair of shoes, and the average annual salary for working-class laborers ran between $250 and $500. So the cash outlay for *Flying Cloud* staggered the minds of many people. Grinnell, Minturn & Company's investment in *Flying Cloud* was substantial and indicated that the partners heading the firm's New York office were desperate to put another clipper on the California run as quickly as possible.

In his autobiography, *My Life in Many States and in Foreign Lands*, George Francis Train, junior partner at Enoch Train and Company, recalled the transaction between his firm and Grinnell, Minturn & Company:

> No sooner was the *Flying Cloud* built than many shipowners wanted to buy her; among others, the house of Grinnell, Minturn, & Company of the Swallowtail Line of Liverpool asked what we would take for her. I replied that I wanted $90,000, which meant a handsome profit. The answer came back immediately—"We will take her." We sent the vessel to New York under

Captain Creesy, while I went on by railway. There I closed the sale, and the proudest moment of my life, up to that time, was when I received a check from Moses H. Grinnell, the New York head of the house, for $90,000.

The crafty Enoch Train had nearly doubled his investment without incurring any additional cost or risk. For old salts along the waterfront it seemed a wise and practical decision for Train to sell at such a high price, particularly given the rumor that the company found itself short of cash. The decision did not seem as wise a few months later, however, when *Flying Cloud* set a world record for the fastest passage ever from New York to San Francisco. George Francis Train wrote in his later years that one of the major regrets he had to endure in his life was the day his company sold *Flying Cloud*.

Chapter 4

White water churned under the transom of the steam tug *Ajax* and whirls of black smoke poured from her stack as she hove taut the towline trailing off the stern. The squat, low side-wheeler moved slowly forward, gradually taking the slack out of the line. As thick as a sailor's forearm and secured to a stout bitt, the cable grew bar-tight and exerted enough of a pull to get *Flying Cloud* under way for the outside passage from Boston to New York.

The outside passage took ships around the treacherous tip of Cape Cod and along the southern shore of Long Island. It was longer than the inside approach to Manhattan down Long Island Sound. But it was safer. At the west end of the sound, the East River, which was actually a tidal strait, posed a significant danger. Ten-knot tidal currents stirred the water into eddies and whirlpools at a narrow stretch called Hell Gate. Acres of reefs throughout the river and the infamous Flood Rock situated in midchannel routinely claimed ships and the lives of those aboard.

As *Flying Cloud* gained momentum, the cable hung in a curve, looped from the bitts on the clipper's bow, down in a bend below the surface of the water, and up again at the bitts on the tug. The tug's skipper glanced aft as he approached Deer Island at the edge of the inner harbor, slowly making his way down President Roads to the Narrows and the open sea beyond the islands of the outer harbor. The clipper tracked well, he thought. She did not wander from side to side, yanking at the towline like an unruly colt. She followed along easily without overtaxing the tug's steam engine in spite of her prodigious tonnage. A small wave formed at her cutwater. Otherwise she scarcely disturbed the sea.

Aboard *Flying Cloud,* Perkins stood at the helm, pleased at the ship's easy motion under tow, despite its being lightly loaded with ballast and having no sail set to keep her steady. It was a good sign. An easy tow meant her passage through the water did not put her in disharmony with it, allowing her to become one with her element. He found her responsive to the slightest shift of the wheel, and he imagined what she would be like under the full press of her ten-thousands yards of canvas.

Standing close beside Perkins, Ellen looked up at him and smiled. His face was radiant; his eyes twinkled like a boy's on Christmas morning. A chance to steer his ship, as odd as it may seem, was rare for a captain, who was considered above sullying his hands on the spokes. At sea, Perkins did not break with the rule. An officer never steered, unless deeming it of vital necessity. With just a skeleton crew aboard, and only for the delivery, Perkins relaxed and enjoyed himself. The voyage to New York was a brief respite before the frenetic days of hiring the crew, loading the cargo, and procuring and stowing the provisions. The process of fitting the ship out for sea marked the start of a long, hard race without end until *Flying Cloud* arrived back in New York the following year laden with China tea. It was only a matter of a day before the hard work began.

Ellen, too, appreciated the grand moment, the first time the clipper took to the sea, as she and her husband were charged with the safekeeping of the largest clipper ship afloat in the world. It all seemed unreal, the way events had unfolded after their return aboard *Oneida* just over a month ago. It had been a tense time for both of them while the company men engaged in their financial maneuvers. Competition for the command of *Flying Cloud* far outpaced that for any other ship on the Boston and New York waterfronts. Though Perkins was well regarded at Grinnell, Minturn & Company, it was by no means certain that he would be given the ship. But for the influence of Creesy's friend Francis Hathaway, he might not have gotten the job.

On April 13, Emily Creesy had written a letter to her brother that mentioned *Flying Cloud*. One passage in particular contained an intriguing revelation about how important Francis Hathaway was in determining Creesy's future. She wrote: "Perkins will start for New York in the *Flying Cloud* on Friday. She will be towed down by steamboat, so he will probably arrive Saturday, even doubtless Ellen will come with him. As Mr. Hathaway has bought an interest in the ship, it is more than probable that Perkins will be master."

On April 15, *Flying Cloud* had slid stern-first down the ways of Donald McKay's yard, flags snapping to the brisk northeast wind. A crowd of spectators, the gentlemen in swallowtail overcoats and high hats, the ladies in full skirts covered delicately with black shawls or partially hidden under coats, gathered at the water's edge. Onlookers perched on rooftops and viewed the scene from the yards of ships anchored nearby.

Built up under her was a cradle, greased smooth for a slick run down the ways. Scores of yardmen armed with sledgehammers banged away at the blocks supporting the keel. As she settled onto the cradle, she began to move, the wooden supports creaking and groaning under the weight. The heavier the load, the faster she moved, until at last with a rush, her flags suspended stem to stern on poles rigged for the occasion, *Flying Cloud* surged into the choppy water of the harbor to the cheers of thousands.

Poet Henry Wadsworth Longfellow may well have been present at the launching ceremony. He was an avid admirer of the clipper ship, and he regularly visited McKay's yard to watch the construction. In his poem "The Building of the Ship," which he wrote in celebration of a later McKay vessel, *Great Republic*, Longfellow described the excitement that occurred when a clipper ship was launched.

Then the master,
With a gesture of command,
Waved his hand;
And at the word,
Loud and sudden there was heard,
All around them and below,
The sound of hammers, blow on blow,
Knocking away the shores and spurs.
And see! she stirs!
She starts,—she moves,—she seems to feel
The thrill of life along her keel,
And, spurning with her foot the ground,
With one exulting, joyous bound,
She leaps into the ocean's arms.

And lo! from the assembled crowd
There rose a shout, prolonged and loud,
That to the ocean seemed to say,—
"Take her, O bridegroom, old and gray,
Take her to thy protecting arms,
With all her youth and all her charms!"

The launch did not mark the end of work on *Flying Cloud*. She was towed to a pier where swarms of men raised her masts and set up the miles of prestretched rigging to hold them in place. Heavy hemp ropes called shrouds supported the masts from the sides, and similar ropes called stays supported them from front and back. The men hoisted in place the yards, long spars set parallel to the surface of the sea upon which the square sails were set. They ran the running rigging, the lines used to work the sails. Among the most important of these lines were the braces used to pivot the yards to enable the sails to catch the wind.

A clipper ship's masts were not one long pole. Each was composed of three individual spars. Starting from the bow and working back were the foremast, mainmast, and mizzen mast. These lower spars weighed many tons. On top of these were the progressively

Spar Plan of a Full-Rigged Ship

On a full-rigged ship, the three sections of each mast are collectively termed mizzen mast, mainmast, and foremast. The bottom sections of each mast go by the same name. In this illustration, the yards on the mainmast are identified in sequence. Though they are not labeled, the yards on the mizzen mast and foremast go by the same names as those on the mainmast, only with the prefix of either mizzen or fore.

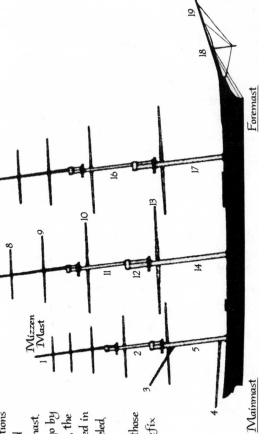

Mizzen Mast
1 Mizzen Topgallant Pole Mast
2 Mizzen Topmast
3 Spanker Gaff
4 Spanker Boom
5 Mizzen Mast

Mainmast
6 Main Topgallant Pole Mast
7 Main Skysail Yard
8 Main Royal Yard
9 Main Topgallant Yard
10 Main Topmast Yard
11 Main Topmast
12 Main Topmast Doubling
13 Main Yard
14 Mainmast

Foremast
15 Fore Topgallant Pole Mast
16 Fore Topmast
17 Foremast
18 Bowsprit
19 Jibboom

ILLUSTRATION BY
MARGARET WESTERGAARD

lighter and shorter topmasts and topgallant pole masts. The masts overlapped where they were fastened together, and the overlapping sections were called the doublings. In addition, the bottom of the masts sat just above the keel, which meant that a good portion of each lower spar was belowdecks. On *Flying Cloud,* eighteen feet of these masts were belowdecks. Taking into account the overlapping at the doublings, the three sections of *Flying Cloud*'s foremast soared 113 feet above the deck, the mainmast 127 feet, and the mizzen 102 feet.

Attached to the masts were the yards that held the sails outward to the force of the wind. These were fixed to the masts with heavy iron fittings leathered and greased on the inside to allow the yards to move easily up and down, at the pulling or the slacking of the halyards, tyes, and lifts, depending on which yard was being worked. They swung around the mast to shift the sail's position relative to the wind. The lower yards were fixed in place. They could not be raised or lowered, but they could rotate like the upper yards.

On *Flying Cloud,* the main yard assumed massive proportions. It was the largest of them all and at its thickest point in the center its bulk measured twenty-two inches in diameter. From the slim, tapered yardarms on each end of the yard the spar extended eighty-two feet. When squared, as the sailors termed it when the yards were set perpendicular to the hull, the ends thrust outward twenty feet on each side of the ship. Above the main yard on each mast, shorter yards supported the successively smaller topsails, topgallants, royals, and skysails.

Attached to all but the highest yards were studdingsail booms to extend the spread of sail. When fully bellied to the wind with all studdingsails set, the clipper's profile as viewed from fore or aft assumed a distinctly lofty and triangular shape. With her masts in place, *Flying Cloud* could take on her complete dress and make ready to move out into the world.

Ellen craned her neck to gaze aloft at the towering masts and the neatly squared yards. The sails, furled tight and shipshape, waited at the ready in the event they were needed if *Ajax* broke down or a storm came up. The skeleton crew aboard numbered enough to sail

Sail Plan of a Full-Rigged Ship

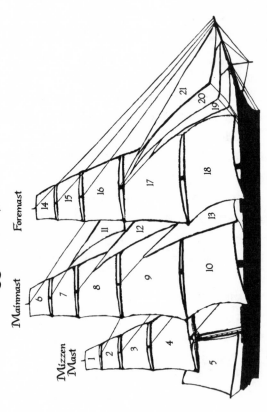

Mizzen Mast   **Mainmast**   **Foremast**

<u>Mizzen Mast</u>

1 Mizzen Skysail
2 Mizzen Royal
3 Mizzen Topgallant
4 Mizzen Topsail
5 Spanker

<u>Mainmast</u>

6 Main Skysail
7 Main Royal
8 Main Topgallant
9 Main Topsail
10 Mainsail or Main Course
11 Main Royal Staysail
12 Main Topgallant Staysail
13 Main Topmast Staysail

<u>Foremast</u>

14 Fore Skysail
15 Fore Royal
16 Fore Topgallant
17 Fore Topsail
18 Foresail or Fore Course
19 Fore Topmast Staysail
20 Jib
21 Flying Jib

ILLUSTRATION BY
MARGARET WESTERGAARD

Flying Cloud out of trouble if necessary, though not enough to efficiently handle all the sails. A month remained before they expected to set off for San Francisco, then on to China, and many tasks remained. As long as all went well, *Ajax* would get them to New York expeditiously and with minimum bother and cost to the company.

Ellen shifted her gaze to the poop deck. It was quite clear of clutter. The helm station with the wheel and the binnacle that housed the compass was situated just forward of the taffrail. A wooden grate in front of the wheel provided extra traction for the helmsman. Her eyes settled on the lazaret hatch and moved forward to the beautifully finished skylight. In the great cabin the sun shone through the glass panes and gave the room's elegant woodwork an added warmth and luster. Two brass-banded capstans used to haul the ship into or out of a wharf stood on each side of the deck forward of the mizzen mast, and beyond the mizzen at the very front edge of the poop there rose the roof of the portico over the entrance to the cabins below. These were reserved for the ship's officers, the steward and cabin boy, and the passengers.

Down stairways on each side of the poop deck was the main deck, also known as the weather deck. It was a much busier place for the eye, and Ellen took time to better acquaint herself with the details. Aft of the mainmast was a big double-action capstan and a hatch to provide access below. Forward of the mainmast was another hatch and the white deckhouse for one watch of the crew. Soon coops, pens, and sties for the livestock carried on any long voyage would surround the deckhouse and make the ship sound like a barnyard at times. Water casks would also be lashed outside the deckhouse. Miles of lines crisscrossed above and below and terminated along each side of the ship at the pin rails and at the bases of the masts. The lines were neatly coiled and suspended from the wooden belaying pins, which were sanded and varnished to a smooth gloss.

Forward of the main deck up at the bow was the raised topgallant forecastle deck. It provided a roof for the forecastle, where the other watch of the crew would live. Atop this deck was another

Furling a Square Sail

Aft view of a partially furled sail

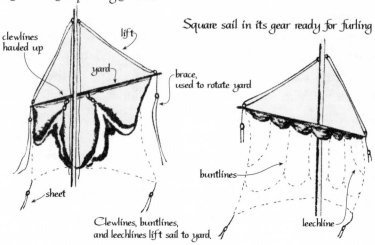

Square sail in its gear ready for furling

clewlines hauled up

lift

yard

brace, used to rotate yard

sheet

Clewlines, buntlines, and leechlines lift sail to yard.

buntlines

leechline

Basic View of Studdingsails As Seen from the Stern

Studdingsails added greatly to a clipper ship's sail area. However, they were time-consuming to rig and take in. They could only be used with the wind directly astern or aft of the beam. In rough seas, the lower studdingsails would dip into the crests as the ship rolled, putting excessive strain on the gear. Most commanders only set studdingsails in fair weather, but Captain Creesy kept them up even in bad conditions.

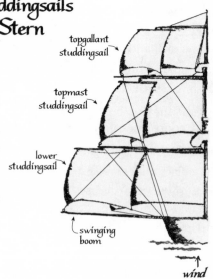

topgallant studdingsail

topmast studdingsail

lower studdingsail

swinging boom

wind

ILLUSTRATION BY MARGARET WESTERGAARD

capstan and other equipment such as the catheads used to hold the anchors when the ship was inshore. However, its most compelling visual feature was the soaring bowsprit and jibboom that protruded from inside the forecastle below to jut far out beyond the bow. The bowsprit was twenty-eight and a half inches in diameter and extended twenty feet from the bow, and the jibboom added even more length. It was divided at sixteen feet for the inner jib and thirteen feet for the outer jib, with five additional feet at the end. As *Flying Cloud* rode to the first swells, the jibboom seemed to scratch the sky.

The details overwhelmed Ellen in their sheer number, causing her eyes to dart from one place to the next in an effort to take it all in at once. The pearl-colored bulwarks and blue waterways contrasted well with the unfinished pine decks, the tar seams still bold and newly blackened, unworn from countless days of sanding and cleaning. Every morning, the sailors brought out Bible-sized blocks of sandstone to sand down the decks. They called these stones prayer books and referred to the exercise of sanding the deck as holystoning. Eventually, the work transformed the surface of the wood to a smooth, white sheen as soft as fine cloth under bare feet. Holystoning was part of shipboard life, as much as washing down the decks, painting, and mending sails. Ellen looked forward to returning to the sea routine that gave each day a sense of continuity.

She watched the islands outside Boston Harbor slowly pass. *Flying Cloud* rolled as the swells increased to a moderate size. The rise and fall of the bow was barely noticeable. The much lighter tug well ahead rolled far more and pushed up a wide bow wave. The last buoy marking the shoals beyond the Narrows dropped astern. The channel between Lovell Island and Gallops and Georges Islands, the only deepwater approach to Boston, became indiscernible among the patchwork of rocky islets. The vast array of rock ledges and bars and the long expanse of shallows to the east formed a network of natural breakwaters in the outer harbor.

Inside, past President Roads, the inner harbor beyond the mud flats at the edge of the city ranked as one of the better-protected

Points of Sail
Some points of sail are more favorable than others.

As a square-rigged ship, Flying Cloud could not sail very close to the wind. She could only sail within approximately 60 degrees of the true wind direction, meaning she was close-hauled or sailing full and by. This was the slowest point of sail. In fact, during storms a square-rigged ship was not always able to make headway while close-hauled.

On courses which put the wind farther aft of the bow Flying Cloud picked up speed. Her best point of sail was a broad reach, or sailing with the wind off the port or starboard quarter. With the wind blowing from that direction all the sails would remain full and at a perfect slant to create forward motion.

When the wind blew directly over the stern, Flying Cloud was running before the wind. While it might appear that this would be her best point of sail, it really was not. The sails of the mizzen and mainmast blanketed the foresails, meaning they received less wind and were robbed of power. As a consequence, Flying Cloud did not sail as fast running as she did on a broad reach.

Points of sail diagram labels — port (left) side: wind / close-hauled; wind / close reach; wind / beam reach; wind / broad reach; wind / running. Starboard (right) side: wind / close-hauled; wind / close reach; wind / beam reach; wind / broad reach.

Ship labels: bowsprit, forecastle, port bow, starboard bow, fore, main or weather deck, aft, port (left), starboard (right), poop deck, port quarter, starboard quarter, stern.

ILLUSTRATION BY MARGARET WESTERGAARD

havens on the coast. It differed from its rival New York both in configuration and accessibility, with Boston finding its approaches more difficult because of Cape Cod and Nantucket Shoals. Both ports, however, shared a universally held attraction to moneymakers and spenders. In the previous year, more than 400,000 immigrants had arrived in the United States, many of them Irish, and they went to work in the burgeoning industries. They often put roots down close to the docks.

At sea the invigorating crisp air smelled fresh and pure, and it carried with it a faint taste of salt whenever Ellen licked her lips. The warm cloak of the land faded astern in a pleasing, comforting way. Ellen turned her thoughts to more immediate business, fixing her point of departure to serve as a starting-off point from which she referenced her navigation as the ship progressed along the coast. She brought up from below a small compass housed in a beautifully varnished box. She held the compass up and sighted through two pins fixed at the front edge of the box until Boston Light appeared between them. The compass needle lined up with the lighthouse gave her a reading in degrees, and she was thus able to establish what navigators call a magnetic bearing, the direction of a terrestrial object in reference to the observer. She plotted the bearing as a line of position starting from the lighthouse and tracking outward across the chart. She knew *Flying Cloud* was somewhere on this line.

Ellen's next step in establishing their exact location, known as a fix, involved taking two more bearings on objects at different angles. She plotted the lines of position on the chart. They formed a triangle, and she knew *Flying Cloud* was somewhere inside it. The tighter the triangle, the more accurate the fix on their point of departure. Even the most basic of navigational endeavors required an understanding of geometry.

The practice of coastal piloting was as much second nature to her as the ability to walk on a pitching deck without losing her balance. She carried out her duties whether they were needed or not at the moment. The navigating was the responsibility of those aboard *Ajax*. Nevertheless, the moods of the sea changed rapidly, and she thought it prudent to be prepared in the event they had to cut loose from the tow. It was standard practice to establish a firm fix at the outset of any voyage, and she would have been negligent had she not done it.

Ellen went below to the officers' cabin and sat down at a table, where she kept a rectangular piece of slate and some chalk. She noted the ship's position and course and the time on the slate. As the day passed, the notations provided an accounting of where the vessel was at a given time, the intended route, and the speed through the water. The information was needed to deduce the ship's location. At the end of the sea day, the pertinent facts were entered into the ship's logbook as a permanent record. Ellen was, however, still missing one last bit of information to make necessary navigational calculations. She did not yet know *Flying Cloud*'s speed.

In times long past, well before the advent of modern navigational aids, mariners judged their ship's speed in a very primitive way. The navigator strolled up to the bow and tossed a wooden chip into the sea. With a sandglass he timed how long it took for it to drop astern, and did the arithmetic necessary to figure out how many feet per minute the ship made good through the water. If the ship was one hundred feet long and it took ten seconds for the chip to pass by, the ship was traveling at six hundred feet per minute. The navigator multiplied six hundred feet per minute by sixty to come up with the total number of feet traveled in one hour, which in this case would be 36,000 feet. He then divided this number by 6,080, the equivalent of one nautical mile, and the answer gave him an approximate speed of six knots, or six nautical miles covered in the space of one hour. These concepts often baffled even very experienced seamen, who were, for the most part, illiterate. The man who had command of these basics, as well as a working knowledge of celestial navigation, was in high demand on the waterfront.

Navigators of Ellen's day were able to determine a vessel's speed much more easily. They used a device known as a log. Instead of a chip, a wedge-shaped piece of hardwood weighted with lead on the base of the angle was attached to a long line wound up on a reel. At intervals of fifty-one feet, the line was marked with knots. The log was dropped in the water, and the number of knots that came off the reel equaled nautical miles when timed with a thirty-second sandglass. Thus, if five knots came off the reel in thirty seconds, the ship was traveling five nautical miles in one hour, or five knots, in the proper terminology. (It is not proper to say a ship sails at five knots per hour, since five knots means the distance covered in one hour. The addition of "per hour" is redundant. If one ever were to say "knots per hour" in the presence of an experienced seaman, one would immediately be termed a lubber, greenhorn, or farmer.)

In actual practice, however, the knots on the log line were tied at intervals of forty-eight feet, short of a true nautical mile, and a twenty-eight-second sandglass was used. This ensured that the navigator slightly overestimated the ship's speed and that his reckoning was ahead of the ship's actual position. This was a big advantage when coming up on a coast because the chances of making landfall ahead of expectations were greatly reduced. In the opposite scenario, if the navigator underestimated the ship's speed she arrived before expectations, and that could land the ship on a reef in the dark of night. That unfortunate navigational error was called overrunning the reckoning.

After finishing her work in the officers' quarters, Ellen returned to the poop deck to enjoy the beauty of Boston's outer islands. As she expected, the tug bore off far enough to seaward to clear Minots Ledge and shaped a course for Pollocks Rip off Cape Cod. As the tug settled in to a steady cruising speed, Ellen ordered the log streamed to establish the vessel's speed and made a note of it. At the change of the watch, the crew repeated the process, thus providing an accurate reading of how fast they traveled during a specific time period. With the speed of the ship known, Ellen multiplied it by the amount of time that had elapsed since her initial fix off Boston Light. In this way, she determined how far the ship was along the intended course. This process is known as dead reckoning, short for deduced reckoning, which essentially means the navigator makes an educated guess as to where the ship is.

At sea, these simple procedures for deducing position represented just one of Ellen's methods. The far more complex world of celestial navigation, using the sun, moon, planets, and stars to guide her, demanded much more knowledge and years of practice with a sextant. For now, though, Ellen's sextant remained safely ensconced in its felt-lined case below in the captain's luxurious stateroom, along with several chronometers and other clocks needed for navigation. The chronometer was a highly sophisticated clock set to keep Greenwich Mean Time, a reference to the time in Greenwich, England, at longitude zero. It was used in working out the sights she took with her sextant. Soon both the sextant and the chronometer would see daily use, but for the moment celestial navigation was not needed. Land was not far off. The chain of lighthouses and lightships along the coast from Nantucket to Block Island, Montauk Point to Sandy Hook, all served as signposts, and if fog settled in, as it often did in springtime, soundings provided clues concerning the ship's position.

In addition to the ship's log, Ellen counted among her navigational tools an ancient device known as a lead line, which sailors called a navigator's third eye. Merely a long line attached to a large, cylinderlike sinker, the lead line was used to determine the depth of the water. The lead was tossed overboard, and when it hit bottom, markings on the line indicated in feet or fathoms the precise depth of the water.

The lead was also able to provide information about the ocean floor, whether it was sand, mud, or gravel. A hole was bored in the base of the lead to hold a wad of fresh tallow placed inside just prior to throwing the lead into the sea. When the lead was brought to the surface, the gunk stuck in the tallow showed the nature of the bottom.

Matching the charted depth at the ship's dead-reckoned position with a sounding and the right bottom composition provided a fairly accurate means of confirming a ship's actual position. Changes in depth and bottom composition yielded valuable clues when the weather came in thick enough to hide the jibboom. Many a time Ellen had conned ships through thick weather, matching the depths of the water in the ship's immediate assumed position with the depths marked on the chart. In these waters, grainy yellow sand meant they were in Great South Channel; black mud, off Block Island; mussel shells in blue ooze, the hollow bowl in the depths off Sandy Hook at the approaches to New York Harbor.

The pilotage of a vessel she had learned from her father, a successful captain in the coastal schooner trade currently aboard the fifty-ton *Californian*. Well known in Marblehead, John Prentiss had created something of a stir by teaching his daughter navigation, walking her through the fundamentals of reading a nautical chart and the basics of dead reckoning. From these and other rudimentary tools of a mate or ship's master she moved on to the art of finding her way across the empty sea using a sextant and chronometer.

An only child until her early twenties, when her mother, Elenor, gave birth to her sister, Abby, Ellen had formed a special bond with her father. She was the boy he never had, and as a forward-thinking man he saw no crime in educating his daughter in the ways of the sea. Even if she never applied the skills he taught her, the very fact that she had mastered the mathematics and comprehended the rather difficult concepts associated with celestial navigation could only help her in life. Such a mastery of knowledge further sharpened her already keen mind.

Ellen studied hard and endured many frustrating hours practicing with her sextant, a sophisticated optical protractor used to measure a celestial body's angle of elevation above the visible horizon. This angle is referred to as an altitude. The act of using a sextant to obtain the altitude of a celestial body is known as taking a sight or an observation. It was just one of many factors that went into the daily tracking of a ship's position when well offshore.

At first, when she just started out with the sextant, Ellen trundled from her home to a place at the water's edge with a good view of the sky and took sights at noon, then returned to the house to run through her calculations. More often than not she discovered errors. But gradually she was able to shoot the sun accurately from shore. She moved on to the next step, taking sights from a small boat, and ultimately from the deck of her father's schooner. While she learned to use the sextant, she continued to work on mastering the concepts of plane and solid geometry, as well as spherical trigonometry.

Ellen's girlfriends in Marblehead wondered why she went to the trouble to deal with any of it, but she had her reasons. The mathematics challenged her mind, and as she learned she found great satisfaction. Her mastery of navigation ultimately allowed her to experience a level of freedom and responsibility rare for a woman of her day. Her knowledge of the sea as well as the complexities of navigation was one of the reasons Perkins had fallen in love with her. She was not the average, simple girl from Marblehead, but a woman whose wit and intellect matched his, and she kept him interested long after he had grown bored with other females who had come and gone in his life.

In Marblehead the old homes closed in, creating a maze of paths around hills and ledges. Many were built with observatories or cupolas on the highest floor, where wives paced, eyes fixed on the empty horizon beyond the neck, waiting for the right ship to come in. Ellen was all too familiar with the waiting. She had seen it as part of a woman's daily life in a seacoast town. She had vowed never to get caught up in the stultifying practice. Yet for many years she had done just that—waited for a change, a shift of fortune, that might never come. Those were lonely times. When Abby was born, Ellen helped her mother, kept the house clean, and cooked the meals.

Time passed with no sign of change, no harbinger of a chance to find her way independently in the world. Beautiful, intelligent, from a good family, she did not lack in suitors. But none captured her fancy, nor offered her the freedom she desired, until she met Perkins when he had come home for a brief rest between voyages. At twenty-six years of age when they were married on June 3, 1841, she was considered dangerously close to spinsterhood. But with Perkins her age did not matter. In fact, they were both born in Marblehead in 1841, just six months apart, and that somehow made them closer, more equal than if he were much her senior.

The afternoon of April 26 faded into twilight, the dunes of Cape

Cod lost in the coming dusk to the west. *Flying Cloud* moved quietly through the water, leaving flickers of phosphorescence in her
wake as the last of the light over the mainland disappeared and a
splash of vivid starlight spread out over the mastheads in thousands
of blinking pinpoints. The masts and yards rose up in slender black
shadow, blotting a fingerlike pattern of darkness against the constellations above. The steady churn of *Ajax*'s paddle wheels carried
back to those aboard the ship, a reminder that they were not yet
alone on the broad Atlantic.

Chapter 5

As April gave way to May, the northwesterlies of early spring diminished in frequency, heralding the arrival of the prevailing southerly winds of summer along the northeastern coast of the United States. The chill gradually left the water at the beaches. The sun rose a few minutes earlier every morning and set a little later every evening.

Far to the south, below the equator, on the barren coast of Patagonia, the days grew shorter and the bite of the west wind seemed more bitter than in the previous months of what was in South America late summer and early autumn. The Antarctic ice pack progressed northward into Drake Passage. Immense icebergs calved from glaciers drifted in the easterly current of the Southern Ocean in greater number. The westerly gales so common in Patagonia gathered strength with the coming winter.

Below a latitude of 40 degrees south the west winds blew across the South American continent with such ferocity sailors referred to the area as the roaring forties. The area below a latitude of 50 degrees south, the region of Cape Horn, was even worse. The sailors called that the furious fifties. The gales now occurred with a regularity that turned the dark, gray sea into an alpine range of undulating water. Waves rose to heights of sixty feet and circumnavigated the globe, rolling forever around the Southern Ocean with no land to drain their power.

In New York and Boston, while the skippers of coastal craft relaxed and enjoyed the nice weather, the clipper fleet put to sea as fast as possible. The good season for the passage from New York to San Francisco grew short. Since the Creesys' return to the city aboard *Oneida,* nine additional clippers had set sail from Boston and New York headed for the Golden Gate, and more prepared to leave every day. At her berth at Pier 20 on South Street, at the foot of Maiden Lane, *Flying Cloud* swarmed with burly stevedores and longshoremen loading heavy casks and crates that contained the cargo and provisions. The men used the main yard as a derrick to lower everything into the expansive hold for proper stowing. The hooves of horses and the iron-rimmed wheels of drays clattered on the flagstones, mingling with the gruff curses of the men at work on the dock.

Just upriver the shipyards exhibited the hustle-bustle of the city as well. At the yard of William Webb, son of the man who had taught Donald McKay the basics of shipbuilding, the 2,006-ton, 230-foot clipper ship *Challenge* was launched to great fanfare on May 24. A rival of McKay, Webb built her to best *Flying Cloud* as the largest merchant vessel on earth and to outdo her in speed. On either side of *Challenge* were the slightly smaller *Comet* and *Invincible.* The skeletal frame of *Sword Fish* had begun to take shape as the process of planking proceeded. In Williamsburg, Brooklyn, *Eagle* and *John Stuart* also stood partly finished. More than ten thousand men worked in the New York yards, and many a common man found his family's standard of living greatly improved because of the clipper fever.

Day by day, *Flying Cloud*'s hold filled up. One third of her cargo space had been engaged prior to setting off from Boston, and in the intervening time the rest had quickly been snapped up at prices as high as sixty dollars per ton. Crates of crockery, tins of butter and cigars, bales of cotton, spools of twine, casks of flour, brandy, and whiskey, boxes of books, apples, rice, soap, cheese, candles, shovels, and boots, the cargo covered virtually every commodity likely to fetch a profit in San Francisco. At the completion of the loading, Perkins's freight list totaled 336 entries and amounted to $49,416.34 in costs to the shippers, about the same price Enoch Train had originally paid for *Flying Cloud*. In today's dollars, the freight costs equaled $900,000.

Taking on fresh water kept a dozen men busy pumping full the enormous cylindrical iron tank set abaft the mainmast on the keelson, where the weight least impacted the vessel's trim. *Flying Cloud*'s water tank held 4,800 gallons, and the ship carried seven casks that held 1,490 gallons more. In recent times, laws had been passed stipulating how much water a ship must carry for each passenger and member of the crew, among many other regulations. The sea, long a place where captains laid down the law according to their whims, now increasingly came under the laws of the landsmen, which some liberal-minded advocates deemed progress. Among them was Richard Henry Dana, famous for his account of a voyage to California first published in 1840 in his book *Two Years Before the Mast*. Conservative merchants and captains, however, considered the new laws a hindrance to the most efficient operation of a vessel.

A clipper the size of *Flying Cloud* required a crew of at least sixty men, good, sea-hardened Jacks able to climb the ratlines to the skysails in minutes to shorten sail in the thick of a nighttime blow. Men who knew how to handle the lines and sails of a full-rigged ship, men who could stand a long trick at the wheel and still keep a good course, these men made the difference between a fast passage and failure. The true Jack, the sailorman whom all captains prized, the man without fear or malice in his heart, these individuals had become all too rare along the waterfronts of Eastern cities.

The goldfields drew them in the thousands. Full of hopes for freedom and riches, they shipped out for California and deserted sometimes before the anchor was properly set in the bottom of San Francisco Bay. Captains occasionally clapped the crew in irons below to ensure enough hands remained to sail out of port, though this practice was soundly discouraged. Reports of mutinous acts, shootings, stabbings, desertions, drunken brawling, and plain laziness or incompetence among the sailors were surfacing more routinely, causing officers to break the tips off sailors' knives at the start of a voyage to prevent bloodshed. Even so, officers at times resorted to issuing orders with a pistol in one hand and the other a fist. The dedicated sailor with no desire to pan for gold had no trouble finding a berth. Demand for his services had never been higher.

Perkins combed the waterfront taverns for the best men he could find and encountered difficulty. He interviewed the steady stream of would-be crew come down to *Flying Cloud* to apply for a position, most of them not sailors at all but gold-seekers looking for a quick ride to the diggings. Gradually, despite the paucity of experienced, motivated sailors, he brought together a core of able-bodied seamen, ordinary seamen, and boys, numbering fifty-nine, plus four mates, the steward, and the cabin boy. The complement was sufficient to handle *Flying Cloud* under the worst conditions, when all hands must lay to the job with a will and with the know-how needed to accomplish it quickly and well.

In return for their work, the sailors earned an average monthly wage of just ten or twelve dollars. Out of this money they had to buy clothes for hot and cold conditions, foul-weather slickers and pants, seaboots, a wide-brimmed hat, a knife, and other gear for their outfit. They even supplied their own eating utensils, which amounted to a knife, a plate, and sometimes a fork. A sailor's sea chest or duffel bag contained very little, outside of the most basic possessions.

The captain of a clipper in the California trade, however, received an average of $3,000 for a voyage. At the height of his career, Captain Creesy earned $5,000 per voyage, plus bonuses for fast passages. He owned stock in companies in New York and California, as well as a share in *Flying Cloud*. In today's dollars, the captain's salary of $5,000 equals approximately $90,000; the pay of a sailor equals a little over $2,100 for a voyage of one year.

While Perkins hired the crew, Ellen busied herself with the ship's provisioning. The list of supplies covered many pages: salt beef and pork, flour, molasses, and peas, hams, roast mutton, salmon, crackers, vermicelli, tea, sardines, herring, cornmeal, lard, apples, sperm whale oil, onions, oysters, cocoa, oats, yams, castor oil, mustard, starch, butter. The stores eventually filled the pantry meant for the meals in the great cabin served to officers and passengers. She also ensured that enough livestock was brought aboard to enable the crew to eat fresh meat twice a week.

At night in their room at the Astor House, Ellen studied the latest wind and current charts from the Navy's National Observatory. These charts, relatively new in the shipping world, were the inspiration of Lieutenant Matthew Fontaine Maury. Maury compiled the charts based on data contained in thousands of logs from Navy ships and from merchant vessels. The charts provided navigators with graphic representations of the world's winds and currents and showed how the winds changed and shifted according to the month of the year in any given location on the ocean.

With an understanding of the wind patterns and calms and how to use them to advantage, it was possible to shave more than three weeks off a passage from New York to San Francisco. The charts were valuable, however, only if the navigator carefully adhered to Maury's directions whenever weather permitted. There were many captains, including Perkins, who doubted the accuracy of the charts and the science behind them, and he did not mind saying so to his wife. Ellen appreciated Maury's revolutionary thinking. It was the first time someone had applied scientific research and theory to practical navigation. As she read his newly published book, *Explanations and Sailing Directions to Accompany the Wind and Current Charts*, her faith in his conclusions grew stronger. Perkins, too, came to believe in Maury, at least enough to allow Ellen to follow his advice.

At long last, after weeks of hard work, the final steps prior to setting sail were at hand. The putting out to sea, like the coming in to port, had its own set of special routines, milestones to mark the progression of all the jobs required to make a ship right for the open ocean. When the ice cart clattered up to Pier 20 and the stevedores began unloading the huge blocks and stowing them on sawdust in the icehouse in *Flying Cloud's* 'tween decks, it signified the start of the voyage was not far off. Ellen's excitement increased markedly. She supervised the stowing of the ice, milk, eggs, cheese, fresh meats, cream, and vegetables, each in its place to stay cool or nearly frozen. With any luck, the most perishable of these provisions might last for over a month, even while the ship sailed through the tropical heat near the equator off the shoulder of Brazil.

The officers and crew and the last of the roosters, chickens, turkeys, ducks, pigs, and lambs came aboard on Sunday, June 1. At slack water when the tidal currents in the East River briefly diminished at the change of the tide, the men set to work pulling *Flying Cloud* away from the dock. They used large vertical winches called capstans and a series of heavy lines to drag her out into the river. It was tough work. The sailors placed a long bar into the top part of the capstan and pushed forward, backs straining under the load, as the rope turned around the winch's drum and the ship slowly inched backward.

The men had to act as one. Every move required coordination and timing. As they worked, they sang a sea chantey, and the rhythm of the chorus kept their efforts in unison. Their voices carried over the entire length of the ship and mingled with the city sounds ashore, the clap of hooves, the rumble of wheels, the hum of crowds. The sailor's song was as timeless a part of the sea as the cry of a gull or the roar of surf, and there was something comforting in it to Ellen. It reminded her of her freedom, the ability to sail to far-off locales and immerse herself for a time in a world completely different from her own.

As the crew heaved the ship backward away from the wharf, a light line attached to a hawser was rowed out to a steam tug waiting nearby. When the hawser was secure, the lines ashore were cast off and *Flying Cloud* floated in the river. The tug nudged her slowly to the anchorage off the Battery and faced her into the wind. Her starboard bower, an anchor weighing over three tons, dropped to the bottom and brought *Flying Cloud* to rest in the busy harbor. The crew, too, had a moment to relax, as was the custom on Sundays, a day of rest for the men, if conditions allowed.

The following day, June 2, a steam launch brought the eleven passengers out to the ship. They were all loaded down with luggage that somehow had to be stowed securely in their staterooms, which they had chosen when coming aboard in the last few weeks while engaging their passage. Those who knew better booked early and chose the staterooms as far forward and to the centerline of the vessel as possible, a position more stable than the rooms in the far aft portions of the cabins. Some of *Flying Cloud*'s passengers had done just that, and they were later quite happy in their foresight.

The accommodations on *Flying Cloud* were among the best available on any ship. Even the luxury packets sailing between New York and Europe were not superior. However, luxury was certainly a relative term. The aft section under the poop deck contained three separate cabins. On the main deck in front of the raised poop deck was a beautiful portico, a coachroof that provided shelter from the weather. Down through a door and a short stairway was the main area of the officers' quarters. A large table sat in the middle, and on either side were the staterooms for the officers and the steward and cabin boy.

Through another doorway headed toward the stern was the great cabin. This represented the essence of luxury, with its mahogany and rosewood bathed in the abundant natural light from the skylight above. There was an ornate sideboard in which the fine china and dinnerware were kept. In the center of the spacious room was the dinner table. Sandwiched between two staterooms on each side of the ship were richly upholstered settees ideal for reading or for quiet conversations. In the aftermost section were two small apartments, no bigger than the staterooms, and the latrines, known as "heads" aboard ship.

All but the captain's cabin and that of the first officer were each shared by two people, and they were small. They consisted of two bunks, each less than six feet long, fitted with preventers to keep the occupant from flying out when the ship rolled with the swells. There were some shelves and built-in drawers for clothing, and there was space for a sea chest. Fittings held the chest in place in heavy weather. The only natural light came from the portholes. On the whole, a stateroom was meant for sleeping and not much else. Passengers in want of a larger space for relaxing gathered in the great cabin or went out on deck.

The passengers were an interesting lot. Ellen had met many of them while she prepared for the voyage. Though she had not spent much time with any of them, there did seem a good mix of personalities. There was Sarah Bowman and her ten-year-old son, Edward. She was a well-to-do lady married to a fellow who had, like so many others, gone off to San Francisco to establish a retail business in the bustling city. A young man, also quite wealthy, by the name of J. D. Townsend was traveling for pleasure. He and a gentleman from Nantucket, a Mr. Laban Coffin, had booked passage for the entire voyage, just for the excitement of travel.

There was a rather flamboyant Italian, Francesco Wadsworth, quite handsome, and a studious, bookish young man named Willie Hall, both bound for the Golden Gate and the commercial opportunities that might await them. A lady of means, Mrs. Gorham, traveled with her maid, Pearl, and there were the Lyons, two sisters and a brother, bound for the West on business. Ellen Lyon was to be married when *Flying Cloud* arrived, and she expressed great excitement at the prospect. Sarah Lyon, the eldest, seemed to take on the role of their absentee mother. She was watchful of Ellen, and of her brother, Whitney.

Ellen could see excitement and a little anxiety on some of their faces. Most has never been to sea for such a long voyage, and *Flying Cloud* was a new, untested ship about to sail into the depths of winter in the Southern Ocean off Cape Horn. How would the ship sail? How would she respond to the force of a gale, the power of the waves? That *Flying Cloud* was to sail on a Monday was deemed lucky by many of the sailors. Sunday and Monday were the days of the week superstition considered fair for voyaging. Ellen was not a believer in all the sailor's lore, but nonetheless was aware of the positive impact the day had on the crew's outlook for the future.

Standing beside Perkins on the poop deck, Ellen gazed forward over the ship as the chief officer, Thomas Austin, hurried to the forecastle deck at the bow to supervise weighing anchor. Men took their stations at the windlass on the main deck while others, under the second and third mates, made ready to set sail. Perkins glanced at the pilot, who had just come aboard to guide *Flying Cloud* out of New York Harbor, and checked his watch. It was nearly two o'clock. He surveyed the water astern at the entrance of the East River and confirmed that the rips and eddies of the incoming rush of the flood tide had all but disappeared.

As captain, Perkins bore the full responsibility for the safety of the ship and all who sailed in her. He was without equal in authority as he went about the rough and hard business of sailing a clipper at her topmost speed. To help him carry out his duty was the first officer, whose primary role was to execute the captain's direct orders. But more was required of him than efficient obedience. Navigational skills, precision with numbers, an ability to keep good records—these were the characteristics shipowners looked for in a captain, and they expected the first officer to have them too. Aboard *Flying Cloud,* Thomas Austin was the only individual other than Captain Creesy to enjoy a private stateroom, a measure of his importance.

The second and third mates occupied a place just above the sailor, with the latter hardly distinguishable from the ordinary crewman. The fourth mate was the lowest mate of them all. The second and third mates, however, shared a room aft. Life as a less important officer still entailed comfortable quarters relative to the forecastle tucked up at the bow, as well as better pay and food. As second officer, Thomas Smith commanded one watch, consisting of half the crew, and as such he bore significant responsibilities when the ship was in his care. At any time, though, no change of consequence in the ship's course or what sails she set was permitted without consulting the captain first. Even Thomas Austin's rank as first officer did not empower him to make such decisions on his own.

Satisfied that the tide was fair for weighing anchor, Perkins addressed the pilot standing near the wheel. "We'll be getting under way. We've enough wind," he said, "and I'd like to get clear of Sandy Hook bar before dead low water."

The pilot nodded in agreement. "It'll be a passage down of some hours, I think," he said. "It's a fair wind, but weak. We'll have the current with us, but it will be slow just the same."

Perkins scowled and looked off to the west-northwest as if he could will the wind to come up into a stiff breeze, a breeze to send his ship to sea in all her glory. Puffs of air moving across the smooth water of the harbor formed cat's-paws, dark patches of ripples that identified the location of the wind, and the slicks of dead air. In the confines of the nearly landlocked upper harbor, the winds shifted about in baffling fashion. Once they were outside the harbor Perkins hoped there would be better wind.

"Haul short starboard bower, Mr. Austin," Perkins cried through his brass speaking trumpet.

"Haul short, aye, captain," Austin replied, and the men under his command began to work the windlass, a large horizontal winch situated close to the bow. With its immense leverage to aid them, the crew slowly hove in the heavy chain link by link until the cable ran straight down from the side of the vessel. The ship's bow pointed into the wind toward Jersey City, her stern toward the Brooklyn shore.

"Loose all sails!" Perkins yelled. With the wind light and the tide about to ebb, the ship could take full sail without danger. She would make a grand sight for those ashore, a grand sight indeed, he thought, looking over at his wife. Both of them savored the rare quality of the moment, a time they each would recall for the rest of their lives, the getting under way of *Flying Cloud* for the first time. It was like releasing a majestic eagle from the leathers holding its talons to the perch, and sending it out to soar in the heavens unfettered by the ordinary and the mundane.

Mixed with the excitement came the thrill and accompanying anxiety of knowing that the race against time began as soon as the anchor broke the surface of the water. Also, there had been no time for a shakedown cruise to test the vessel and get the crew into proper shape, each man knowing his station and duty. That was left for the maiden voyage. Any problems with the design or rig would quickly become obvious as the elements searched out weaknesses or flaws, as would problems stemming from the crew. Few things at sea were certain, but the ocean's ability to bring to light shortcomings of ship and crew came close. It could be counted on, and it added to the many other emotions that spun through the mind of a captain when a voyage commenced.

Ellen and Perkins were well aware of the wagers many of the gentlemen in the merchant and shipping trade put up in a complex betting network, and that, too, added to the subdued tension. Most common was the bet on how fast the ship made the trip from anchor to anchor over the entire route, the time measured in days and hours. There were subcategories as well. The clippers competed for the best time from New York to the equator, or "the line," as seamen called it, from the line to latitude 50 degrees south, from latitude 50 degrees south to the line on the Pacific side of South America, and from the line to San Francisco. Each of the four parts of the passage held different weather and navigational challenges. Ellen assiduously studied Maury's writings to familiarize herself with a path through the seas quite dissimilar to those on the run to China.

The China route relied on the monsoons to blow the ships back and forth across the Indian Ocean and the China Sea, just as mariners in those parts had done for centuries. Monsoons had their unpredictable elements, but for the most part they blew with a reassuring regularity in one direction, then the opposite way as the season changed. The California run, however, relied on the trade winds, and these were a little more crafty in nature. They tended to move north or south by the month. They varied in strength and direction depending on the season and the ship's location. Winds completely contrary to prevailing patterns were not altogether uncommon.

Although Ellen was familiar with the trade winds, and the calms between them known as the doldrums, this was the Creesys' first voyage on the California run and there remained much that was unknown. No two passages were ever identical. Ships even leagues apart experienced different localized weather—so much hovered in the realm of the unpredictable. The weight of their shared responsibilities manifested in them a nagging presence that remained for the duration of the voyage.

Sailors aloft fanned out on the yards and released the gaskets holding the canvas tight, and the sails immediately fell out of folds like massive, spanking-new white curtains. The men in the tops scurried down on deck, and together the crew hoisted up the heavy yards extending the canvas to full length, shivering and shaking in the wind. Ranged in lines at the pin rails, the decks awash in snake-like coils and bights of rope, the crew sheeted home the topsails, topgallants, royals, and skysails, heaving in time to a double-pull chantey.

The chanteyman's talents usually included an innate ability to emerge as a leader among the forecastle hands very early in a voyage. One had already emerged to lead the men. He sang out the solo of an old, favorite song known to most seamen. He improvised, sometimes quite amusingly, on the lines.

"A Yankee ship came down the river . . ."

In one voice the crew sang out and pulled in unison on the first and third words of the chorus: "Blow, boys, blow."

"Her masts and spars they shine like silver," the chanteyman sang.

"Blow, my bully boys. Blow!"

When all the sails were raised and hove into proper shape, Perkins bellowed through his speaking trumpet, "Brace all aback forward and all full aft for the starboard tack! Heave free the anchor!"

He ordered the man at the helm to steer the ship to the left as the men at the windlass worked with a will, their voices carrying their work song out over the harbor. With the hard upward pull from the windlass and the lateral force from the bow moving to the left, the flukes of the anchor lifted from the black ooze on the harbor bottom. From the forecastle Austin shouted, "Captain. She's aweigh!"

Flying Cloud's bow paid off, bringing the wind more on her starboard, or right side. The three headsails were set and the spanker was hauled out to help put her on course and gather way. The yards on the foremast suddenly braced with those of the main and mizzen, and the sails filled with a series of loud snaps as one after another billowed into proper shape. Slowly, the ship gathered speed and wove a path through the dozens of small craft, schooners, steam ferries, and large merchant ships at anchor and under sail. Up forward, Austin supervised catting the anchor and securing it to the timberheads for the open sea.

Flying Cloud ghosted along the west side of Governors Island and briefly obscured the fortress at the northern end on her way past. Her black hull appeared buried under a cliff of canvas and contrasted well against the white fore, main, and mizzen masts, the varnished natural wood of the spars above, white at the doublings where the masts overlapped. Her black yards tapered thin at the ends gave her a clean, shipshape look aloft. Her figurehead, a white angel on the wing with a gilded speaking trumpet held at the ready, pointed toward the sea, seeming almost to take flight and sound a blast of exuberance for all the world to hear. Only the narrow channels of the lower harbor stood in *Flying Cloud*'s way, the last gauntlet to run before the embrace of the sea took her and all aboard into the unknown beyond the horizon to the east.

Chapter 6

The west-northwest breeze picked up when *Flying Cloud* cleared the lee of the Verrazano Narrows and Staten Island and moved beyond the long spit of Sandy Hook. The pilot safely discharged, the crew scrambled aloft to set the studdingsails. Dozens of men moved nimbly along the yards. Supported by sturdy footropes, they ran out the studdingsail booms, hoisted them in place, and set the sails with the array of lines, the halyards, downhauls, sheets, and tacks. *Flying Cloud*'s lowest studdingsails spread more than forty feet beyond either side of the ship, far enough to catch the tops of the waves when she rolled in rough seas. From the topsails to the royals, she spread canvas enough to slightly lift her bow. With the wind dead aft as the vessel made her way boldly out to sea on an east-southeasterly course, the waves washed in under the transom and imparted a gentle roll.

The purple hills of the Highlands of Navesink and the long, low smudge of blue along the south shore of Long Island gradually faded astern, until the very last of the land dropped below the curve of the earth. The sea and sky merged into an inky expanse off the bow. In the diminishing light, minute by minute, the red lantern fixed to the port fore shrouds and its green counterpart to the starboard grew brighter, like eyes opening to the coming night. The dull yellow glow of oil lamps illuminated the windows of the deckhouse and shone onto the poop deck through the open skylight. Up forward, the silhouettes of sailors off watch, smoking their pipes and talking quietly, appeared now and then in the open doors of the forecastle.

The watches chosen after the ship settled under way divided the men equally under the chief officer, who took the larboard, and the second mate, who took the starboard. At eight o'clock, the quick double ping of the ship's brass bell sounded out in four sets of two rings. Eight bells signaled the end of the dog watch and the start of the night watch from eight o'clock to midnight. As was the custom, the able-bodied seaman chosen among the crew to stand the first two-hour trick at the wheel walked briskly aft to take his place at the helm. Once the helmsman was relieved, the larboard watch could go below. The sailors of the starboard watch emerged from the forecastle, and for a few moments all hands moved about in a cycle that was to repeat itself a thousand times over the next few months, the changing of the watch every four hours.

On a pleasant evening, the night watch passed easily. The helmsman held the ship on course, the lookouts kept an alert watch at the bow. The rest of the men were able to curl up on a coil of line, wedge themselves against the windlass, or find a spot out of the wind in the lee of the deckhouse near the coops, sties, and pens. The practice was not condoned, but more or less winked at. But let the man on watch not see a ship's lights before the chief or second officer, and that sailor would receive a severe reprimand. Aft on the weather side of the poop deck, Thomas Smith, the second mate, leaned against the taffrail and gazed up at the sails to assure himself that they drew fair. The man at the helm peered into the dimly lit binnacle at the compass, keeping Ellen's course. The wheel pulled as the ship rolled and danced with the following sea, the fair wind hurrying them away from home at an average speed of nearly eight knots.

In the great cabin below, a steady flow of cool air entered through the skylight and the portico leading to the weather deck.

The wind carried the last hints of the land, as if to drive home the point that the passengers' world had suddenly changed from an ordinary day-to-day routine ashore to a sort of suspended animation until the ship reached port once more. The steward and the cabin boy, a young Chinese named Ching, served brandy or wine to those who wanted it. Laban Coffin sat with Willie Hall and Mrs. Gorham, nursing their drinks in crystal glasses and swapping stories at the table. Others read alone on the settees under the light of gimbaled lamps.

Several passengers retired early to their staterooms, down with *mal de mer*, the polished tin pails held near, the latrines too far in the event the motion of the vessel won out over their desire to keep their dinners down. Ellen ordered the steward to bring around weak tea and crackers, which the sufferers accepted hesitantly. Among the most miserable was Whitney Lyon. Ellen sat with him for a few moments, then moved on to check on Edward, a likable boy traveling to San Francisco with his mother, Sarah Bowman, to join his stepfather, Charles.

Although Ellen knew little about the passengers, it struck her that most of the women were sailing to join their husbands or to marry, as was the case with Whitney's younger sister. Most had not seen their loved ones in years. The men had followed the gold fever early and instead of heading for the diggings they set up businesses from Portland to San Francisco, even in the Sandwich Islands. For their ladies left behind, the voyage represented the last in a long series of waits. The wait for letters turned into the wait for their arrival at the Golden Gate, a far more difficult proposition. Every mile brought them closer to their new lives and fueled their anticipation.

Ellen gave the passengers her time and ministrations gladly, seeing her role aboard as more than just that of the navigator. Hers was a balancing act, playing hostess, nurse, and wife, depending on what hat was needed at a particular time. As the ship's nurse, over the years she had tended to fevers, toothaches, rope burns, scalds, and broken or crushed fingers. A ship could do a lot of damage to a body, and yet most merchant ships sailed without anyone endowed in the least with medical knowledge and skills. To Ellen, it made no sense to sail without making some provision for dealing with the sick or injured. Whether required or not, Ellen determined to learn enough to do some good. She studied and mastered the basics of medicine, enough to get by. Her abilities and kind bedside manner won her respect among the crew and the passengers.

The presence of passengers was a relatively new experience for Ellen. Few people traveled to China for business or pleasure, which made it rare for anyone but officers and crew to be aboard *Oneida*. The California run was different. Many people wanted to get to San Francisco, and demand for the limited space aboard the clippers was high. Passage on a clipper from New York to San Francisco averaged two hundred dollars, but despite the demand it still cost about half the amount of steamship fares for travel to the Golden Gate via the Isthmus of Panama. The clipper fare was cheaper because of the duration of the voyage and because sail power was less expensive than steam.

Of the five women and six men shipped aboard *Flying Cloud* as passengers, none were of the gold-seeking lot. Working as teachers, shopkeepers, or clerks, or starting their own businesses, the passengers represented the class of folk that would build the nation. All of them would know each other well before *Flying Cloud* sailed into San Francisco Bay, and the knowledge, she hoped, would be a pleasure, rather than something to endure.

Of the three main routes to California—Cape Horn, overland, and Panama—the passengers had chosen the longest way in terms of miles. The passage around the tip of South America was dangerous. Ships sometimes disappeared, an occurrence that drove home the inherent risks involved when sailing sixteen thousand miles through some of the worst oceans on earth. There was also the problem of living packed together in close quarters for nearly four months. During the long voyage the tiny staterooms closed in on the passengers. Every day was a copy of the last, with the same faces at the dinner table uttering the same stories and jokes. The tedium aboard a clipper could eat away at the most sanguine personality. However, the sea offered an assurance of decent food, a berth to sleep in, little fear of disease, and no likelihood of dying from an Indian attack or starvation. The benefits of traveling aboard a clipper outweighed the liabilities, though when the gales of the Southern Ocean raged, many travelers reconsidered the merits of their choice.

The overland route provided no assurances for relative safety and comfort. In late winter and early spring, settlers rode trains and coaches to Midwestern frontier towns like St. Joseph and Independence, Missouri, which served as staging areas for the westward migration. Starting the journey from halfway across the country meant only about fifteen hundred miles stood between the settler and the California coast, but those miles were tough. Long trains of Conestoga-like wagons, known as prairie schooners, crossed the Great Plains, the Rocky Mountains, the vast desert wastelands of Nevada, and finally the Sierra Nevada to reach San Francisco. The trip from the Midwest to California took four to six months. Traveling fifteen miles a day was considered good. Most maps labeled the broad expanse of land between the Mississippi River west to the Rockies as the Great American Desert, for it was largely unexplored territory, untamed and potentially lethal to cross.

There were other overland routes to the south that drew a smaller number of settlers. These travelers took the Santa Fe Trail, with its shortcut through the furnace of Death Valley three hundred feet below sea level. Many never made it out alive. Still others took steamships to Veracruz and rode horses across Mexico to reach the west coast at Mazatlán. From Mazatlán on the mainland just east of Cabo San Lucas at the tip of the Baja peninsula it was an easy steamship passage up the coast to the Golden Gate. The Mexicans were not very welcoming to the Americans. They remembered well their recent defeat at the hands of the United States Army. As a consequence, the Mexicans demanded a hefty price for goods and services, and occasionally bandits robbed and killed the gold-seekers long before they made it to the Pacific Ocean.

The sixty-mile route across the Isthmus of Panama promised the swiftest passage. It also entailed a Faustian arrangement with unscrupulous boatmen and mule drivers, innkeepers, city officials, and steamship ticket clerks, all of whom conspired to make the trip as costly as possible. Malaria, yellow fever, dengue fever, and cholera thrived in the steamy jungle, thick and dark under an impenetrable canopy. Disease killed thousands of the Irish, Chinese, and Africans building the railroad across the isthmus, which was completed in 1855.

In particularly bad years during the gold rush, thousands died en route to or from Panama in steamship explosions, in storms, from disease, and in crossing the isthmus. The isthmus route required riding a steamer from New York and other ports to the mouth of the Chagres River. There the traveler embarked on a frightening trip in a dugout canoe, known as a bongo, through the dense jungle, paddling and poling in the muddy shallows against the river's swift current. At the head of navigation, the traveler walked or rode a mule for the remaining miles to Panama City, where the wait for a steamer from the Pacific Mail Steamship Company commenced. Travelers often lingered for weeks before starting on the last leg of 3,500 miles up the coast to San Francisco. Forty days was considered a fast passage on the isthmus route for both passengers and mail.

By June 1851, the full force of the year's migration was on the move over the various routes to California. The wagon trains stretched for miles on the trails across the Great American Desert, the dugout canoes penetrated the jungles of Panama, and the clippers sailed southward across an empty sea. For the passengers aboard *Flying Cloud*, the first night offshore represented a jump into a new environment vastly different from the one left behind. Ellen knew it took some getting used to. However, she expected the passengers soon to become accustomed to the motion of the ship and find their sea legs, acquiring a bit of the sailor's gait, if only temporarily, as the days stretched into weeks and months.

Satisfied all was well below, Ellen draped a shawl over her shoulders and climbed the stairs to join Perkins on the poop deck. While below with the passengers, Ellen was aware of the muffled clatter of blocks, the snap of lines, the shout of orders. She knew these noises well and paid them little heed. But as soon as she emerged from the companionway onto the weather deck she saw the yards braced to catch the southwest wind that had come up, blowing just right to fully power the sails. The ship appeared to have picked up speed, something she would take into account when deducing the ship's position through dead reckoning before she went to bed.

"The wind still favors us, I see," she said quietly.

Perkins nodded. "I've whistled for more. We'll see if it comes in fresh."

With the wind blowing toward the ship nearly broadside on, it filled every sail. It was coming in off the beam, as the sailors said. The square sails, jibs, staysails, and spanker pulled hard against the masts. The aerodynamic forces at work created lift and forward motion as the wind blew on the back side of the sails and through the slots between them, exerting thrust in perfect harmony with the motion of the clipper. She glided through the water almost silently, a gentle heel to port exposing some of her copper sheathing, already stained a dull green patina from oxidation in the salt water. The earlier west-northwest wind from dead aft lacked the lift of the current point of sail. It pushed against the canvas, masts, and spars, and literally pulled the ship through the water. The foresails, staysails, and jibs filled and emptied, intermittently robbed of the wind's steady influence in the blanket of sails behind them.

"The crew did well bringing her out today," he said.

"It's good to see so many able-bodied seamen among them. You did well in choosing, Perkins. I imagine *Flying Cloud* will be something to handle in a blow. We'll need a good crew."

"She'll be a handful. But see how she sails!" Perkins ran his hand over his beard and looked aloft. He began to whistle quietly as he gave the taffrail an affectionate pat.

Ellen laughed. Every sailor knew that to whistle aboard a ship while moving through the water invited a blow to tear through. Should the ship find an obstinate calm that seemed intent upon a long stay some captains lined their crews up on the main deck to whistle in unison, favoring a hatful of wind to lying dead in the water rolling to the swells. Another superstition held that heaving the captain's old shoe overboard might end a calm.

There were many worries about the supernatural among the sailors. A playful black cat on the pier just before sailing foretold a storm. It was thought there was a gale in a black cat's tail. Cats in general were not welcome aboard ships. The sailors believed them to be closely associated with witches. They preferred to have a dead body in the hold, which in itself aroused deep anxiety. It was thought the dead brought bad luck to all the ship's company. Cats, however, were worse, since they embodied the evil of the world. That they ate the ship's rats and thus kept the vessel from infestation did not enter the minds of the sailors. But nobody ever accused Jack of being smart or logical. The men before the mast were derided among officers as having strong backs and weak heads, and they were treated like peasants.

Ellen did not take these old superstitions to heart. She was too scientific and rational in her thinking to put much credence in the supernatural. She saw the world through a modern lens and sought clarity through knowledge. But she knew Perkins harbored just a hint of belief in the unseen. She, too, at times, humbled at the majesty of the sea, felt reaffirmed in the notion that there was something greater than humanity, a force both beautiful and ugly. There was more than pure science and logic.

Ellen smiled. She remembered the many times aboard *Oneida* when there had been wind enough to lay the rail under, and Perkins still whistled for more wind. He expected it to come in fresh and strong at the bidding of a whistle, as if nature could be trained. They sat together on those long voyages playing chess on the poop deck, the vessel sailing fast, the rigging humming, and the spray flying. There were few times when they were more content.

"You'll have your wind, darling," she said. "It's only a matter of time."

They fell silent and lingered close together, each lost in thought. They were quite alone, except for the helmsman. In deference to the captain, and in keeping with the custom, Smith left the poop deck when Perkins came topside. He found a comfortable place in the ship's waist, where he could observe the crew, the sails, and the beauty of the stars. When the captain and Mrs. Creesy went below for the night, Smith returned to the poop deck. He passed time in solitary contemplation until the larboard watch turned to and Austin relieved him.

Chapter 7

Through the night, *Flying Cloud* sailed ever eastward out across the shallow, gently sloping continental shelf. She reached the last vestiges of North America, the thousand-fathom line, at dawn. The seafloor continued to drop precipitously away below the keel in a series of downward steps that formed huge undersea bluffs cut through with a network of ancient canyons. The great depths imparted a new look to the color of the ocean. The murky, gray-green waters off the coast, dotted with hundreds of fishing craft, gave way to the bottomless blue of offshore waters turned almost azure from the Gulf Stream's tropical influence. No sails broke the horizon in shining peaks of white. Only the vast, smooth surface of the sea met the eyes of those aboard. Alight as it was with the reflection of the sun in a sprinkle of diamonds, it struck Ellen as quite beautiful.

The wind diminished with the rising sun and shifted to the northwest. The ship slowed, until she loped along at only six knots. Though the surface of the sea appeared as polished as black ice, it moved and heaved, in no way solid, or inert. A swell piled up. The northward-flowing Gulf Stream opposed the northwesterly wind. Such a wind, if it blew hard, would kick up nasty waves that rose and fell without seeming to move forward in normal fashion for wind-driven crests. They more resembled the standing waves in a stretch of river white water than the long, organized wave trains found in midocean, and they represented a far greater danger.

But no threat of a big wind emerged throughout the day, nor did it materialize on June 4, their third calendar day at sea. In the absence of a steady breeze, the sails flapped, slatted, and boomed against the masts, a noisy and irritating fact of life aboard the clipper during a calm or in light air. Ellen observed the slow rise of tension in Perkins as the hours of fickle wind stretched on. He paced the poop deck, hands behind his back, and looked up at the sails every few minutes, then off to the northwest, a wistful gleam in his eye.

Ellen understood his impatience. She felt it herself. Every hour counted in each and every day. She needed to turn every wind shift, favorable current, and navigational shortcut to full advantage for *Flying Cloud* to beat *Surprise*'s run of ninety-six days, an eventuality that many ashore in New York and Boston hoped for the ship and her captain. Little did it matter that *Surprise* had sailed during a more favorable season. Seasonal variations in wind patterns eluded most people's level of comprehension. They preferred to match ships and captains without regard to the time they sailed. It was simply easier that way.

The passengers remained oblivious to their captain's dark mood. The fine weather provided ample opportunity for them to ascend from their staterooms to enjoy the sun and balmy air on deck. They lounged in comfortable upholstered chairs reading magazines and novels, sketching, sewing, telling stories, or gazing at the sea waiting for the next meal to break the monotony. All but one or two of them had overcome their seasickness, and in general the spirit of the ship impressed Ellen as peaceful. Friendships had already begun to form. The social intricacies of life aboard ship proved fascinating to watch as they unfolded.

The Italian from New York, Francesco Wadsworth, a very dashing, rather highly dressed fellow, entertained them with his pleasing voice, singing out snippets of Italian operas. He told outlandish stories of fighting duels, being presented to Queen Victoria, and other tall tales he swore were true. His flamboyance matched with

the arrogance of J. D. Townsend, a young man of nineteen sufficiently well off to have booked passage for the pleasure of it and
sufficiently devoid of manners to brag about it. He, too, was full of
stories few aboard believed, but they listened attentively just the
same. His stories helped pass the time, and he seemed not to know
or care that his shipmates regarded him with incredulity.

The demure and very pretty Mrs. Gorham, traveling with her
maid, was bound out West to reunite with her husband. She was all
smiles and very kind, though there was a quiet side to her as well.
She came to dinner dressed as if she were at a formal ball, with
long, full evening gowns, her figure confined in a tight corset. Her
Irish maid, Pearl, joked about her lady's high tastes when she was
not about.

Sarah Bowman was the eldest of the passengers, though she was
only in her early thirties. She had seen something of the world, had
been married to a Southern gentleman of means who had died and
left her with a son to take care of. Edward was a bright young boy,
very amusing, and a delight for Ellen. Edward found himself
befriended by all aboard. The crew, and in particular the second
mate, Thomas Smith, took a liking to him and allowed him free
run of the ship, even the rare privilege of climbing aloft. For the
sailors, having a child aboard was a good omen for a safe voyage. It
was thought that no child was born to die at sea, and by extension
the ship's company would fare well through the worst of storms.
His mother expressed concern about the rough language of the
men, but perhaps unwisely took her son's word that they did not
swear in his presence.

In sharp contrast to the passengers and their leisure, the crew lay
to the multitude of ship's chores. Among the worst, Perkins
ordered the standing rigging checked and tarred down where
needed. Lashed to the stays, a bucket of warm tar slung near, the
crewman dipped his hands into the gooey mess and lathered up the
thick ropes, taking great care not to let even a drop fall to the deck
below. Among other duties, the sailors slushed down the masts
with grease to ensure that the yards were easy to raise and lower.

They unwound old ropes, known as junk, and spun it into yarns to use in a wide assortment of functions.

In his book *Two Years Before the Mast,* Richard Henry Dana tried to dispel the false impression of landsmen that the sailor's life was easy. He provided a concise description of how busy a sailor was at sea, and of his own surprise at the amount of labor required of him when he started as a neophyte on his voyage to California in the mid-1830s.

It may be well to define a day's work, and to correct a mistake prevalent among landsmen about a sailor's life. Nothing is more common than to hear people say: "Are not sailors very idle at sea?—What can they find to do?" This is a very natural mistake, and being very frequently made, it is one which every sailor feels interested in having corrected. In the first place, then, the discipline of the ship requires every man to be at work upon *something* when he is on deck, except at night and on Sundays. Except at these times, you will never see a man on board a well-ordered vessel standing idle on deck, sitting down, or leaning over the side. It is the officers' duty to keep everyone at work, even if there is nothing to be done but to scrape the rust from the chain cables. In no state prison are the convicts more regularly set to work, and more closely watched. No conversation is allowed among the crew at their duty, and though they frequently do talk when aloft, or when near one another, yet they always stop when an officer is nigh.

With regard to the work upon which the men are put, it is a matter which probably would not be understood by one who has not been at sea. When I first left port and found that we were kept regularly employed for a week or two, I supposed that we were getting the vessel into sea trim, and that it would soon be over and we should have nothing to do but to sail the ship; but I found that it continued so for two years, and at the end of the two years there was as much to be done as ever. As has often been said, a ship is like a lady's watch, always out of repair.

Ellen's first established position on June 3 put them 164 miles from New York City, an acceptable distance over the first twenty-

one hours of the voyage. By noon on June 4 the ship had progressed only 145 miles from Ellen's previous fix, a pace equal to
that of an old-time merchantman. However, in the shifty winds
such a bad sailer would have sat dead in the water while the clipper
continued to ghost. *Flying Cloud* crossed the Gulf Stream at dusk,
the demarcation zone between the cold inshore water and the tepid
stream clearly defined both by color and by the chop. In the
predawn glow of another glorious day the wind abruptly shifted
from the west-northwest to come in fresh from the northwest
again, off the left side of the stern. It was an excellent wind angle
for the clipper.

The officer on watch ordered the helmsman to change course
temporarily to keep the wind blowing evenly into the sails. He set
the crew to bracing the yards smoothly around to give a full spread
of canvas to the wind as the helmsman brought her back on course.
On the poop deck, crewmen eased the spanker sheet, and the fifty-
three-foot boom at the bottom edge of the sail swung well out over
the water on the right-hand side of the ship. The triangular staysails
and jibs pulled harder. The quiet of just moments past vanished.
With the gentle wash of the bow wave, the gurgle and swish of the
sea as it hissed under the stern, and the hum of the running rigging
stretched tight, the ship bounded forward into the new day.

The first arrival of the northwesterly fanned the surface of the
ocean into a darkened swath of ripples. In the dim gray light, its
passage across the smooth areas of dead air passed like a curtain,
blotting out the reflections of the stars. As the wind freshened,
waves built. As they grew larger and began to break, the rising sun
caught their endless collapses in flashes of aquamarine, white, and
black. They rolled toward *Flying Cloud* in disorderly patterns.
Groups of larger seas sprang up to sprinkle the poop deck, the
crests murmuring harmlessly under her.

Gradually, as the day progressed the northwesterly settled in on
a slow gathering of gusty strength. The sustained velocities climbed
beyond twenty-five knots, and the sea accordingly roughened up
into an expanse of whitecaps made all the more confusing by the
influence of the Gulf Stream. Powerful blasts of wind buffeted the

waves into chaos, flattening the tops at times. The masts groaned and creaked under the stress and the slender tips bent slightly forward at the skysails. The windward shrouds drew taut and stretched, leaving those to leeward slack. As the gust passed, the rig relaxed under the lighter loads, and so the cycle went from lull to full fury.

Ellen and Perkins basked in the sheer spectacle of it all. The incredible forces at work for the first time on the sails, the masts and spars, and the hull awakened a side of *Flying Cloud* neither had yet experienced. Though they each held high hopes for her as a speedy sailer, the reality of it remained beyond confirmation without a sea trial. The ship's bow lifted, pointing to the puffy white clouds, and settled moments later in the trough, pushing aside a wedge of foam that ran in streaks down the hull to merge with the wake.

"She's magnificent," Ellen said, her voice full of emotion. "She's doing at least nine knots, more in the gusts."

Perkins laughed. "McKay is a wizard. A wizard! Imagine what she'll do with a real wind at her heels."

Flying Cloud surged forward under the force of another strong gust and heeled sharply to starboard. The tips of the lee studdingsail booms sliced through the tops of the waves. The edges of the sails scooped green water, momentarily increasing the strain on the booms, fittings, and lines. Showers of water poured down the length of the booms and flew forward, riding the wind.

Ellen knew Perkins gave no thought to taking in a stitch of canvas. This was no storm. Just a good, fine clipper breeze. The thrill of seeing the ship sail so well instilled in her a deep sense of confidence in the vessel. Just the same, Ellen knew equally well that McKay had sparred *Flying Cloud* with the tallest rig he could get away with. He had no certain means of telling how high he could go without risking the ship's integrity, and in this he was not alone. Her husband had no better idea of how much *Flying Cloud* could stand than McKay.

Ellen had come on deck to prepare for the last of her morning observations, the noon sun sight to determine the ship's latitude.

She wedged herself tightly in the lee shrouds, the four-pound sextant in her right hand, her left hand free to manipulate the instrument when she was ready to take the sight. Perkins stood by with a timepiece ready to note the precise time and the measurements Ellen read from the sextant when she completed her observation.

Ellen began taking sights a few minutes before estimated local noon, the time the sun reached its highest point in the sky. This differed from noon local zone time set on the ship's clock. The sun could, and often did, reach its highest point at times other than noon local zone time. It was just another of the many complicating factors she had to take into account. She steadied herself as best as she could and sighted the horizon just below the sun through the eye-protecting shades of the index mirror. With her left hand, she moved the mirror to catch the image of the sun and brought the reflection down until the lower edge of the orb kissed the horizon. She fine-tuned the reading as she swung the sextant through a short arc to obtain the minimum reading that occurred when the sextant was perpendicular to the horizon.

"Mark!" she said firmly.

Perkins noted the time and the measurements as she read them from the markings on the sextant. Ellen repeated the process until her sextant readings reached the highest point for the sun's altitude and began to descend, indicating with certainty the passage of the sun over their meridian and its subsequent steady setting to the west. Down below at the table in the officers' cabin, she worked through her calculations and corrections to find their current latitude.

Latitude provided Ellen with a position either north or south of the equator in degrees and minutes, with one minute being equal to one nautical mile. Longitude provided a position east or west from the prime meridian that ran through Greenwich, England, and that was marked as zero. Ellen recorded *Flying Cloud*'s position in reference to the ship's latitude in degrees and minutes equal to the distance north or south from the equator, and, in terms of longitude, east or west of Greenwich, also in degrees and minutes. It was possible to break the position down to seconds, but in practice, celestial navigation in Ellen's day assured accuracy only to within an average of five nautical miles.

Based on her observations taken earlier in the day and their most current latitude, Ellen was able to plot *Flying Cloud's* position on the chart. She advanced the lines obtained from her two earlier observations forward in time to noon. The two lines intersected at an angle. Combined with her latitude, the lines formed a triangle. She knew *Flying Cloud* was somewhere inside it and could thus come up with the ship's latitude and longitude. Later in the day she took additional observations and advanced her noon latitude to get a new running fix. In this way, so long as there were no clouds obscuring the heavens, she could accurately track the ship's progress along the desired course. If the sky was not visible, she relied on dead reckoning.

In Ellen's time, it required hours of intense concentration to break an observation down and convert the resulting information into something useful. She typically filled a large sheet of paper with figures just to work out a single sight. Later advances perfected celestial navigational techniques, and the compilation of sight reduction tables streamlined the procedures, reducing the time required to work out a sight to mere minutes rather than hours. The improved techniques and the advent of modern sight reduction tables made it possible for a person with limited math skills to navigate with a sextant, but only highly skilled practitioners with years of experience could do it in the days of *Flying Cloud*.

Perkins leaned close over Ellen's shoulder as she went through her figures and plotted their position. When she finished, she looked up at him. "Two hundred twenty-eight miles from noon to noon."

He grinned and examined the chart. By Ellen's plot the ship was about 270 miles due north of Bermuda. For the next several days no major course changes would be necessary. According to Maury's sailing directions, *Flying Cloud* must sail east-southeast to a longitude of 40 degrees west before turning south for the run down to South America. Ellen worked out her courses to take them to the designated spot.

The northwester blew fresh all night into the morning of June 6, rushing *Flying Cloud* along. The steady rumble of water at the bow lulled the starboard watch to sleep in the forecastle, the easy rise and fall of the bow a further inducement to slumber. Occasionally, *Flying Cloud* buried her bow deep and sent patters of spray over the forecastle deck. The rigging moaned in the higher gusts as the wind continued to build. It was a low, haunting sound that never remained consistent in tone or duration, but wavered in and out of mind as one alternately became aware of it and dismissed the auditory presence.

At noon, Ellen found *Flying Cloud* had made good a run of 298 miles. Ellen and Perkins beamed at each other with pride. For the last twenty-four hours the ship had averaged a speed of twelve and a half knots, faster than most vessels afloat. Since their departure five days ago, *Flying Cloud* had sailed 830 miles to the east-southeast. In the last two days, the clipper had matched or exceeded the best speeds of the steamers in the transatlantic fleet.

In the early 1850s, clipper ships were the fastest vessels in the world. But steam power, particularly on the three-thousand-mile transatlantic run between New York and Liverpool, was starting to show great promise. Like the owners and captains of the swift clippers, those with a financial interest in the steamships cruising on regular schedules back and forth across the rough waters of the North Atlantic pushed for speed. Fortunes were to be made by the men with the fastest ships, whether driven by sail or steam.

In 1840, a Nova Scotian named Samuel Cunard put the first efficient and well-run transatlantic steamship line into operation. He had won a lucrative subsidy from the British Admiralty to start his enterprise with the express purpose of carrying mail between England, British North America (Canada), and the United States. Cunard began with four nearly identical ships 207 feet in length and displacing two thousand tons, a shade more than *Flying Cloud*. These ships cruised at eight knots, and though they got passengers to their destinations faster than might be possible on a sailing packet, the ride was anything but comfortable.

The hiss and rumble of the engines was ever present. The noise blocked out the sounds of the sea one heard under sail. Smoke poured from the stack and covered everything above decks with a fine layer of soot. When large waves hit the ship broadside on, the paddle wheels rose clear of the water to churn the air, creating a frightening din. At such times the helmsman momentarily lost control of the ship. Many passengers stepped ashore vowing never to put to sea in a steamer again.

The comfort of the passengers was considered secondary in importance to making a fast passage. Speed was everything. There were attempts at luxury in the saloons, warm with the glow of finished hardwoods and gilded trim, furnished with comfortable upholstered chairs, brass lamps, and Oriental carpets. But for the most part the accommodations were spartan. Author Charles Dickens remarked that on a voyage aboard *Britannia,* one of the first Cunard liners, his stateroom was an "utterly . . . profoundly preposterous box," so small that the odds better favored persuading "a giraffe . . . into a flower pot" than stowing his wife's baggage inside. Conditions were often so rough men gave up trying to shave during the passage.

After several failed attempts, the United States fielded its own fleet of steamships, beginning in 1850. These were the steamers of Cunard's arch rival, Edward Knight Collins. The Collins liners were larger than Cunard's, at over 280 feet and displacing close to three thousand tons. They were also more comfortable and much faster. Although Cunard's ships were capable of cruising at ten knots by 1850, the Collins liners routinely cruised at thirteen knots. Captains drove hard even when faced with headwinds and waves that sent spray flying over the entire length of the ship. Running full ahead in storms resulted in frequent damage.

While the clippers raced against each other around Cape Horn, British and American steamships raced each other across the North Atlantic, and it was quite a fierce competition. Passage times were recorded down to the minute. It was possible by early 1851 for a steamship to cross the Atlantic in just ten days, something previously unheard of. In 1852, *Baltic,* a Collins liner, became the first mail ship to sail from Liverpool to New York in nine days, thirteen hours. Her record on that westbound crossing remained unbroken for a dozen years.

Despite the clipper boom, shipbuilders were starting to see increased demand for steamships. One of the leading builders in New York, William H. Brown, who had built two of the big liners for Edward Knight Collins, ranked among the richest men in the city, in large part because he saw merit in steam and pursued it. Steamships were still primarily made of wood, but iron ships were also in operation in the 1850s. Iron, then steel replaced wood, because metal allowed larger and larger ships to be built. The same progression occurred with sailing vessels. In addition, the screw propeller began replacing the cumbersome side wheels as a means of propulsion. Improvements in engine technology increased the fuel efficiency of the steam engine, reducing the amount of coal required to fire the boilers.

While the steamships were capturing ever more of the transatlantic trade, the sailing packets serving the same routes were doing a brisk business as well. They carried freight on the eastbound runs from New York to Liverpool and other ports. On the return trip, the ships' holds were crammed with immigrants fleeing famine in Ireland and economic and political unrest on the European continent. An immigrant paid twenty dollars for a place in steerage. Many died in the crowded, unsanitary conditions in the hold—so many, in fact, that the old packets were known as "coffin ships."

The early days of the sailing packets began in 1818 when the Black Ball line started providing regular service between New York City and Liverpool. The average passage eastward took twenty-three days, and the passage back against the westerly winds took forty. In 1851, the average westbound passage, the rougher and more difficult leg of the trip, still took approximately thirty-five days under sail. In fact, the actual sailing time for packets on the transatlantic route in the early 1850s went up, not down, because most of the vessels were getting old and could not be driven as hard as when new.

The luxury steamships had already surpassed the sailing packets in the best part of the transatlantic trade by 1851. Although the packets were to hang on for many more years, their decline was steady and sure. Nevertheless, it was easy to ignore the progress that the emergence of the steamship represented, particularly with regard to the clipper ships, which were nearing the peak of their supremacy on the high seas at hauling freight long distances. The grand sight of a clipper spoke to the romantic side of human nature. The utility of the steamer did not. Most people along the waterfront failed to see the demise of the American clipper ship coming. It was not far off, though, only six years in the future as *Flying Cloud* made her way eastward on her maiden voyage.

The boisterous weather *Flying Cloud* encountered on June 6 compelled most of the passengers to remain below in the great cabin, or in their staterooms. As a consequence, the dinner hour shortly after noon represented the highlight of their day. Ellen and Perkins usually ate with the passengers after making the noon observation and entering the previous day's progress in the log. Both social in nature, though Ellen more so, they enjoyed the lively banter at the table.

Up forward in the deckhouse, the cook sweated over the large cast-iron stove in the kitchen, which was known as the galley. Gray smoke poured from the stack atop the roof of the deckhouse and streamed away in the wind. When the day's main meal was ready for the officers and the passengers, the cook sent for the steward and the cabin boy to collect it. The two men trundled platters of roast chicken, boiled fresh vegetables, just-baked bread and cakes, and other delicacies to the ornately carved mahogany table in the great cabin. During bad weather the danger of dropping the meal on deck caused the steward to tread with care on the seemingly endless number of trips it took to muster a complete repast. On very rough days, he appeared almost to dance as he headed across the main deck to the companionway leading below.

As they sat down to their meal under the warm glow of the sun shining through the skylight, the passengers heard an urgent shout from the poop deck. A tremendous bang rang out, one that would have stirred the memory of a woodsman in the forest after an ice storm, the branches tearing from trunks in explosive volleys. The passengers gasped in surprise as the commotion increased, and just above their heads they heard still more crashes and shouts and the stamp of feet on the deck. They all stood up at once and looked at Perkins.

"All of you stay below," he said calmly. He shot Ellen a worried look as the ship slewed around broadside to the seas and heeled well over to starboard, knocking some passengers into the table and causing others to lose their footing. The fine china dishes smashed against the fiddles on the table and the crystal wineglasses tipped, spilling the contents. Several of the passengers cried out again in surprise as Perkins raced through the cabin and up the companion-way stairs. He looked aloft, confirmed his worst fears, and lay to with a will to save his crippled ship.

Chapter 8

Huddled together in silence at the door of the portico and braced against the violent motion of the ship, Ellen and the passengers gazed aloft. The crew scrambled to carry out the rapid succession of orders Perkins shouted from the poop deck. It was as if the entire ship's company had stepped through a boundary to another world, tiny in its sphere and terrible in its chaos. The routine comfort, the security that all was well, departed to leave them at the mercy of an element completely indifferent to the design and ingenuity of mankind and his lofty creations.

The main topgallant pole mast hung suspended in the lower rigging amid a tangle of black and tan lines nearly a hundred feet above the deck. It smashed into the main topmast and topsail yard with every roll of the ship. The impact carried over the shouts of the men, the rush of the wind, and the thunder of the sails tearing loose from the skysail, royal, and topgallant yards still attached to the mast. Tattered streams of canvas blew downwind, making a terrible, thunderlike noise. The destruction appeared odd, juxtaposed as it was against the backdrop of pale blue sky flecked with puffy clouds scudding along in the upper levels of the atmosphere. A fair-weather blow always conveyed a sense of the surreal. The mind accepted that grim, low clouds and a barrel of wind went hand in hand with calamity. But it less easily accepted the prospect of disaster on a sunny day.

The mizzen topgallant pole mast also toppled from its supports at the mizzen topmast eighty feet above the deck. The vast network of lines that had held it upright kept it from falling completely, and the lower rigging also helped keep it trapped in midair, about sixty-five feet over the heads of the people on the poop deck. Its extreme end pointed toward the sea. Both masts had come down due to a failure in the rigging.

When a critical stay or shroud on the main topgallant pole mast gave way, the spar could not withstand the force of the gusty wind against the sails. As it fell, it tore loose the stays and shrouds of the mizzen's upper mast, causing a chain reaction that followed seconds later and set the stage for the destruction of every successive weak link in the rig. At any moment tons of solid pine, iron fittings, hemp, blocks, and canvas might plummet to the deck, taking with it the rigging and spars below. As Ellen watched, the crew on the foremast, now high above the main, struggled to take in sail. *Flying Cloud* righted herself. Perkins ordered the helmsman to steer dead downwind. Ellen feared for the men at times like this. A ship in serious trouble could kill in an instant, its power out of control, a wild expression of brute force staggering to the mind.

Every crewman aboard hurried to bring the ship back under control. They had to disconnect the tangle of lines from the damaged spars and send the entire rigs for both the main and mizzen upper masts down to the deck for repair before the wreckage aloft pounded the still-unharmed lower masts and rigging to pieces. The stress on the main and mizzen topmasts twisted and worked the spars. They could not hold up for long. The entire crew, the steward and Ching, the cook and the carpenter, and all the officers, sixty-six men in all, struggled to put the ship right. Their first task was to secure and send the broken masts down before more damage occurred. It was a race against time. Ellen was unsure of the outcome.

Up on the main topmast, sailors balanced on the footropes of the main topsail yard ignored the hard-and-fast rule of the sea—

keep one hand for the ship, and one for the man. With both hands they grabbed at the flailing lines of the topgallant pole mast as it swung near and tried to haul it in and lash it tightly to the rigging. Before they could send it down, they had to subdue it, and that was not easy to accomplish. Even with the ship's lower sails reduced and the ship moving slowly through the breaking seas, the motion aloft sent the loose topgallant pole mast gyrating and careening against the spars and lines that offered some semblance of support. As the sailors worked, more of the remaining lines holding the main upper mast broke in a series of gunshot-like reports.

Suddenly, the men felt the main topsail yard start to give way. Several of the lines holding the yard in place parted under the strain of the wreckage bearing down on them. The main topsail yard came adrift and banged against the topmast. It threatened to toss the men still clinging to it into the sea. Carefully, but as quick as cats, the sailors climbed off the yard and back down the ratlines a safe distance away from the airborne battering ram.

"Lay to there, boys!" Perkins cried. "Get back up there to secure that yard!"

The men hesitated only a moment. Down below on deck their shipmates worked the lines still attached to the main topsail yard to hold it as steady as possible against the topmast. This bought time for the rest of the sailors as they rushed back up to the yard and tied it against the mast to prevent further damage. After that danger, the men returned their attention to the effort to secure the twenty-eight-foot topgallant pole mast and prepare to send every broken piece of the main rig, which weighed well over a ton, down to the deck for repairs. Other crewmen set to work on the twenty-two-foot mizzen topgallant pole mast. Weighing just under a ton with all of its gear, the uppermost spar on the mizzen required fewer men to lower it to the poop deck. But the job was dangerous just the same.

"My God," more than one passenger murmured.

Ellen turned to them, ready to offer a few words of comfort. But what could she say? "We can do no good here," she said quietly after a long pause. "We must leave it to the captain and crew."

One by one the passengers went below to sit nervously together, wondering what might happen next. Ellen sat with them and tried to reassure those who seemed most worried. The noise above deck, however, did nothing to reassure any of them.

Outside the commotion intensified. The mizzen topgallant pole mast, together with its yards, was slowly secured at great risk to the men. They had to balance in the rigging while trying to avoid being crushed as the spar swung and grated against the mizzen topmast. They rigged block and tackle to lines attached to the topgallant pole mast, and men below hauled away to lift the spar off the lower rigging. Additional lines were rigged to control the mast's movement. Once the mast was immobilized, the crew loosened the rigging attached to it and the yards and prepared to lower the rig down to the deck. They did the same with the main topgallant pole mast and its yards as well. All the while Perkins stormed and shouted at them not to cut away anything unless it was absolutely necessary.

"Mind your blades, boys. Don't let me see you too free with them!" he bellowed.

His concern was for the rig, not the men. He had to save every piece of it if he was to ensure a speedy repair. The ship carried extra spars, but they were blanks, timbers not yet shaped for a precise use. There were not many of them aboard, and he could not afford to lose time in fashioning complete new topgallant pole masts and yards, even if that were possible. The only chance he had to keep the ship going with such a fair and stiff breeze was to send the damaged masts down quickly without damaging them further.

The men aloft worked with a will, their curses and cries, grunts and growls lost to the wind. Although time seemed to stretch on forever, every minute feeling like an hour, the work went quickly. They had the spars secured and with great care they sent them down to the deck.

The last danger involved sending down the seventy-four-foot main topsail yard. One of the heaviest yards aboard the ship, it weighed over two tons. Its prodigious length and enormous weight required all the skills of the men both aloft and on deck. If the men lost control of it as they sent it down, it might well punch through sails and slash through the stays and shrouds supporting the top-mast. But they succeeded in their work without further mishap.

Once all the spars were on deck, Perkins glared at the wreckage. Above stood the remains of the main and mizzen masts and their topmasts. The accident had robbed him of more than half the sails, and the ship sailed more slowly as a result. He cursed under his breath at the sight, lifted the speaking trumpet to his lips, and cried, "Lay aloft and make all possible sail!"

As tired as they were, the crew climbed aloft one more time and released the gaskets on the sails they had furled just after the dis-masting. The sails billowed out with the wind in resounding booms as the yards were hauled up and braced to best advantage. The jibs and spanker reset, *Flying Cloud* gathered way under seven fewer square sails than had been set less than two hours earlier. She had also lost the use of some of her staysails. Her profile looked mis-shapen, with the foremast high and stately, its thin topgallant pole mast soaring to the clouds. The main course was all that flew from the mainmast, and on the mizzen, the topsail and spanker. Despite the reduced number of sails, the ship picked up speed in the strong, gusty wind, and the wake stretched out astern in a ribbon of white eddies and whirls.

A moment of quiet descended on the ship, as so often occurred after a clash with the sea. It was a slow dawning of just how vulner-able the ship and by extension her people were even when storm winds remained blessedly locked away in a far-distant weather sys-tem. The fragile nature of the ship crept into the mind and stayed there, and that was the very thing a sailor faced time and again, and lived with for the duration of a passage. For the passengers, without the benefit of experience, the dismasting cast a sense of foreboding over what had formerly been a happy-go-lucky spirit. Traveling in luxury aboard the finest clipper afloat perhaps had its liabilities after all. The outcome of the voyage looked a lot less certain.

The sight of all the wreckage on deck made the situation look worse than it was, at least to some of the passengers. The slender pole masts were gouged and scraped. Iron and wooden fittings were torn loose and hung from the spars amid ropes wound up in tangles that appeared impossible to sort out. The yards lay askew on top of the masts at various angles, with the sails ripped from the attachments to the yards in many places. The main topsail yard looked long enough to serve as a mast, and indeed it was. Parts of its huge sail blew loose and billowed in the wind. Still, the rest of the rig was intact.

Below in the great cabin, Edward hugged his mother tightly. His fear was obvious to all the passengers as he cried, wishing he was back with his Aunt Kate in Massachusetts. Whitney Lyon and his two sisters sat on the lee settee and stared up through the skylight as if expecting a revelation. The usually ebullient Francesco Wadsworth had nothing to say, nor did J. D. Townsend. Willie Hall wrote madly in his journal, oblivious of the others. Mrs. Gorham looked decidedly shaken, as did her maid. Only Laban Coffin, originally from Nantucket and well familiar with the ways of the sea as an experienced sailor himself, appeared as calm as Ellen. With the topgallant pole masts and main topsail yard down on deck, he knew the ship was safe and could proceed on her way in all haste while repairs were made.

Dismastings were not uncommon among the clipper fleet. One could cite a long list of damaged ships putting into Rio de Janeiro or Valparaiso for repairs. No year passed without finding scores of clippers and other sailing ships in trouble, and most of them made it to port despite the adversity. *White Squall,* which had sailed from New York the previous September, had lost a goodly number of her masts only three days out of the harbor. The mishap cost her the main topmast, the most important spar other than the mainmast, which served as its support. *White Squall* also lost her topgallant pole masts on the mizzen and foremast. She took over a month to reach Rio for repairs.

John Bertram sailed from Boston on January 10, 1851, and sprung her mainmast and bowsprit in the Southern Ocean. She put into Valparaiso for repairs. The day after *John Bertram* put to sea, Grinnell, Minturn & Company's *Sea Serpent* set sail and sprung her bowsprit four days from New York City. Like *Flying Cloud*, *White Squall* and *Sea Serpent* suffered damage while still in the general vicinity of the Gulf Stream, the first of many hazards on the way to the Golden Gate.

Most of the passengers failed to understand they had unwittingly signed on as passive spectators to a race of enormous proportions, both for the high stakes involved and the sheer size and power of the vessels thrust into the battle against nature and time. They were part of a very risky game of money, power, and fame on the part of the captain as well as the owners of the ship. The loss of a couple topgallant pole masts and the danger to the crew counted little when taken in the context of the bigger picture, and neither did the passengers, though few captains admitted it.

Had Captain Creesy been driving *Flying Cloud* too hard? Should he not have ordered the crew to shorten sail in such a big wind? Many of the passengers may have entertained these questions, but they did not voice them, at least not in front of Ellen. It was not proper to question the judgment of the master.

The northwest wind blew on through the rest of the afternoon. Every sail drew hard. Yet the ship still sailed well under her best speed, without her towers of sail. Perkins did not rest, nor did the crew. As soon as the ship was put back on course, he ordered the first mate, Thomas Austin, to supervise the men in making repairs. He stayed on the poop deck and kept a watchful eye to see that no man slacked off, not even for a minute to draw a cup of water from the scuttlebutt, a barrel of drinking water lashed on deck for the men. Ellen joined him, but eventually left him to his own thoughts.

Both watches of the crew toiled until the sun slipped beneath the dark horizon well near nine o'clock that evening. The task of putting *Flying Cloud* right involved a multitude of jobs large and small. Though they had worked hard, much remained unaccomplished. Broken into details, some of the able-bodied seamen, the most talented and experienced sailors aboard, worked as riggers. They measured hundreds of yards of standing rigging for the stays and shrouds that could not be salvaged, each line with its own specific length and width. Additional yards of running rigging for the halyards, braces, lifts, slings, sheets, and dozens of other lines needed to handle the sails required close attention.

The men removed the sails from the yards, taking care not to cut any line they could untie. Some of the sails were beyond salvage, mere tatters of torn canvas. But others could be made serviceable again. Those the sailmaker and his assistants set to repairing. Other men brought spare sails up on deck and secured them to the yards to replace the ones that had been destroyed. On all the yards, the men rigged the necessary lines used to control the sails. Still more crewmen checked the main and mizzen topmasts and all of the rigging to spot any additional damage.

The crew went back on watches of four hours on and four hours off, and the ship settled into its nightly routine. Exhausted, and still hungry after a cold meal of salt pork and hardtack, the crew off watch fell into a deep sleep. The passengers retired early, ending a day they would always remember. They, too, were hungry, since the cook had been too busy to heat a proper supper, and their dinner had gone uneaten in all the excitement.

Ellen sat alone at the table in the officers' cabin and listened to the sea washing past outside the hull. The ship rode easily under her greatly reduced spread of sail, with just a gentle heel to starboard, despite the sustained strength of the wind. The dull yellow light of the gimbaled lamp cast moving shadows as it swung from the beams above. She heard someone snoring, but could not tell whether it was the steward and cabin boy asleep in their stateroom, or the second and third mate asleep in theirs. It was a rare time when no one was about, a time when she could enjoy moments alone without being on call to wear one of her many hats. She needed a few minutes to collect her thoughts, but peace did not come. She busied herself in working out the ship's position.

The ship's estimated speed was pretty vague on this particular day. There had been no time to regularly stream the log. She was reduced to the ageless method of navigation by dead reckoning. She guessed at the ship's estimated speed and multiplied the average by the number of hours since her last fix to obtain an estimated distance run. Based on her figures, the ship would make only one hundred miles or so to noon the next day, a loss of precious distance.

Ellen smoothed her dress as she stood up from the table and retired alone to her stateroom. As she lay in the soft berth under the blankets, wondering when Perkins might come below, the events of the day settled over her like a damp cloak, depressing her spirit. She pulled the blankets close to her chin against the cool of the summer night. She snuggled down in the sheets and tried to let sleep come with its blissful escape. Above her on the poop deck, Perkins stood watch, in addition to the first officer. Perkins paced the deck and barked orders at the men to trim the sails to take full advantage of every subtle change of the wind.

Chapter 9

Unable to sleep for most of the night, Ellen yawned and glanced out the porthole in her cabin. Finally, the weak light of the rising sun painted the sky to the east a dull gray. She got dressed and went up on deck, anxious about the next round of repairs to the ship. All hands were gathered at the base of the mainmast listening to Thomas Austin as he gave the sailors their orders. In moments such as these, she became a spectator, apart from the ship's crew and her officers. The passivity of her position, while she understood its rationale, nevertheless failed to correspond with her typically active role aboard. Above her, alone at the forward rail of the poop deck, Perkins looked down on every member of the crew save the helmsman, his jaw set, his eyes as clear as the water in the shallows of a lagoon, the wind tousling his hair round the rim of his cap.

The crew silently dispersed, each man ready to execute his duty to the best of his ability and counting on his shipmates to do the same. The sailors worked in teams. Some of the men climbed up to the main topmast and rigged the block and tackle needed to lift the topgallant pole mast one hundred feet above the deck to its proper place. Others ran a heavy line through the hole in the base of the spar about to be hauled up to create a massive sling. Installing the spar would be a tricky undertaking, one involving all hands in a well-timed effort. The threshold for error was low, and every man knew it.

Thomas Austin stood ready, eyes on the poop deck. At the captain's order, he shouted, "Ready, boys?"

"All ready, aye!" the men replied.

"Sway away, my bully boys, heave, ho, heave!" Austin cried.

The first mate's strong voice carried over the length of the ship. On the second "heave" the men reached forward, grabbed hold of the lines that formed the sling, and as one they heaved with enough strength to move the mast off the deck a few feet. As they worked, they swayed back and forth in a stationary dance, their muscles bulging, their breathing timed to the rhythm of a sea chantey.

The chanteyman sang: "Oh, the ladies of the town, hio!"

The sailors hauled and replied: "Cheer'ly man."

"All soft as down, hio," the chanteyman continued.

"Cheer'ly man."

The mast swung upright on its base like a long, slender finger. It was essential that the men raise it parallel with the other spars to avoid damage to the lower rigging. Blocks creaked and lines vibrated as the load increased. The men began to sweat, despite the cool of the early dawn.

"In their best gown, hio!" the chanteyman sang.

"Oh! Hauley, hio! Cheer'ly man!" The mast rose higher.

As the main body of the men hauled the mast upward, other sailors hauled and eased the new and salvaged rigging, already secured in place, to keep tension on all the lines and prevent the mast from gyrating about when the ship rolled. She continued sailing fast on her course, and the motion was rough. The higher the mast rose, the more it swayed. The men shouted and swore in their struggle to prevent the mast from tangling itself into an inextricable jam as it ascended farther and farther from the deck through the maze of lower rigging.

Slowly and carefully the men at the bottom of the topmast high above the deck fit the base of the main topgallant pole mast into place and lowered it into position at the mount. They drove home a large bar of iron called a fid to snug the mast in tight. Next they secured the standing and running rigging, a task that consumed the bulk of the day. Once in place, the stays and shrouds were tightened to just the right tension, using the configuration of blocks known as deadeyes. It took days before all was as it had been, taut and tight and nicely tarred.

Throughout Saturday, June 7, the men continued to work. They sent up the mizzen upper mast next and set to work on the yards. At sundown, all hands yearned to fetch their supper from the galley and stretch out on their berths to rest. Yet, as tired as they were, at one point or another as the regular watch was set, each man stopped to gaze up at the soaring masts and graceful yards of the clipper, so nearly restored to her full abilities thanks to their collective efforts to make her whole again. There was a sense of pride in a job well done among many of the men. They took compliments from the passengers with a wink and a smile, and stood tall in front of the officers when Perkins made it known through the first mate that he thought every man Jack had served well and true.

Perkins ordered a measure of grog, a mixture of rum and water, for the crew that night. Grog was distributed every Saturday night aboard naval vessels, but aboard a merchant sailer such as *Flying Cloud*, it was given only as a treat after the crew completed a job to the liking of their captain or when bad weather merited a boost of the crew's spirit. Perkins also ordered the cook to prepare their Sunday duff, a pudding made from boiled flour, with extra molasses, apples, and raisins, considered a delicacy among the oldest hands, who knew enough to appreciate their captain's kind gestures.

The northwester gave its last and surrendered its influence on the sea to a light west-southwesterly breeze that brought the wind off the stern, a point just as fair as the previous wind direction. It continued to shift in fluky puffs that gathered strength from the south and east. The sky to the south paled under a gauze of high cirrus clouds, a harbinger of the new weather system about to take over their part of the ocean.

The work on the ship continued at daybreak on the second day after the mishap. There was still much to do before *Flying Cloud* was put right. The main topsail yard was hoisted and secured, and a spare topsail was set. Once the topsail was drawing well, Perkins ordered every other sail set, including the studdingsails. Booms were run out, and the halyards, sheets, and tacks were rigged. Sail after sail spread to the wind until every stitch of canvas flew aloft in tiers of white, golden with the sun and crossed with strands of black shadow from the lines hung slack down their fronts. As *Flying Cloud* surged forward, some of the passengers clapped their hands and cheered among themselves. The wind bellied out the sails. All aboard felt her accelerate, and leave behind with every passing mile the danger and hardship of the preceding two days.

The gentle southerly wind blew broadside to the ship for the next three days, ushering in a tame sea ideal for fine sailing. The wind had power enough to move *Flying Cloud* along at a steady eight to nine knots, mile after mile, as the watches changed to the ring of the ship's bell. As the bell rang, the meals were prepared, served, and eaten. The small waves driven forward on the heel of the wind did not show any crests. They rolled short and squat to slap merrily against the clipper and caused no reduction in her speed. The weather came in humid and hazy, and for the first time the sailors worked with their shirtsleeves rolled up and the ladies came on deck with parasols to shade them from the sun.

The time passed easily for all but one aboard. Sarah Lyon stayed tucked below in her stateroom, weak, pale, and unable to consume anything more than broth and a scrap or two of bread. She had been ill since their departure, and Ellen began to worry that her condition might be more serious than a simple case of seasickness. She checked in on her periodically, hoping to see an improvement. But if anything Sarah's condition worsened.

Sarah's brother, Whitney, was fond of reading poetry to Ellen. During those fair-weather days they sat together on deck in the company of any other passengers in need of a diversion, which usually accounted for most of them, and read verse with exaggerated flourishes. He was also something of a jokester, able to nudge a smile from everyone at the dinner table. In a quiet moment, as Ellen gazed out at the passive sea, Whitney asked her about his sister, concern in his voice.

"I'm very worried about her, Mrs. Creesy," he said. "Isn't there anything you can do?"

"There is medicine aboard that may help," Ellen said. "But let's give your sister a little more time."

Such emergencies always left Ellen feeling doubtful about her abilities. She was no doctor, and her studies went only so far. The subject of human illness remained quite mysterious, and even the most learned texts offered little practical guidance to a self-educated would-be practitioner. Many physicians, in their attempt to explain the origin of malaria, argued the disease stemmed from inhaling bad air. The mosquito's role in its spread was still undiscovered. This was just one of many misconceptions of the time. Even basic sanitary practices during surgery failed to find favor in all but the most rare progressive medical institutions, and the use of ether as an anesthetic was a brand-new practice. Knowledge gleaned from her studies gave Ellen confidence in dealing with obvious emergencies such as broken bones, burns, lacerations, and toothaches. But it did not extend to the diagnosis or treatment of an illness of unknown origin.

Mariners did devise a way around the general lack of medical knowledge among the officers of a merchant vessel. Some ships carried medicine chests whose bottles were numbered. The chest came with a book containing lists of symptoms that corresponded with a particular illness. Remedies were included in the text and listed a number that the ship's doctor matched to a similarly numbered bottle in the medicine chest. The sick sailor simply said what bothered him, and the doctor looked through the book to find an ailment that seemed to fit. Reading ability was the most important consideration in these cases, not medical experience. It gave the individual acting as doctor a fighting chance to help. The so-called "cookbook" system was also used aboard American privateers during the Revolutionary War. The ships were too small and too underfunded to afford the luxury of a trained surgeon.

The bottles in Ellen's medicine chest contained a rather limited range of remedies. Morphine to reduce pain, quinine for malarial fever, camphor to act as a stimulant, and ipecac for use as an emetic were among the drugs carried on ships and on the frontier. There were also botanical remedies such as organic cough powders. Ellen thought it possible Sarah's system needed purging to clear out the illness, whatever it was. For this she had calomel, a mercury-based cathartic used as a laxative. By its more scientific name the fine, taste-less white powder was known as mercurous chloride. On June 11, Sarah's condition was no better. Ellen gave her the drug and fer-vently hoped for a quick recovery.

The 11th of June stood out for another reason, apart from Sarah's worsened condition. *Flying Cloud* drew near where Maury advised Ellen to turn south for the run to the equator and then on to Cape São Roque, the easternmost extremity of South America. Any vessel headed south to Rio de Janeiro or Buenos Aires or to California around Cape Horn had to clear Cape São Roque first. *Flying Cloud* was just forty-eight miles north of the designated turning point in midocean about 1,500 miles east of Bermuda and 900 miles southwest of the Azores. Ellen felt quite satisfied with herself for bringing the ship close to the exact loca-tion Maury suggested for the course change. As he had written, it was as if there were now a sign posted in the vast, empty sea pointing the way to the fastest passage to the Southern Hemi-sphere.

The clippers followed paths across the oceans that placed them in the best position to find a fair wind. That most often meant sail-ing much longer distances in directions that seemed contrary to the logic of sailing a direct course from point A to point B. Cape São Roque was approximately 3,600 miles from New York on a direct line to the southeast. But a southeasterly course did not favor a square-rigged sailing ship. Instead, Ellen had to steer eastward until she was lined up north-south with Cape São Roque. Only then could she turn south. The indirect route from New York to the shoulder of Brazil was about 4,200 miles, or 600 miles longer than the direct route.

Ocean Winds
North & South Atlantic
April – June

The variables, trade winds, and doldrums shift location with the seasons.
Navigators took this into account when planning voyages. Sometimes there
were surprises. Flying Cloud failed to find the northeast trade winds.

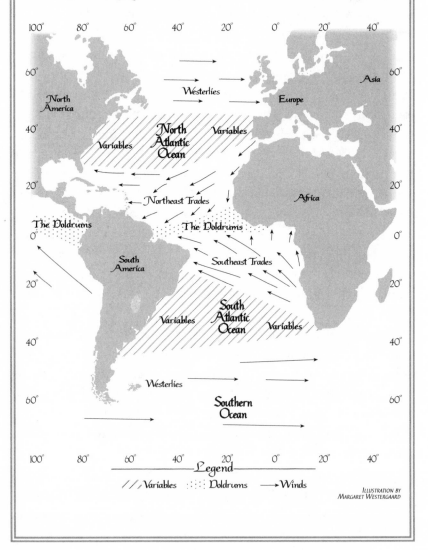

ILLUSTRATION BY
MARGARET WESTERGAARD

Sailing eastward took the clippers through the variable winds that exist between latitudes 25 and 35 degrees north of the equator. Sailors called this area of light, unsteady wind the horse latitudes. The name dated back to the days of the explorers. Their slow ships were sometimes becalmed for so long that drinking water ran short. When there was not enough water for the horses and other livestock to drink, the crews killed the animals and threw the carcasses overboard. The clippers passed through the variables to get east. It was a necessary evil. However, beyond their influence, the clippers picked up the northeast trade winds that blew below the horse latitudes. Once through the northeast trades, there was another area of calms known as the doldrums.

Throughout the voyage, Ellen charted her courses to ride from one belt of steady winds to the next, and she avoided the variable winds and calms as much as possible. She learned from Maury that variable winds, the trade winds, and regions of calms resulted from differences in atmospheric pressure and air temperature, as well as the influence of the earth's rotation. Differences in air temperature and barometric pressure created wind. Warm air rose and drew cooler air in from other locations, which generated movement of the air. She learned that air also flowed from areas of high pressure to areas of low pressure.

In the Atlantic Ocean, there was an area of permanent high pressure known as the Azores high. Low-pressure areas existed on either side of it. Air from the Azores high flowed out to the low-pressure cells, thus setting up a fairly consistent pattern of winds. As the earth rotated on its axis in an easterly direction, it influenced the direction of the winds as they traveled from areas of high to low pressure. This set up the northeast trades, which were so named because of their vital importance to ships engaged in commerce. The system of trade winds both north and south of the equator shifted as the seasons changed with the movement of the sun.

Maury's understanding of the worldwide circulation of wind patterns and his theories of why they existed and why they changed and shifted through the seasons intrigued Ellen. The changing angle of the sun and barometric pressure from one place to the next, the influence of deserts and ice sheets, and many other factors entered into Maury's theories. Similarly, he explored the ocean currents, mapped them, as he did the winds, and tenaciously probed their origins. Maury wrote of the doldrums: "The calm belts of the sea, like mountains on the land, stand mightily in the way of the voyager, but, like the mountains on the land, they have their passes and their gaps."

The analogy focused the concept with the precision of a prism to break light into distinct bands all the easier to see and understand. The idea that the doldrums varied in width and moved north and south was relatively new. That they did so in accordance with the sun and its subsequent ability to heat one part of the world with more vigor than another was quite new. The connection between the sun's changing position in the sky as the seasons came and went and variations in wind patterns had never been fully explained to mariners. The impact of these variations on the day-to-day navigation of a vessel remained beyond the understanding of most captains. It took Maury to link the scientific discoveries to the practical matter of using them to help ships better navigate the world's oceans at the fastest rate of speed. His thinking was as revolutionary as the clipper ship, something unique, exciting, and also a bit frightening because it seemed to subdue the sea with science.

As Ellen studied the text of Maury's book, she noted his repeated warnings to apply his sailing directions with common sense. He warned mariners not to chase wind or blindly follow a course, but to react as the weather and wind dictated. He cautioned that his findings should be used as a guide only. The sea, he said, was always revealing new mysteries. It could never be fully explained outside the context of a higher being, because it was the higher being that had created it.

Maury's new route to the equator differed greatly from the traditional path mariners had followed for centuries. Common wisdom held that a ship should make easting well beyond Cape São Roque. The cape was known for its contrary winds and strong westward-setting currents, at least according to common knowledge, all of it anecdotal. As a consequence of steering too far east to

Ocean Currents
North & South Atlantic

Flying Cloud rode the Gulf Stream eastward before turning south. Off South America, the Brazil Current helped the ship's progress. The Falkland Current slowed the clipper.

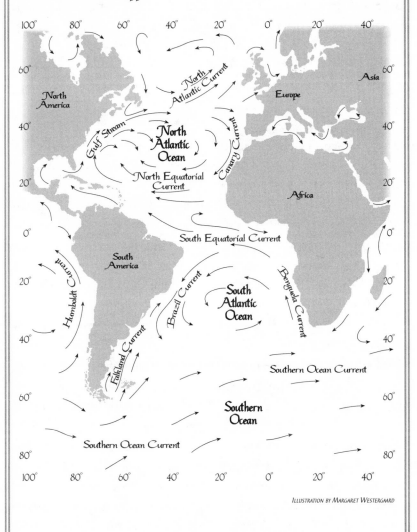

clear the cape, ships remained in the variables longer than necessary and hit the wider belt of the doldrums close to Africa, where they drifted becalmed, sometimes for weeks. As a vessel progressed southward to Cape Horn, the angle to the prevailing southeast winds in the South Atlantic proved too acute for optimal sailing. A ship was not making enough westing for an efficient passage around Cape Horn.

According to Maury's findings, the winds and currents near Cape São Roque were not a hindrance. The anecdotal evidence, he said, was patently flawed. There was no reason to give the cape so wide a berth, no reason to sail south down the middle of the South Atlantic, only to face the roaring west winds in the higher latitudes well east of the Falkland Islands and a very long slog around Cape Horn.

The new route promised fairer winds, calmer seas, and a faster passage. However, it was still in the early stages of testing. Few, if any, of the other clippers under sail in June 1851 had Maury's newly published book. Adhering to Maury's sailing directions demanded faith in science, faith in a modern way of seeing the world that many a mariner found difficult to accept. The wind had fallen light through the previous day, and on the course Ellen needed to steer to reach her turning point it blew well forward of the beam, or at an unfavorable slant for the sails. It required some convincing on her part to justify to Perkins the need for a more southerly course regardless of the unfavorable wind angle. But he went along with her.

While Ellen was more prone to embrace new ways of thinking, Perkins, too, was keenly intelligent. He understood Maury's reasoning, to the point where he was conversant with his wife on the new theories, which they talked about over a quiet game of chess on the poop deck. If following Maury's directions meant a fast passage, then, by God, follow them he would. The sailing directions could be the very edge he needed over the rest of the fleet headed for California. Ellen ordered *Flying Cloud* brought around to a course of south 5 degrees east, or nearly due south, and began her run for the equator more than eighteen hundred miles away.

Back in New York, business went on with regard to *Flying Cloud*. Grinnell, Minturn & Company drafted a short letter to S. Griffitts Morgan, the company's agent in California engaged to sell the freight the ship carried in her hold.

June 11, 1851
Dear Sir,
Captain Creesy sailed for your port on June 2 and we think he has had a fine run down the coast. She [*Flying Cloud*] makes freight about $50,000. As all the bills of lading are not in we cannot send the freight list by this mail, but we hope to have it completed in time to dispatch by the next mail.
Sincerely,
Grinnell, Minturn & Company

Chapter 10

*F*lying Cloud sailed slowly southward toward the equator against a light southwesterly wind that came in fitful puffs. The ship crept along at an agonizing two knots, drifting in the swells, the sea the color of pewter under a hazy sky. Her distance made good over the preceding twenty-four hours stood at only fifty-four miles. But as the afternoon of June 12 passed into early evening, the wind came from a more easterly direction. It gradually increased and gained enough strength to move *Flying Cloud* at a respectable rate. The ship heeled gently to the wind, canting the deck as she cut through the water. Every sail drew fair.

The spray pattering over the forecastle deck no longer stung with a chill as it sprinkled the cheek. Instead its warmth heralded the ship's approach to the tropics, a world of azure waters and coral atolls, soft, puffy trade wind clouds, and gentle, balmy breezes. As *Flying Cloud* sailed southward, the days grew longer. The sun soared ever higher overhead the closer the ship came to the equator. They sailed to meet the sun as it traveled toward them on the last legs of its northward journey, culminating in the longest day of the year in the Northern Hemisphere at the summer solstice, just several days ahead. Soon the ship would pass under the sun perpendicular to its daily east-to-west track and leave it behind to chase the wake as it traveled south again to eventually diminish the cold of the southern winter. In the Pacific, *Flying Cloud* would once again catch up to the sun and leave it astern on her way to the Golden Gate.

Between June 12 and June 19, *Flying Cloud* covered 1,591 miles, much of it due south. Since leaving New York the ship had traveled a distance about equal to sailing from the Battery to Cornwall on the southern coast of England, a distance of over three thousand miles. For five days the ship exceeded runs of two hundred miles from noon to noon, making an average speed of ten knots during the sustained southeast by easterly winds. The weather came in fair, a fine blue sky made interesting with a display of passing clouds. The clouds occasionally blocked the sun and caused the air close about to feel cool and inviting.

The ship's approach to the equator represented the final stages of the first leg of their journey and the start of the second leg, one far more dangerous. As the ship sailed down the coast of South America to Patagonia and beyond, she would literally sail through the seasons. The days would grow shorter and the sun would hang low over the horizon, even at noon. The cold winds of the southern winter in high latitudes would cut through woolen pea jackets, sweaters, and shirts. The anticipation of what lay ahead added moment to the sense of closure presented at the approach to the line.

The passengers, all of them well, including Sarah Lyon, talked of the ship's remarkable speed, how the captain and crew kept her driving hard. They talked of home, of places they had been, and their prospects out West. However, overshadowing their general good cheer and running like an undertow through the conversation was a nagging worry made all the more urgent when they gazed above at the mainmast, and the repairs made to it on June 14.

A crewman had discovered the mainmast badly cracked about a foot below the hounds. Located toward the top of the mast, the hounds were huge shoulderlike supports for the topmast and topgallant pole mast above. Damage just below the hounds meant that the entire rig might not hold up in heavy weather. Perkins went aloft himself to inspect the mast. It could be repaired, he told Ellen, but he expressed his concern about the gales off Cape Horn.

The mainmast measured three feet in diameter, rose eighty-nine feet from the keelson, and weighed nearly thirteen tons. It was not a solid piece of timber, as were the topmasts and topgallant pole masts above. To achieve its mammoth dimensions, the mainmast was composed of pine staves fitted together to fill out the mast diameter. The pieces were held in place with thick iron hoops that had been heated to a red glow, quickly run up the mast, and shrunk in position. Buckets of cold water sloshed on the hot iron contracted it and bound together as one unit the individual parts of the mast. The mainmast served as a solid foundation for the topmast and topgallant pole mast, keeping the weight aloft as low as possible. A ship could survive the loss of a topgallant or topmast at the height of a storm. However, if the mainmast carried away it more than likely meant the end of the hapless vessel.

The crew once again set to work repairing the ship. The carpenter fashioned thick wooden staves and nailed them vertically around the deep cracks where the mast joints had separated. The iron hoop, broken during the dismasting, had allowed the cracks to work farther up and down the spar. How the damage had gone unnoticed until the 14th was a question no one could answer. In place of the iron hoop, the carpenter wrapped the staves tightly with stout line, and, in a fashion, splinted the mast as if it were a broken leg. There was little else the carpenter could do. The remedy promised only to prevent further damage. It did not add significantly to the mainmast's strength, which had already been permanently compromised.

In addition to the uneasiness concerning the mainmast, the passage to the line presented something of a mystery to Ellen that inclined her to think the sailing season of 1851 was quite unusual, at least in the month of June in their part of the Atlantic. The persistent southerly winds baffled her, and Perkins as well. Their experience in the China tea trade routinely brought them down the length of the Atlantic, through the northeast and southeast belts of prevailing winds to the Cape of Good Hope off the southern tip of

Africa. The trade winds in the ship's present position were supposed to come from the northeast, not from a southerly quarter.

Assert the wind will blow from a given direction in a specific location and time, and it surely will blow in the reverse of all expectations. Although the Creesys knew the trades sometimes proved inconsistent, the question of where the northeast winds blew at this particular time became a puzzle to solve. Could the fair wind be just over the horizon? With the ship sailing well, close-hauled though she was, little temptation arose to change course to chase it.

On June 17, Ellen awoke as she always did before dawn and together with Perkins went up on deck to take the first observations of the day. Her routine involved taking as many as seven different sights, though that many were not always needed. Sometimes she took observations for fun, as a way to pass the time and to occupy her mind. If the moon happened to show itself during the day, it delighted her. Perkins and she, both with sextants in hand and assistants to help, shot the sun and moon at virtually the same instant, speeding up the process of getting a fix.

At such times Ellen converted her numbers and measurements for both observations into lines on the plotting chart. Sights taken through the day provided additional lines, and when she had three lines crossing at wide angles they formed a triangle, the sailor's cocked hat, with the ship somewhere inside it. Shooting only the sun, she took sights at various times during the day as the sun's angle relative to the ship changed, thereby obtaining the three lines she needed to fix her position. Those taken earlier in the day she advanced across the chart to cover the distance sailed from the time the sight was taken, arriving at her cocked hat, if her work was done well.

Taking an observation demanded that the desired celestial body reveal itself at least 22 degrees above the horizon, where the refraction of light through the earth's atmosphere caused the least amount of distortion. Ellen had to be on deck ready to begin her work fifteen minutes before sunrise or fifteen minutes just after sunset. Only in those two short windows of time could a star, planet, or the moon be captured in the mirrors of the sextant and brought down to the edge of the earth to obtain its altitude, the first step in a chain of processes that ultimately helped determine the ship's location. Without sufficient light the horizon merged with the sea, making it impossible to measure accurately the altitude of a celestial body.

On this day as the Creesys came on deck, the predawn clouds foretold a change of the weather. Layers of cirrus clouds formed a pale white backdrop tinged with the blue and pink of early morning. Mottled bands of altocumulus below the cirrus clouds partially obscured the stars. It was a special time of day, the ship quiet, at peace. The animals stirred awake to add the sounds of a farm to the sounds of the sea and wind, the creak of wood as the ship worked and flexed, the intermittent luff of canvas.

The juxtaposition of the sounds of a farm aboard the ship with the murmur of the sea made an impression on Sarah Bowman as well. She wrote about it in a letter to her sister, Kate: "You don't know how odd it seems of a morning, when comfortably seated in my rocking chair on deck—when gazing over the broad ocean, to hear roosters crowing, hens cackling, turkeys gobbling, pigs grunting, and lambs bleating. There is an immense amount of livestock on board and our ice house is still well stacked with fresh provisions—so no danger but we shall fare well enough let us have ever so long a voyage."

Ellen waited for the star she selected to emerge and hang suspended for a few moments in a scrap of clear sky. When the opportunity came she efficiently ran through a series of sights to assure herself of obtaining the best average for her calculations. Because a star provided a very small target, Ellen inverted the sextant and, once she had the star caught in the mirror, brought the horizon up to meet the tiny speck of twinkling light. If the clouds came in thick to obscure the sun, she would have a satisfactory sight to help her with the dead reckoning for the day. A wise navigator always took advantage of an opportunity to obtain an observation. Every bit of data served as a piece in the puzzle of determining the ship's position.

But of all the day's work, it was the noon hour that ranked as the most important in terms of her records, the daily tally of miles made good in the log, and the changing of the course steered, if she deemed a change necessary. It also stood as an important part of the daily lives of all aboard on a psychological level. At noon the progress of the ship became tangible, a confirmation that they indeed sailed toward their destination. When sailing across an empty sea, day after day, week after week, the world seemed to stop, and forward motion seemed almost too abstract to comprehend in an environment composed solely of water, clouds, and sky, with the ship as its center. Without a landmass against which the forward progress of the ship was visually obvious, the ship could just as easily have been standing still while the larger world moved forward. The noon routine grounded the voyage in reality, turned the abstract to the concrete.

The first rain of the voyage fell on June 17, and it continued to fall in showers and squalls for several days. The squalls, embedded in the low rain clouds, appeared as dark bands amid the overwhelming gray. The sea below the dark layer of overcast churned white with short, steep crests. The ship roared and surged through the seas when the wind howled as a squall approached, screamed overhead, and passed on, sometimes in twenty minutes, sometimes longer. The captain drove through each successive disturbance without shortening sail, eyes constantly aloft, looking for the first sign of weakness in the rig. The ship bucked and pitched at the height of the windstorms, and settled down soon after they passed. Breakneck bursts of speed interspersed with periods of slow sailing and violent rolling to the swells became an irritating and occasionally nerve-jarring fact of life.

On June 18, the wind finally came in fresh from the northeast with more rain, and over the next eighteen hours it blew the ship ever closer to the edge of the doldrums, then faded into a faint southeasterly come in hard off the bow. So much rain, the contrary southerlies, and now the northeasterly in the backyard of the doldrums? The trade winds seemed out of balance. Somehow the weather patterns had been disturbed, altered.

It was possible the entire system of northeast trades and the calms at their southern edge had moved inexplicably north of Maury's projected latitudes. If that was the case, Ellen's tactics for crossing the calms at their thinnest location might not work. It was also possible they were caught in a large, unsettled low-pressure system blown across from Africa. The possibilities simply fueled more questions. The uncertainty of it all, and the high stakes, for both career and finances, added to the anxiety as *Flying Cloud* sailed toward the belt of calms sailors had hated for centuries. The intense heat, the relentless rolling of the ship and slatting sails, and thunderstorms that materialized from nowhere taxed the patience of virtually any sailor.

Flying Cloud faced another complication besides the weather in her approach to the doldrums. Ellen observed on Maury's current charts the presence of an easterly current near the ship's latitude of approximately 7 degrees north. The narrow band of water moved counter to the general circulation of currents north of the equator, where the rotation of the earth imparted a clockwise motion to the circulation pattern. Currents circulated in the opposite direction in the Southern Hemisphere.

The southeasterly headwind, which seemed intent upon dying at any moment, presented a danger. With so little way on, the easterly current threatened to push the ship into the wider, more turbulent section of the doldrums east of longitude 30 degrees west. At their present position, it was possible that *Flying Cloud* might find herself drifting for days, maybe weeks, in the fickle airs and calms. The width of the doldrums in June varied between one hundred and four hundred miles and grew dramatically wider as it approached the African coast. On top of the seasonal shifts to consider, the location and width of the calms changed on a daily basis. This injected an element beyond prediction and put Ellen uncomfortably close to navigating by guess.

Ellen recommended a radical course change from south 45 degrees east to south 63 degrees west, or a shift in course of over 100 degrees, to compensate for the current and put the southeasterly wind at a much more efficient slant while there was still enough strength in it to move the ship. To hesitate might mean delays, but to act could also put the ship well westward of her desired course if she overcompensated. Ellen and Perkins weighed the consequences of keeping on or changing course, and chose to gain some westing with the idea that they soon would be becalmed as they entered the doldrums and thus would be unable to fight the current. Perkins ordered the ship put on her new course.

With the wind blowing fair almost directly toward the left side of the ship, *Flying Cloud* jogged west southwest. Her bow faced the Amazon Basin more than a thousand miles away. Not long before, navigators bound for Cape Horn had never willingly sailed toward the Amazon, even if such a course might in the end favor a faster passage south. With the new knowledge of the area, however, it made sense to Ellen. Just as Ellen had predicted, the wind gave out early the next morning. It shifted to the south, south-southeast, and went calm, and repeated the cycle with different variations of wind direction. At intervals it boxed the compass, covering all the cardinal points in maddening puffs and lulls that induced the captain to tack the ship six times. Tacking meant the ship's bow turned through the direction from which the wind blew. It sometimes took all hands more than an hour to complete the maneuver in the light winds.

Throughout the day, dark clouds lined the horizon and the rumble of thunder echoed in the dull, heavy air. In minutes, a line of fierce squalls tore at the sails and all hands on watch tumbled to and trimmed with a will. Just as quickly as the squalls came, they disappeared. The sea calmed down and resumed its oily, slick swelling and rolling. As the ship drifted in the calms and sailed in the squalls, she moved deeper into the doldrums. Ellen could only wonder if she had made the right choices. Was Maury right? Had he found an elusive pass through the doldrums, the fair way to San Francisco? And could she find it in such an unpredictable sea?

Chapter 11

A broad expanse of calm ocean reflected and shimmered in the blazing sun all around *Flying Cloud*. The water was a deep silver blue that seemed to magnify the heat. The long, gentle swells lumbered under the ship and rolled her. Any slack line, loose block, or limp sail created a confusion of bangs, snaps, and thumps. The yards creaked and shimmied in their fittings at the masts. The stays and shrouds tightened and slackened as the spars worked back and forth, the whip effect most pronounced high above at the mastheads. The quick, hard pulls of the masts against the ropes supporting them stressed every part of the rig. Ellen and Perkins looked uneasily aloft at the damaged mainmast.

The ship drifted forty miles to the eastward with the current on June 21, accounting for half her total run from noon the previous day. The change of course to the west-southwest together with the last of the southerly wind brought *Flying Cloud* to a longitude of 34 degrees 3 minutes west, enough to compensate for the easterly current. In the preceding twenty-four hours, the current returned the ship to about the same longitude she had been on before heading toward the Amazon Basin. Ellen's plot of the clipper's track revealed a nearly perfect triangle, with the westernmost longitude as its apex. Ellen changed course once again to a new heading of south 72 degrees east that put the ship on a slant identical to the southeasterly trend of the upper Brazilian coastline terminating at Cape São Roque. When *Flying Cloud* arrived at the cape, Ellen intended to follow the land south all the way to Cape Horn.

The calms prevailed through the next day, and the ship drifted an additional twenty miles to the east, covering only fifty-two miles noon to noon. The sailors kept busy pouring water over the sails to close the fibers of the canvas, the better to catch the intermittent puffs that teasingly darkened the water a mile off, then disappeared. The stronger puffs skimmed across the water like shadows, turning it momentarily black with a patch of ripples and a breeze come in fresh enough to tempt the officer on watch to order the men to the braces.

A general sense of torpor settled over the passengers. They sat listlessly on deck under an awning. The shade provided a welcome cover from the hazy sun that burned hot enough to melt the tar on the standing rigging. Sarah Lyon and Laban Coffin talked quietly together, as they had with growing frequency. It appeared that a romance between them was taking root and might well grow to something more. Mrs. Gorham and Ellen Lyon sat reading, the latter thoroughly engrossed in a magazine called *The Young Ladies' Friend*.

As usual, Willie Hall scribbled away furiously in the journal he was keeping of the voyage. It was a chronicle of events and the people aboard the ship. He often shared his writings with Sarah Bowman, who took an interest in the young man and his ambition to become a writer. Meanwhile, her boy, Edward, had made fast friends of the sailors and spent much time forward and aloft, with special dispensation from the mates and the captain. The officers turned a blind eye to the sailors when they joked with him and told tall tales of ships and the sea. Edward sat near his mother, playing with bits from his collection of small items. These were gifts from the sailors—sperm whale teeth, pieces of tortoise shell and mother of pearl, flying fish wings and balls of twine.

To help break the monotony, Perkins allowed several passengers to take one of the ship's boats out, with members of the crew at the

Navigating the Doldrums

On June 20, Ellen Creesy kept Flying Cloud on a westerly course, but the ship made little headway. A strong current pushed the clipper 40 miles to the east, and another 20 miles the next day.

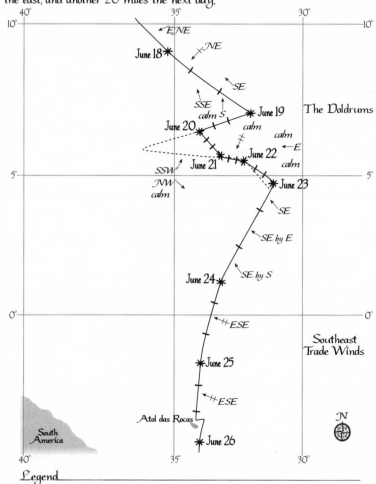

Legend

＊ noon position
∼ divides nautical day
- - - course steered between fixes
—— course made good between fixes
wind direction: ←— one–third of day ←+ two–thirds of day ←++ entire day

ILLUSTRATION BY
MARGARET WESTERGAARD

oars. They tried their hand at fishing and met with success. They caught a shark, adding significantly to the excitement of the day. The creature topped the conversation at the supper table that evening and inspired the men to tell gruesome stories about shark attacks. The shark's appearance served as a change from their usual observations of the colorful Portuguese man-of-wars, a species as ancient as any in the sea, and the squads of flying fish that leaped from the depths to soar dozens of yards on the updrafts of the waves.

The flying fish did not perform their aerial acrobatics for pleasure. They fled the jaws of larger fish intent upon devouring them. Nature gave the fish a means of escape, although it was temporary. The flying fish could leave their watery element, take to the air, and thus have a chance at life. But the flight only prolonged their days if they plunged back below the waves far enough away from the predators.

During periods of fair weather, or calms, the coops for the chickens, roosters, and turkeys were run out well over the side on long poles. The boys of the crew climbed the ratlines armed with buckets of seawater. They doused the coops to clean them, raising the occupants to a cacophonous welter of cackles and caws that seemed much louder than usual in the quiet air—strident, and out of place. The boys also set to cleaning up after the other animals, the pigs, lambs, and sheep. They saw to the worst job aboard, taking care of the pharmacies, as the older sailors called it, a euphemism for cleaning out the latrines.

Aboard a sailing vessel in naval or merchant service, boys ranked as the lowest members of the crew, because they lacked experience as sailors. They could not be counted on to know how to handle the many lines needed to control the sails, or how to work a marlinespike, a sharp metal tool used when working on the rigging. They did not know how to furl or shorten sail while perched on a yard in the face of a blow. They were not even permitted to steer, except on calm days when the trick at the wheel might teach them something without harming the ship. To the boys fell tasks such as slushing the masts, picking oakum, filling the scuttlebutt. They were not, for the most part, actually "boys." A boy, in fact, could be a green hand of thirty or more, and there were a goodly number aboard *Flying Cloud*, because of the shortage of experienced seamen on the nation's major waterfronts.

Their duty done, the sailors sought what shelter they could from the sun. With no breeze to move the stifling humid air, it was too hot to linger in the deckhouse or belowdecks in the forecastle. They hid away in the shadows behind a hatch coaming, deckhouse, capstan, or spar. Hours passed. Above the deck, the sails dried slowly. The dark patches of moisture on the sails faded and constricted into fine layers of salt.

"Lay aloft to sluice the sails!" the officer on watch shouted, always aware that Perkins was nearby.

With carefully squelched curses and groans, the crew climbed aloft and heaved up buckets of brine to soak the canvas. The water rained from the yards and the flaccid bellies of the sails and pattered loudly on deck and into the sea. The evening brought no relief from the heat. The off watch slept on deck. The men were not concerned about the likelihood of a wetting from an occasional squall. The cool rain was welcome. The men even welcomed steady rain during the prevailing calm, an Irishman's hurricane, as they called it. It was a disparaging remark, based on the Irish propensity to exaggerate things. Sailors were not selective in whom they insulted.

The ship inched southeast toward Brazil. Gradually, the clipper sailed and drifted to a position about as far east as Ellen deemed wise. She changed course to south 26 degrees west. The new course took them back slightly to the west to line up for the approach to Cape São Roque. The day's run to noon amounted to just fifty-three miles. A good deal of the progress, such as it was, resulted from the diminishing easterly current.

On the third afternoon in the doldrums, the first teasing puffs of the trade winds of the Southern Hemisphere appeared and blew toward *Flying Cloud* from the southeast. They came in tiny patches and at first no one paid any attention. But the moving air spread out over the smooth surface of the sea in larger and larger areas until the entire ocean off the port side of the ship darkened into a deep blue flecked with silvery ripples of light dancing on the water. The stale, still air quickly dissipated, and the fresh, pure smell of the sea flowed over the vessel, clearing out the cabins and deckhouse.

The passengers below in their staterooms hurried up on deck and joined the others at the rail. With the ship broadside to the freshening breeze, the crew trimmed the sails for a beam reach, swinging the yards around to present the most sail area. The canvas, lifeless just moments before, fluttered. As the wind filled it, the canvas boomed out with a pleasing snap. The thirty-star American flag flying at the end of the spanker gaff lifted to the breeze and streamed off to leeward.

The gurgle of water at the bow grew louder. As the ship picked up speed, the passengers rejoiced in the steady murmur of the sea against the hull. They let the wind stream over their faces like the cool wash of a mountain brook. It tousled their hair and dried their sweat-dampened clothes. Almost giddy at the prospect of freedom from the inertia that had pervaded every waking moment of the past few days, Ellen joined the passengers at the rail, smiling broadly as the wind breathed life into the ship and began the voyage anew.

Flying Cloud averaged nine knots through the night, and by noon, June 24, she was out of the doldrums and just ninety-seven miles from the equator. Clear, dry weather with puffy cumulus clouds splashed against a light blue sky replaced the steamy, squally weather of the doldrums and elevated the spirits of everyone aboard. The entire ship's company, seventy-eight souls, buzzed with excitement over their remarkable luck. Only three days in the doldrums. Few ships ever made it through so quickly.

At the ship's present speed, she would cross into the Southern Hemisphere at around ten o'clock that evening just twenty-one sea days out from New York over a course of 3,780 miles. There was much talk about crossing the equator among the members of the crew, some of whom were intent on initiating the green hands in the ancient ritual. Though initiations were seldom allowed on merchant ships, when passengers were aboard and the captain agreed, the crossing was an occasion of much sport for all hands, sport that might have struck a landsman as cruel. The Old Man, however, upon receiving the crew's request for a bit of skylarking, firmly quashed any hope for it. On a well-disciplined merchant ship, he said, order was maintained at all times. *Flying Cloud*'s crew would cross the line without prank or ceremony, or face the dire consequences of disobeying a direct order.

In the old days, though, the green hands routinely received a hazing upon crossing the line, and they still did aboard ships of war. It was a rite of passage almost every old-time sailor had endured, and it served to relieve the frustration and boredom when becalmed in the doldrums. The green sailors, or lubbers, who had not yet crossed the equator were blindfolded and summoned on deck one by one to sit before the court of Neptune, king of the sea. Triton, Queen Amphitrite, and the humpbacked and horned devil Davy Jones were all in attendance, played by seasoned members of the crew. A sea lawyer, shorthand for troublemaker, was also part of the ritual. His job was ostensibly to defend the lubber, but the objective was really to dig him deeper in trouble with Neptune. The officers of Neptune's court dressed in costumes consisting of beards and wigs made from unraveled old ropes, worn-out coats, and pieces of junk wood to serve as tridents. The lubber was seated on a plank set over a tub of brine, and Triton or Davy Jones questioned him.

"What is your name and occupation?" Triton grumbled.

When the sailor opened his mouth to answer, a swab soaked in a solution of soap, caustic soda, and water, affectionately referred to as soogy-moogy, was promptly thrust into it. This usually disinclined the sailor to answer any more questions.

"Are you a lubber, or a sailorman?"

If the sailor failed to answer, which most of them did, one of Neptune's court dashed him with a bucket of water or prodded him with a stick. When the questioning was done, they swabbed more soogy-moogy on the lubber's face and shaved it off with a razor, at which time Neptune proclaimed him a true sailorman for having come across the line. He was promptly pushed into the tub of brine, and the next victim was hauled up from below for his bit with the court. The green hands were told they could expect to feel a bump as *Flying Cloud* crossed the equator, and more than a few of the ignorant lads believed it.

After supper, the passengers gathered on deck to enjoy the relative cool. They sang songs as the sun sank low and made its sudden dip below the horizon. The reds, pinks, purples, and blues blended into colors of ever transforming shades and textures, and the blink of stars twinkled faintly through the fading light of the sun. Their old friend Polaris, the North Star, had given way at last to the stars of the Southern Hemisphere. The Southern Cross appeared off the left side of the ship and slowly began its nightly ascent across the black dome of sky. Of all the constellations to the south, the Southern Cross was the best known. Its crosslike appearance was a great comfort to the early explorers, reminding them of their religious faith. It was as familiar a sight to the people of the Southern Hemisphere as the Big Dipper was to individuals living north of the equator.

When *Flying Cloud* drew near to the shoulder of Brazil, Ellen changed course to due south, aware that they were sailing into an area of ocean that required close attention to navigational details. A strong westward-setting current attempted to push the ship too far inshore, where the winds were less steady and there was the chance the ship might get forced downwind of Cape São Roque. Although the easternmost coast of Brazil was bold and dropped sharply to great depths not far offshore, dangers lurked close in. The going was also not completely clear out at sea. In particular, the navigator making the approach faced a dangerous obstacle, the Atol das Rocas, a shoal that rose suddenly from the seafloor about 120 miles northeast of Cape São Roque, right in the path of *Flying Cloud* on her present course.

Part of a chain of banks and seamounts extending two hundred miles northeast of Cape São Roque, the Atol das Rocas was a desolate protrusion of rock and sand inhospitable even to the seabirds. No lush palms swayed in the breeze. No clear lagoon inside a protective coral reef provided shelter in a storm. There was no fresh water to speak of, just low grass swept in the wind on two sandy mounds nine feet tall at low tide and practically invisible until the flash of breakers loomed off the bow. In storms, the entire area was a deathtrap of seething combers piling up on the shoals to break in thunderous procession, and boiling currents that kicked up a confused cross sea. Even on a calm day the swells broke with a magnificence that spoke to the soul, arousing a primal connection to nature and a healthy respect for its power.

Ellen ran through her sights with extra care, thankful that the weather was fine, visibility seemingly unlimited and sea conditions moderate, which went far in assuring the best accuracy with the sextant. Steering due south, the east-southeast wind blew gently just forward of broadside on. *Flying Cloud* moved sleekly along, responsive to the slightest touch of the helm.

Based on her noon calculations, Ellen put the ship on a longitude of 33 degrees 26 minutes west and on a latitude of 1 degree 56 minutes south, or about 120 miles due north of the Atol das Rocas. She plotted the exact longitude of the Atol das Rocas and noted that the ship would pass the danger about twenty-three miles to the east, a safe enough margin. But there was the westerly current and the leeway to account for from the east-southeasterly wind.

As the wind pushed against the ship's sails from the side, it moved the vessel laterally across the sea as well as forward, causing leeway. Ellen estimated that at their present rate of speed the ship would require approximately twelve hours to come up to the Atol das Rocas. In that time it was possible for the ship to get pushed by both current and wind off her course onto the hazard. The predicting of future events based on the knowledge of the moment was the essence of her art, as was the thought and challenge that went into taking just the right action in response at just the right time.

The following twelve hours represented a game of timing, a delicate blend of mathematics and artful guessing. As the ship moved forward and made leeway to the west, the Atol das Rocas would creep closer and closer to a point dead off the bow. It would be dark when the ship reached the Atol das Rocas's parallel, the breakers ahead difficult to see. Ellen had to know exactly at all times the ship's margin of safety and what time to order a course change before the ship approached within a league, or three nautical miles, of the edge of the shoals east of the islands. As the ship slowed and sped up, the estimated time of arrival changed on an hourly basis. Ellen factored all these considerations into her work tracking the ship throughout the day.

Ellen could have ordered a course change to sail the ship midway through the sixty-mile slot between the Atol das Rocas and the Fernando do Noronha Archipelago, another patch of islands to the east. But that ran against her mandate, her covenant with Perkins to get them to San Francisco without delay. Aboard a merchant vessel in the not so distant past, sailing mere miles off course made no difference, nor did days lost on a cumulative basis every time the commander grew lax. But *Flying Cloud* was sailed much like a rich man's racing schooner, her captain and crew tense and finely tuned to coax every half knot of speed from her hull.

Instead of changing course, however, Ellen maintained it through the day. Her observations confirmed her thinking. The ship was indeed being set into the Atol das Rocas at a speed sufficient to put them slowly in danger as the hours passed. Still, she steered due south, into the darkening night.

Chapter 12

The deep sea was a place of relative peace for Ellen, despite its occasional fury. With *Flying Cloud* sailing far from land, there was plenty of sea room and little to worry about. If a storm came up, the ship could ride it out without Ellen having to concern herself with the hazards generally encountered close to a coast. Most of the days aboard during much of the voyage passed in a comforting routine as the plots Ellen marked on the chart stretched out in a trail of small dots against the white paper that graphically represented the empty ocean all around the clipper. Nearly every day since their departure from New York had shown progress as the ship sailed onward.

The closer *Flying Cloud* drew to a coast, however, the more Ellen needed to take into account a number of variables that complicated the navigational equation. The circular, rotational tides of the deep ocean subsided and became defined tidal streams flowing around islands, off headlands, and into and out of bays in a timeless cycle. These tidal currents forced a ship off course, and it required careful navigation to avoid trouble. Under the influence of the tide and inshore shoals, the waves grew short and steep, and often dangerous in storm conditions.

Regardless of how much Ellen wanted to reach a hospitable port at the end of a voyage, she knew an approach to any shore offered a cold welcome to the person responsible for guiding the ship. Navigation close to shore presented far more of a challenge than simply gliding day after day across an ocean. Inshore work was also much riskier.

As the ship neared the Atol das Rocas, the first hints of their closing with the land emerged as the swells shifted direction and piled up now and then in disturbed bunches. In the darkness, Ellen and Perkins could not see the surface of the water, just the sprinkle of reflected starlight on the smooth black sea and the flash of phosphorescence in the wake. But they could feel the ship's motion change as they neared the Atol das Rocas. The presence of land in the midst of nothing caused the swells to break and wash out from the shores, setting up a variation in the wave pattern that translated to a more discernible pitch as the ship sailed on. Like the Polynesians of the Pacific, Ellen used sea changes as an additional way to confirm the ship's position. In time the waves would grow more chaotic as the ship closed with the islands, but they would not sail much closer.

At midnight, when the watch changed and all hands were on deck, Perkins ordered the crew to prepare the ship for turning. The crew scrambled to their stations. Working more from their sense of touch than with their eyes, the men grabbed the appropriate lines and stood ready to do their part in turning the ship away from the Atol das Rocas. This involved the somewhat complicated maneuver called tacking. On their present course, the wind blew over the port, or left-hand side of the vessel. Changing course and sailing away from the Atol das Rocas required the ship to tack, turning her bow right into the wind to position the ship to catch the breeze on the opposite side of the bow, the starboard or right-hand side.

The sailors remained quiet, waiting for the captain's order. Some of the crew stood at the bow to pull the triangular jibs set on the bowsprit over to the other side of the ship. Other men on deck manned the braces, the sturdy ropes used to pivot the yards around the masts. Still more men lined up on the poop deck to tend the enormous fore-and-aft sail known as the spanker. Thomas Austin

Tacking a Square-Rigged Ship

Tacking: turning the bow through the wind

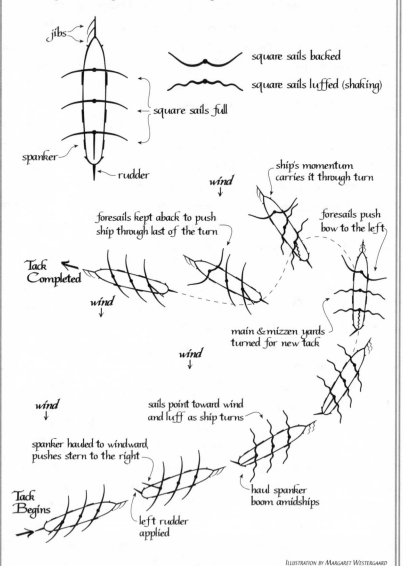

jibs

square sails backed

square sails luffed (shaking)

square sails full

spanker

rudder

wind

ship's momentum
carries it through turn

foresails kept aback to push
ship through last of the turn

foresails push
bow to the left

Tack
Completed

wind

main & mizzen yards
turned for new tack

wind

wind

sails point toward wind
and luff as ship turns

spanker hauled to windward,
pushes stern to the right

haul spanker
boom amidships

Tack
Begins

left rudder
applied

ILLUSTRATION BY MARGARET WESTERGAARD

supervised the men responsible for the sails on the foremast, and Thomas Smith those handling the sails on the main and mizzen masts. Men nimbly climbed aloft and readied the staysail sheets for the new tack. Each triangular staysail, set between the masts, had two lines, called sheets, connecting its lower end to the deck. As the ship turned, each line had to be brought over to the other side to clear the standing rigging. Shouts from alow and aloft indicated all was ready for the maneuver.

The ship sailed silently on as Perkins faced the wind, gauging its strength and direction by its soft, warm touch on his cheeks and the skin on the back of his neck. To tack at night demanded attention to detail. It was difficult to see the sails and to ascertain the wind's direction as the ship turned. He ordered the helmsman to run *Flying Cloud* off the wind at a broader angle to pick up speed sufficient to turn the ship. The clipper gained momentum fast.

"Ready about!" Perkins shouted.

"Ready about, aye, sir!" the mate replied.

Perkins turned to the helmsman. "Down helm," he said, and the ship turned smoothly toward the eye of the wind. Straight and true she turned, the sails rumbling, lines snapping, blocks banging and creaking. The quiet of moments ago vanished in an instant as the ship fell out of harmony with the wind and slowed in the water. The vessel pointed straight into the wind, the foresails, still braced for the port tack, blanketing the main and the mizzen. The canvas shook but could not draw, and under the reduced load the braces went slack. The men hauled with a will. Their shouts rang out in the night. The yards swung neatly around the mast to catch the wind from the new direction. The ship slowed nearly to a stop, but there was enough momentum to carry the bow through the rest of the turn. The main and mizzen sails filled with a loud snap, and the force of the wind aided the crew as they braced the yards of the foremast around.

Executed perfectly, the maneuver brought *Flying Cloud* in a wide horseshoe loop to a northeasterly course. The wind now blew over the right side of the bow. The Atol das Rocas lay off the stern, and every minute put the danger farther away. The slight disturbance of the swells disappeared and the ship was again beyond the influence of the land, at peace on a gentle sea.

Flying Cloud sailed clear of the Atol das Rocas and at two o'clock in the morning Ellen determined the ship was in a safe position to turn back to a southerly course. All hands were called and the ship was smartly tacked south in the light tropical breeze. For the next few days, *Flying Cloud* continued her run south with the fair wind coming in just forward of the mainmast, a fine point of sail that carried the ship down a meridian of 33 degrees west on a course parallel to the northeastern tip of South America, Cape São Roque. The past four days since leaving the doldrums tallied up a total of 744 miles, steady progress that boded well for the run to Cape Horn.

Based on Maury's sailing directions, Ellen planned to sail west to a longitude of 35 degrees, where she would run south keeping well offshore but not going any farther east than their present meridian until she reached Cape Frio, a bold headland just above Rio de Janeiro. Maury's directions for Cape São Roque to Cape Frio were written in his dense, elongated scientific prose full of tangential offshoots that undoubtedly baffled many a navigator. It was possible to ignore Maury's reasoning, not to know the why behind the directions, but that diminished their value, at least for Ellen. To gain a thorough understanding of why Maury suggested one route and advised against another required a concerted effort to absorb all he had to say about the ocean currents, the winds, the atmosphere, and other phenomena.

Ellen understood that Maury's directions kept the ship squarely in the favorable Brazil Current, which flowed southward at a good clip until it gradually weakened beyond Cape Frio. With this current, Ellen expected to make good progress. The course also kept the ship from the unsteady land and sea breezes close to shore and the treacherous tidal currents that could run a vessel aground on the islands and off-lying shoals that extended beyond the desolate beaches of Porto Seguro. Maury's explanations made it clear that the new route was in close harmony with the natural elements for good reason. An understanding of how to put them to use made fast passages possible.

On June 27, Ellen ordered a course change to south 27 degrees west to take her closer to shore. *Flying Cloud* loped along in the diminishing east-southeasterly wind, and on the first night watch from eight o'clock to midnight the last of the trade winds died out altogether. A southerly breeze began to blow and slowly shift toward the bow in fitful puffs and longer spells of steady air. The shifting wind direction did not favor the square sails. Even though the yards were braced at the best possible angle to catch the wind, *Flying Cloud* could not sail on the desired course. The ship lost headway and rolled in the swells at the northern edge of the variables, a large wedge of unpredictable winds. In June off the east coast of South America, the variables sometimes extended north of Cape Frio and south below Buenos Aires.

Calms broken with the occasional relief from the southerly wind gave way to squalls and unsettled weather to the south and southeast. The sky darkened under a thick mat of clouds laced with dark black and dull gray. The ocean took on a similarly leaden appearance and the air grew cooler. The more experienced sailors aboard looked aloft and cursed. It was Sunday, a time to mend and wash clothes, read, or just sit on the forecastle deck, backs against the capstan, smoking and telling stories. It was their custom and right to relax on Sundays when the weather allowed, but as the seasoned hands expected, the wind slowly freshened into a stiff south breeze and put an end to any hope for a break in the constant work.

Flying Cloud sailed close-hauled, meaning the wind blew at an angle over the bow. Under those conditions, a sailing ship tilted, or heeled, as the sailors called it. Unlike when the wind blew over the stern and pushed the ship along, sailing close-hauled relied more on the lift the sails provided. The air pressed against the sails, and in the gusts it pushed the ship over until the rail on the low side plunged underwater. The motion aboard became very rough as the clipper rose to meet the short, steep waves that quickly formed. Sheets of spray flew over the bow and pattered on the forecastle deck.

Looking off to the southeast, Ellen observed the blur of rain descending from the bottom of a particularly dark bank of low clouds. The rain linked the sea with the sky, marrying the two in a tumultuous whirl of energy. She glanced nervously at Perkins, then at the jury-rigged mainmast. The first gust of the squall whistled across the water and hit the ship with an incredible burst of power. She reeled under the pressure of the wind, dug the tips of her leeward yards into the tops of the waves, and took solid water over the rail. The next gust nearly pushed the ship over on her side. Ellen hung on tightly to the windward shrouds of the mizzen mast, clenching them till her knuckles went white. As the ship accelerated, the wind whipped strands of her hair and billowed the soft material of her dress. She felt the first pellets of rain, cool and startling to the skin.

Before Ellen had time to go below for her rain gear the sea metamorphosed into a raging fury of short breaking crests. The wind screamed in the rigging and kept *Flying Cloud* pressed hard over, exposing a large expanse of her dull green copper sheathing and some of her rudder. Rain slashed through the air in whirlwind twists. It beat against the sails and deck and stung Ellen's cheeks. The wind was strong enough to take her breath away if she looked into it full on.

Perkins shouted to the helmsman struggling to keep control of the wheel. He ordered the man to steer *Flying Cloud* so that the wind blew more from astern, enabling the vessel to keep upright on an even keel and speed along with the squall. *Flying Cloud* slowly righted herself, helped to her feet in a lull, and tore through the waves as all hands trimmed her sails to catch the full force of the wind. She parted the waves in roaring masses of foam and spray that drove far out on either side of the bow and over the forward rails.

"All hands! All hands! Lay aloft to shorten sail," Perkins cried through his speaking trumpet. "We'll take her down to topgallants and reefed topsails to relieve the masts," he shouted in Ellen's direction.

Like hers, his eyes were constantly looking upward. The strain on the rig was unimaginable in the highest gusts, some of which exceeded fifty knots, and the wet sails increased the weight, further taxing the stays and shrouds. The ship was over-canvased for such winds, and each burst laid her over on her side. The windward stays and shrouds thrummed and vibrated, every fiber of hemp stretched to its maximum.

The crew worked the lines needed to lift the skysails and royals close to the supporting yards. The canvas thundered and shook in the driving rain, blots of white confusion against the gray backdrop of the sky. Next the sailors lowered the yards down the mast to their proper place when no sail was set and secured them. In minutes, the lightest, most able men climbed the ratlines to where they terminated at the bottom of the topgallant pole masts. The sailors climbed the rest of the way to the skysail yards on a narrow rope ladder that swayed precariously in the wind.

Timing the moment to the roll of the ship, the first man hoisted himself up on the main skysail yard 125 feet above the deck. He planted his feet firmly on the footropes and pressed his body to the yard as he moved out toward the end on the windward side of the clipper. His two companions followed him. Starting from the center of the skysail, they hauled and beat the canvas into submission, furled it, and secured it with gaskets. As they worked, every roll of the ship almost pitched them overboard. At those heights, the velocity of the wind was far greater than it was on deck. It clawed at their bodies and snatched their breath away. The rain blinded them.

Lower down on the masts, dozens of other crewmen worked on taking in the topsails. These were among the largest sails aboard the ship, and in a blow the flapping canvas was capable of whipping a man off a yard in seconds. Topsails possessed power enough to snap bones, or cut off limbs if a man got his arm or leg caught in lines suddenly under load. Most of the sails could be made progressively smaller through a process known as reefing, which was similar to furling a sail, only some of it was left set when reefed and all of it was taken in when furled. The larger sails could be reduced, or reefed, in three stages. The single reef reduced the sail area only a little, the double reef a little more, and the third, or close reef, was as small as the sail could get without being furled. Reefing gave the captain options when the wind got up, allowing him to set enough canvas to sail fast even during gales.

More than a dozen men lined the main topsail yard to put in the single reef Perkins had ordered. The sailors hauled up part of the sail, rolled it into itself, and tied the partial furl in place, leaving most of the sail still set. Other crewmen took in the main and fore courses. These were the big, billowing sails that made up the lowest tier on the masts. The sound of the flogging canvas reminded Ellen of gunshots. Combined with the scream of the wind in the rigging and the roar of the sea, it was a fearful sound.

For the first time since leaving New York, *Flying Cloud* sailed with reefs in her topsails. With only topgallants and single-reefed topsails flying, the masts looked naked. Under reduced canvas, the ship's motion grew less violent. She went back on her southwesterly course without smashing into the waves as much, but also without making much headway.

Flying Cloud continued sailing under shortened sail through Monday, June 30, zigzagging to windward in a nasty sea made disorderly in the gusty, squally conditions. The waves piled up in pyramids that collided and collapsed in a rumble audible above the wind. As the breakers rolled toward the vessel, momentarily obliterating the horizon, it seemed as if she might be overwhelmed. When the waves dashed against the hull and flooded the deck, the clipper hesitated, staggering under the weight of tons of water. But the water quickly drained from the decks, and she rose to meet the next onslaught and sped south toward Cape Horn.

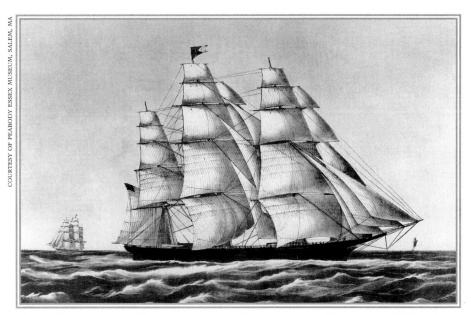

Flying Cloud *was and still is the most famous clipper ship in the United States. While her lines were not that different from those of other clipper ships, she showed time and again an almost magical ability to sail swiftly. Much romance and lore surround this ship. However, what remains clear is that she performed well beyond the expectations of her builder, Donald McKay; her owners, Grinnell, Minturn & Company of New York; and her captain and navigator, Josiah Perkins Creesy and Eleanor Creesy.*

At the time of her launching, Flying Cloud *was the largest merchant ship in the world. She was 235 feet from bow to stern and carried approximately 10,000 square yards of canvas. Several thousand people came to Donald McKay's shipyard in East Boston on the day she was launched, April 15, 1851. None of the spectators could have foreseen that she would remain interesting to people throughout the world 150 years later as a result of her unbroken record runs from New York to San Francisco over 16,000 miles of open ocean.*

This woodcut appeared in the Boston Daily Atlas *shortly after the launching of* Flying Cloud.

DONALD McKay

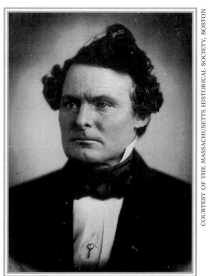

In 1826, McKay emigrated from a coastal town in Nova Scotia to the United States at the age of sixteen. He worked his way up in the world of shipbuilding to become one of the most well known and respected men in his trade. McKay built thirty-one clipper ships between 1850 and 1858. His most famous ship was Flying Cloud. *McKay's shipyard was located in East Boston. Old-timers along the waterfront said he used to prowl among the ships under construction late at night and embrace the bows, imparting his spirit to the timbers and blessing the ships with good luck.*

At the height of the gold rush, as many as ten thousand men worked in the shipyards of New York. In Boston, a major rival in both shipbuilding and shipping interests, a similar number of laborers swarmed about the great hulls as the construction process progressed. Donald McKay's shipyard was among the most prolific of all. A clipper ship could be built in an average of ninety days. Seasoned timber was in such short supply that many clippers were built with green wood, which greatly diminished their hull integrity and reduced their years of service.

This photograph provides a good view of Donald McKay's shipyard, as the clipper hull of Glory of the Seas *neared completion in 1869.*

Boston Harbor was one of the busiest ports in the United States in 1851, though not as full of hustle-bustle as New York, and it offered one of the best natural harbors on the East Coast. Many fine ships were built there, including Flying Cloud. This illustration shows the harbor in 1854, long before the flats were filled in to make room for the growing city and, ultimately, Logan International Airport.

Flying Cloud did not cause much of a stir among residents of New York City while loading for California in preparation for her maiden voyage. She may have been the largest merchant sailing ship afloat, but even larger clippers were under construction in the East River shipyards, most notably Challenge. However, after her record voyage, Flying Cloud was the talk of the town. Her passage made headlines in major cities throughout the United States and Europe.

This painting shows Flying Cloud moored at the pier at the foot of Maiden Lane on the East River. She boasts a studdingsail painted with an advertisement noting that she will soon sail for California.

JOSIAH PERKINS CREESY, JR.

Captain of Flying Cloud, *Creesy was among the more forward-thinking commanders of his day. He shared the responsibilities of running the ship with his wife, Eleanor, who served as navigator. While many wives of captains went to sea with their husbands, few took on official duties as Ellen did. An exhaustive search failed to turn up any images of her, so despite her accomplishments she remained overshadowed by her husband, quite typical of the relationship between men and women in Victorian times and in later times as well.*

LIEUTENANT MATTHEW FONTAINE MAURY

When Flying Cloud *set off on her maiden voyage on June 2, 1851, Eleanor Creesy made a concerted effort to obtain a copy of Maury's* Explanations and Sailing Directions to Accompany the Wind and Current Charts, *published earlier that same year. Maury's work in charting winds and currents led to new sailing routes between New York and San Francisco that significantly shortened the passage.*

Maury was a mentor for Eleanor. She read his works, studied his charts, and factored his revolutionary thinking into her tactics for navigating Flying Cloud *on her record-setting passage from New York to San Francisco in eighty-nine days, twenty-one hours in 1851. In 1854,* Flying Cloud *broke her own record on the same route, arriving in just eighty-nine days, eight hours, a passage no other square-rigged ship ever surpassed.*

An aerial view of lower Manhattan in 1849, looking southward from Union Square toward the Verrazano Narrows. Notice the large number of sailing ships on the East River and the Hudson River, known at the time as the North River. New York Harbor in the early 1850s was the busiest port in the United States, largely because of the transatlantic packet trade with Europe. Raw materials such as cotton were shipped to New York on coastal packet ships and sent across the Atlantic to England, France, and Germany. Packet ships returned to New York with an abundance of manufactured goods.

Early lithographers used to send their equipment up in balloons to obtain aerial shots such as the one shown here. It was a time-consuming and often frustrating endeavor.

Ships putting into San Francisco Bay after a long voyage around Cape Horn were often abandoned and left to rot in the harbor. Crews anxious to get to the gold fields jumped ship by the thousands. Some captains clapped their crews into irons belowdecks to prevent them from escaping, though the practice was soundly discouraged.

At 11:30 A.M. on August 31, 1851, when Flying Cloud *sailed through the Golden Gate and came to anchor off San Francisco, as many as eight hundred ships were anchored in the harbor. The derelicts were stripped of their wood and canvas, which was used to build temporary shelter for the residents of the city. The ships were also converted into piers and boardinghouses, and some of the planks were used to construct sidewalks.*

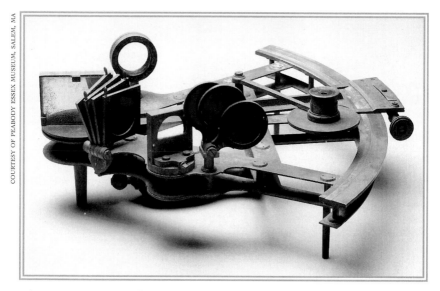

The sextant was one of Eleanor Creesy's most important tools for navigation. An optical device used to measure a celestial body's angle of elevation above the horizon, the sextant enabled Eleanor to find her way across thousands of miles of empty ocean. Most navigators carried a spare sextant. If the primary instrument broke, the navigator could still locate the ship's position at sea.

An early form of sextant called an octant was in use as early as 1731. Two men are credited with its development at roughly the same time, John Hadley of England and Thomas Godfrey of Philadelphia.

The modern compass card is broken up into 360 degrees. North is zero and the degrees increase in number clockwise until reaching 359. This type of compass card was first suggested for use in the United States Navy in 1901 and was implemented a few years later. Prior to that most compass cards were broken into four quadrants of 90 degrees each, as shown.

Eleanor Creesy directed the helmsman to steer courses based on the four-quadrant compass card. For example, on a modern compass a heading of 100 degrees would be 10 degrees past due east, which is 90 degrees. Eleanor would have directed the helmsman to steer south 80 degrees east. To find the proper course, look at south, marked zero, and count 80 degrees counterclockwise to east. This course would equal a heading of 100 degrees on a modern compass.

When Flying Cloud *hit heavy weather, violent seas frequently roared over the lee rail. The crew rigged lifelines from one end of the deck to the other to grab as a wave boarded the vessel, preventing them from washing overboard. In bad conditions, it was too dangerous for the passengers to venture out on deck.*

The photograph above shows the power of the sea at the height of a Cape Horn storm. It was taken from the deck of a windjammer, a type of sailing vessel that came after the age of the clippers.

Clipper ships were designed with very sharp bows that had little buoyancy. The knifelike bows meant the ships could sail swiftly, but in heavy weather waves would sweep across the forecastle deck. Hapless crewmen often were washed overboard.

Above is a windjammer with the forecastle deck awash in a storm off Cape Horn. Flying Cloud *weathered severe storms on her way to San Francisco in 1851.*

Clipper ships bound from New York to San Francisco had to round Cape Horn from east to west against the prevailing westerly winds and the huge waves sailors call graybeards. The wind and waves could delay a clipper ship for days or weeks.

Above, a Cape Horn sea rolls in toward the stern of a windjammer. When a wave washes up behind a ship, sailors call it a following sea, and with the wind astern it is known as a downhill run. If Flying Cloud *had been unlucky, she would have had to sail into waves as high as or higher than the one shown here.*

The storms off Cape Horn were well known to sailors. The high winds and waves often sank ships with great loss of life. This scene reflects the horror many sailors encountered off Cape Horn in the days of sail.

Chapter 13

The weather system behind the fresh southerly winds and squall lines gradually died out and left *Flying Cloud* trapped in a series of light, variable winds that remained stubbornly against her. The ship fought for every mile as she made her way slowly along the tropical lowlands of northeastern Brazil. The poor sailing conditions forced Ellen to turn the ship closer to shore in hope of finding better wind. She would have preferred to follow Maury's sailing directions without deviation, but she reminded herself that his data were not infallible. At all times the sea demanded a sensible, practical hand at the helm and a willingness to change course when conditions merited.

Flying Cloud turned inshore toward a part of Brazil that had supported settlements as far back as the mid-1530s, when Portuguese colonists founded a little town that grew to become the busy port of Bahia, present-day Salvador, and other cities as well. The wet, steamy climate proved ideal for growing sugarcane, and it became the primary export during the early period of Brazil's development. The discovery of gold and diamonds in the east-central interior in the early 1700s sparked additional settlements. The sheltered and beautiful harbor at Rio de Janeiro in southeastern Brazil bustled with activity. In 1800, it was the nation's largest city, with a population of 100,000.

Beyond the lowlands of the northeast, in the vicinity of Rio de Janeiro, the coast rose majestically from the beach in a long, steep slope called the Serra do Mar. Rising from the sea past Cape Frio, the blue, flat-topped mountains of the highlands, veiled in mist, appeared on the horizon and grew more distinct. The Brazilians called them the fingers of God. Close to the harbor of Rio, tall conical and mounded rocks jutted from the ocean and from the dense forests surrounding the city and covering the hills. The 2,300-foot Corcovado peak presented a stunning backdrop for the town and Botafogo Bay. The Brazilian Indians called the area Guanabara, "Breast of the Sea."

Southeastern Brazil was a far better place than the northeast for growing a wide variety of crops and for raising cattle. The port of Rio served as the key business center. Since 1822, when Brazil achieved independence from Portugal, the southeastern region had proved very attractive to settlers. Despite the steady growth of Rio with its crowded markets and the sprawl of whitewashed homes with red-tiled roofs, the land was an untamed frontier. Opportunity called individuals with spirits like those of the pioneers moving westward across the prairies of the United States.

In the early 1850s, Brazil was undergoing a time of growth and prosperity under the rule of Pedro II. Railroads were built to connect coastal cities to inland towns. Factories began manufacturing goods, reducing the need for expensive imports. Thousands of German, Portuguese, Italian, and Spanish immigrants established and worked the coffee plantations, known as fazendas, situated on fertile plateaus beyond the highlands and blessed with a climate cooler than the rest of Brazil. Coffee became the main export.

A popular drink of the day, known simply as "Rio" coffee, combined two of Brazil's most common products. A small cup was filled to the brim with sugar and a hot, thick, bitter coffee was poured over it. It was the custom to down the concoction in a single gulp. The sugar balanced the bitter taste of the coffee and the mixture was evidently quite good.

Some of the passengers aboard *Flying Cloud* wondered if Captain Creesy might put in to Rio for repairs. There was idle talk and conjecture on the subject. At the moment, however, the ship still sailed far north of Cape Frio. No decision was expected for several more days.

Ellen's new course brought the ship very close to the coast. At noon on July 3, *Flying Cloud* was only thirty miles from the beach, sailing across a wide bank of shallows extending 120 miles offshore. Early that morning, the ship sailed from ocean more than a mile deep onto a shelf that rapidly shoaled to only sixty feet well to the east of the ship's current position. Prudence dictated posting extra lookouts at the bow and taking soundings periodically to gauge the water depth. No chart ever revealed all the dangers. There was always the chance the ship might fetch up on a high ridge of sand or coral.

Off to the west, the coast of Brazil loomed visible on the horizon, a low dark smudge topped with a layer of thick white clouds. The water shimmered a deep green, the sky a light blue. With the gentle breeze the ship moved easily through the water, fast enough to foul the deep-sea lead line used for soundings offshore. Perkins ordered the crew to take in the studdingsails. When the crew finished their work with the studdingsails, he ordered them to turn the main topsail yard to position the sail to catch the wind from its front side. The canvas blew back against the mast and acted as a brake to slow the ship.

Four crewmen brought a large tub filled with hundreds of feet of line up to the mainmast, where they dropped it heavily on deck. Letting the line run free, they passed it forward outside of all the rigging to the man waiting at the bow with the deep-sea lead, a slender, heavy sinker weighing more than twenty pounds, which he tied to the end of the line. The men each took a coil and spaced themselves along the windward side of the vessel, ready for their orders. Stationed at the cathead to take the depth, Thomas Austin glanced aft at the men and shouted, "Stand by. Heave!"

The man at the bow heaved the lead and cried, "Watch, ho! Watch!"

The lead broke the smooth surface of the sea with a loud splash and dragged the line after it. Taking great care to avoid rope burns, the first man let the line run from the coil he held. When the last of his coil was about to go over the side he repeated the cry, "Watch, ho! Watch!"

The rest of the men followed the first, and the line went suddenly slack as the lead touched bottom. Austin peered over at the line and noted one knot just above the water, the first mark at twenty fathoms. Additional knots, leather strips, and rags of various colors tied down the length of the line denoted other specific water depths. "By the mark, twenty," he shouted, and the men repeated his call to ensure that the captain heard.

The handline used inshore had a much lighter lead for frequent soundings, but the crew sounded just once with the deep-sea lead. The sailors immediately hauled the line in. At twenty fathoms, they had 120 feet out, and several minutes passed, the men hauling in and carefully coiling the line in the tub before recovering the lead. Austin examined the tallow placed in the hole at the base of the lead and found it packed with a reddish mud. He reported his findings to the Creesys as the ship was put back on course and slowly gathered speed.

The land remained in sight throughout the day, and its appearance awakened a longing in all aboard. In some of the crew it kindled a deep desire to be put ashore. The Old Man, they thought, drove the ship too hard. He was too ready to carry sail when it should be shortened. With the damaged and jury-rigged mainmast, any sensible man would put into Rio de Janeiro for repairs. These and other complaints were voiced by a handful of the men of the starboard watch in the cramped, dark confines of the forecastle.

Ellen and Perkins considered the matter of the mainmast in the privacy of their cabin. Now that the ship was only several days' sail from Rio de Janeiro, the subject arose more frequently between them. The danger of sailing on to the higher latitudes in the depths of the southern winter with the mainmast sprung hovered in both their minds. Scarcely a day went by without a worry that there was no way to tell how much the mast could withstand, and when the ship drove hard the anxiety increased. Yet for Perkins not to drive on hard contradicted the essence of what a clipper ship was, what he was as a captain. Up to now he had bravely run the risks and Ellen had supported his decisions. However, the time had come to decide whether to put into port for repairs or to keep sailing south toward Cape Horn, and that presented a more complex issue.

A fast passage meant much to them on a personal level, and to Grinnell, Minturn & Company and all others with an interest in the ship. The high financial stakes factored into the mix of emotions. Ellen's desire to see Perkins further excel as a captain weighed against the risks involved in keeping on, and the possible consequences for all aboard if the worst happened. On the one hand her husband had a duty to get *Flying Cloud* to San Francisco as quickly as possible, and on the other he had the lives of the passengers and crew to consider, a moral obligation to take them into account. It was, therefore, not without considerable misgivings that she lent her quiet support to the decision to sail onward. There would be no repairs, at least none in Rio de Janeiro. Their course south of Cape Frio would put the next major ports, Montevideo and Buenos Aires, even farther out of the way.

When *Flying Cloud* reached the coast of Patagonia there would be no safe harbors where repairs of the kind required to fix the mainmast could be made. Their only recourse if serious trouble arose lay in plotting a course to the Falkland Islands. Situated about three hundred miles east of the Strait of Magellan, this group of approximately two hundred islands was one of the most isolated outposts in the South Atlantic. France, Spain, and England all laid claim to the Falklands at one point or another over a period of more than two centuries, but no nation appeared ready to fight to keep them. The islands remained largely uninhabited while the mainland of South America continued to develop. Occasionally, the islands served as penal colonies for both the Spanish and the British.

The two largest islands were known simply as East and West Falkland and were separated by a sound. Scattered around these were the many smaller isles, most of them barren wastes of rock and peat bogs. In fact, the entire group of the Falkland Islands offered little to attract any kind of settlement other than a penal colony. One of the key characteristics of the place was the singular lack of trees of any kind. The land rolled in low sloping hills covered with brown grass punctuated with high protrusions of dark rocky peaks and ridges more than a thousand feet above sea level. Wild horses and cattle, introduced by the French in 1764, lived on East Falkland. Wild hogs and rabbits existed on the islands as well, but the most common animals were the seals and the seabirds, for which the islands proved an ideal habitat.

The abundant seal population drew many sealing vessels to the shores of the Falkland Islands. Small parties of men landed on the beach, established a base camp, and proceeded to club the creatures to death as quickly as possible. The skins were dried and packed for shipment to major cities in Europe and the United States, as fur hats and coats were then very much in vogue. One hapless captain of a sealing vessel, Charles Bernard, wrote of being marooned with several crewmen in the Falklands during a voyage in 1813 in his book, *Narrative of Sufferings and Adventures*. He described the islands as utterly bleak:

> The islands present nothing but darkness and desolation to the eye; their sole vegetable productions are a species of coarse, long grass, and scattered patches of tushook, which every where abounds upon all the islands on this coast. They are surrounded by numerous reefs and keys, which oppose a perpetual barrier to the approach of vessels; and woe to the unhappy mariner whom contending winds dash against this inhospitable region! for here he will find deliverance from the waves to be only a prelude to a more lingering and awful death.

The Falklands were inhabited at the time *Flying Cloud* sailed. However, there were no trees to cut and no access to skilled craftsmen, to sailing there was a course of last resort. Clippers did put in to the islands when trouble arose, but only to find shelter while the crew jury-rigged broken spars and severed rigging to make their ship seaworthy enough to limp back to Buenos Aires more than a thousand miles to the north.

Thus, *Flying Cloud* had reached a turning point in the voyage. To sail on might well invite disaster. Ellen simply had to have faith that Perkins was right in choosing to sail on, that his decision was not based solely on financial considerations and his ambition but also on a firm belief that the mast would hold. It was a belief as equally based on faith as hers was in his motivations and judgment. The uncertainty of the situation weighed heavily on her. The stakes of the race suddenly appeared exponentially higher.

The wind continued light throughout the day, but gradually it swung to a more easterly quarter, bringing it nearly abeam. It settled in at barely a whisper from the east-northeast early Friday morning, July 4.

When the sun rose, no land appeared off the starboard side of the ship. They were alone, drifting and sailing in fitful winds under an overcast sky broken occasionally with rays of sunlight filtered artfully through tears in the cloud cover. The splashes of light caught the eye and held it. The sea sparkled and glittered in sharp contrast to the dark water in the shadow of the clouds, oily and thick with sediments washed up from the shallows below the keel.

The day started just like any other when the ship sailed peacefully, at ease in her element. The crew on watch cleaned and holystoned the deck, filled the scuttlebutt, coiled any loose lines neatly on the belaying pins, and fed the livestock. The log was streamed at the start of the forenoon watch at eight o'clock and the ship's speed was marked on the slate, five knots. All appeared typical, except for the cook. Always busy preparing three meals a day for seventy-eight people, he was even more so on this morning. With help from the steward, cabin boy, and some of the crew, he slaughtered chickens, a turkey, and a hog for the day's feast in celebration of the seventy-fifth anniversary of the birth of the United States. It was a day all aboard looked forward to as a break in the routine of daily shipboard life.

Toward midmorning the fragrant odor of baking bread and roasting pork wafted out of the open door of the galley. Crewmen and passengers alike found every excuse to wander near, linger a few moments to savor the flavorful air, and move on, lest they annoy the cook. Only Ellen, who had planned the menu, or one of the cook's assistants ventured into the galley.

While he prepared the feast for the cabin, the cook also worked up a special mess for the crew from the leavings of the hog, augmented with good pieces of salt pork and boiled potatoes. For dessert he boiled some flour, mixed in a goodly dose of molasses, and added bits of apple to give the pudding more body. It was as fine a duff as any sailor could wish for.

At eleven-thirty, the usual time for the crew's dinner, a crewman appeared at the galley door with his kid, a large wooden tub. The cook hoisted all the food for the watch from the stove and deposited it in the kid. Up forward, the men gathered around with their tin plates, which they provided for themselves as part of their outfit, and sliced off chunks of the fresh pork with their sheath knives. The sailors did not use silverware, nor napkins of any kind. They wiped their mouths on the sleeves of their warm-weather cotton shirts and their hands on the seat of their denims. Their meals, as simple as they were, required none of the refinements of civilization.

The sailor's usual diet consisted mainly of salt pork, salt beef, or salt fish and hardtack, a hard bread baked at low heat. There was little the cook could do to make the food taste good, and that was why the men appreciated and waited for their Sunday duff the week long. Along with the occasional ration of grog, it counted among their few comforts.

When a new barrel was opened, the first bits of salt pork or beef to wind up in the kid were those pieces with fat on them. These were juicier than the leanest cuts, which the sailors called "old horse." If the meat was bad enough, the crew swore it really was an old nag, not a steer or a hog, that sat in a puddle of cool, viscous grease, and, as for virtually every occasion, they had a favorite verse to sum up their opinion of the meat. When a truly bad specimen appeared in the kid, one of the sailors reverently picked it up, held it in both hands as if it were a baby about to be baptized, and solemnly said:

> Old horse! Old horse! what brought you here?
> —From Sacarap to Portland pier
> I've carted stone this many a year,
> Till, killed by blows and sore abuse,
> They salted me down for sailors' use.
> The sailors they do me despise,
> They turn me over and damn my eyes,
> Cut off my meat, and pick my bones,
> And pitch the rest to Davy Jones.

A common story passed around the waterfront told of a beef dealer who was caught selling horse instead of beef. The unscrupulous man was sentenced to remain in jail until he himself ate his foul wares. The outcome universally amused sailors throughout the world, regardless of whether it was true or not, and the story spread from forecastle to forecastle from Canton to Cape Town.

While the crew enjoyed however they could their Fourth of July dinner, under Ellen's watchful eye the steward and young Ching set the table in the great cabin. They folded the linen napkins and laid out the silverware. They set out crystal glasses and bottles of claret, champagne, Madeira, and brandy. Silver serving bowls and china platters they placed on the sideboard ready for the meal. With the easy motion of the ship in the near calm, the dinnerware stayed put. Admiring their work, the steward and Ching checked once more to see that all was right, every detail attended to, as the captain's wife had ordered.

"Everything looks wonderful, just wonderful," Ellen said, and smiled at the men. They thanked her politely and went forward to help the cook. Ellen followed them up the companionway stairs to the weather deck, where she joined Perkins and mingled with the passengers, all dressed in their finest clothes out of respect for the occasion.

The men without significant means, Willie Hall and Whitney

Lyon, wore simple suits—brown-and-white-plaid pantaloons, plain vests over white shirts, black cravats tied in a loose bow, and light cotton jackets. Wide-brimmed felt hats topped them off. The more dashing of the men wore white piqué trousers, embroidered vests, and flashy knee-length, tight-fitting coats with full skirts, set off with high hats. Laban Coffin and Francesco Wadsworth both sported diamond pins, which the ladies admired.

The ladies of means, which accounted for Mrs. Gorham and Sarah Bowman, dressed in fancy gowns with V-design bodices and full lower skirts. Sarah and Ellen Lyon dressed in tasteful but simple plaid or checked calico dresses with wide, low necklines, straight bodices, and a narrow waistline.

Perkins dressed in his customary tight-fitting gray coat, dark pants and vest, and white shirt with a black cravat. He cut a stern figure among the more colorfully adorned men, revealing in his dress a conservative side to his nature. On this day, he allowed himself to relax a little. He looked down at his wife, whom he had arm in arm. Artificial flowers decorated the delicate bun knotted at the back of her neck. With her hair pulled back, the gentle contours of her cheeks, fine brows, hazel eyes, and angular nose accented her smile. Her formal gown was of pale green satin with sheer white lace. The bodice hugged just above her shoulders and came down in a wide V neckline decorated with a bow, and the skirt flowed outward from her waistline to its full potential.

The rapid pings of the ship's bell momentarily silenced the witty exchanges of jokes and puns and the social banter. The steward summoned them below to the table. The passengers gathered together to make their toasts to God and country, to the good ship, to her captain and navigator, and to a fast and safe run to the Golden Gate. Willie Hall, whom they chose as orator of the day, read a poem he had written for the celebration. No sooner did the verse end than they all set to with a will on the vast spread laid before them—roast turkey and chicken with a rich oyster sauce, roast pork and boiled ham, potatoes and vegetables, and bread and butter, the latter nearly the last of the supply in the now nearly empty icehouse. For dessert they had English plum pudding, tarts, fruits, and nuts.

Throughout the meal the young aspiring writer, Willie Hall, earned for his efforts at poetry good-natured jests and praise from his fellow diners. A shy man, Hall smiled meekly and played along as best as he could. His quiet personality stood in sharp relief against those of the other male passengers, the boisterous and outgoing Francesco Wadsworth, J. D. Townsend, Whitney Lyon, and Laban Coffin.

"A toast to the poet of *Flying Cloud!*" one of the men boomed, and they all lifted their glasses and toasted Willie Hall. They repeated the cycle when the glasses needed refilling, which was often.

Seated side by side, Laban Coffin and Sarah Lyon spent much of the dinner talking together. Sarah's laugh, her smile, her eyes held Laban's attention. A success at sea and in business by his late twenties, Laban could afford to satisfy his wanderlust. Some of his wealth he had dug himself from the goldfields of California, and he was determined to enjoy himself. He spent much time sailing to exotic ports to savor the change in scenery, culture, and food.

The voyage aboard *Flying Cloud* marked the fourteenth time he would double Cape Horn and his fourth visit to San Francisco. This voyage, it seemed, held something more for him than the pleasures of travel. In Sarah he saw a possibility that had thus far remained in the background of his life. The thought that he might share his days with this companionable, intelligent lady from Roxbury began to surface in his mind at regular intervals. For her part, Sarah let herself hope the handsome Laban Coffin's interest in her would not fade soon after they reached the Golden Gate.

Ellen leaned close and whispered to her husband, "It seems as though Cupid has paid a visit to *Flying Cloud*." She laughed softly and glanced over at Laban and Sarah.

Perkins smiled, raised his eyebrows. "Perhaps," he said. He surreptitiously clinked his glass against hers. "May his aim be true."

Chapter 14

A lobe of shallow water arched southeastward from the main bank off the Brazilian coast and created a large, deep bight in the ocean floor north of Cape Frio. Under the sea the face of the shoal resembled a cliff more than a mile high. Unseen currents running deep below the surface churned up a nutrient-rich mix, and consequently the water near the steep drop-off teemed with life of every variety—krill, shrimp, bonita, and, most impressive, whales. They all converged to feed in a timeless natural cycle.

Whales followed paths through the seas every bit as precise as the clipper's, navigating by a means mysterious to mariners. They chased their food with the seasons, and when the time was right they waited off hospitable coasts to feed or to tend their young. Thousands of miles away, off the rocky shores of New England, where it was summertime, the whales returned to the cold waters. Humpback, finback, right whale, and the white-sided dolphin swept close in to feed off banks very similar to the one *Flying Cloud* was about to leave astern as she passed over the drop-off into the deep sea.

A pod of whales suddenly surfaced around *Flying Cloud*. They sounded and breached, struck the sea with their massive tails, and spouted great blasts of air that sounded like escaping bursts of steam. The passengers, sated and lethargic from their feast of hours earlier, leaped to the rails and pointed at the visitors. Edward Bowman shouted in delight as one of the whales swam close to inspect the hull.

"Thar she blows! Thar she blows, fine off the larboard bow," he cried, proud to show he knew the lingo of the crow's nest, just as the sailors had taught him.

The whales cavorted around the ship for a while, swimming close and seeming to look up at them with human curiosity. Though massive, they swam with a gentle grace that inspired awe. In one moment the sea boiled with the whales as they played, and the next, the water showed no sign of them. The whales sounded and disappeared as suddenly as they had come, to search elsewhere for their nourishment.

The whales provided a moment of pleasure for the passengers. It was natural to view the creatures with curiosity. However, it was equally natural for the passengers to consider whales on a par with farm animals. The leviathans were meant to serve man's needs. That they were magnificent was of little importance. Whale oil fueled lamps and lubricated machinery. Oil bailed from the heads of sperm whales was used to make candles. Ground whale bone was commonly used as fertilizer. The bonelike ribs in the mouths of baleen whales—those that strain the sea for plankton and krill, as opposed to toothed whales like the sperm and orca—were used for a wide variety of applications such as corset stays and skirt hoops, buggy whips and fishing rods, as well as stiffeners for umbrellas and hats.

Although life aboard a clipper ship was hard for a sailor, the men who set off in ships to hunt whales endured a truly desolate existence. Voyages lasted three or four years and often took sailors down around Cape Horn and up the entire length of the Pacific Ocean to the Arctic before enough oil was collected to fill every cask in the hold. When a whale was sighted, men chased it in swift rowboats. After the whale was harpooned, it dragged the boat as it tried to escape. That was called a Nantucket sleigh ride, and it was quite dangerous. Exhausted, the whale was easier to kill.

After the kill, the men towed the whale back to the ship, stripped off its blubber with huge spadelike knives, and boiled the blubber to render the valuable oil. Many sailors recoiled at the stench rising from the tryworks, which was essentially a large brick furnace built on deck. Still other sailors, however, thought nothing of dunking bits of raw dough in the boiling oil to make doughnuts.

In return for their work, the sailors received a small share in whatever profits the ship made at the end of the voyage. If the ship did well, the whaler might receive a bit more money per year than his counterpart on the clipper ships. But if the hunt went badly (one in ten voyages lost money), the wages could equal less than a hundred dollars for each year aboard the vessel. The whaling captain's share of the profits, though far more than a sailor's, seldom matched the annual salary paid to a clipper captain. The captain of a clipper had little in common with his whaling colleague. One man was a racer, the other a hunter.

The whaling industry had nearly reached its zenith, producing annual yields of approximately five million gallons of sperm whale oil, ten million gallons of train oil (oil distilled from blubber, as opposed to oil bailed from the heads of sperm whales), and five million pounds of bone. The industry's slow decline was not to begin until 1859, after petroleum pumped from wells assured a steady supply of a less expensive and more easily obtainable substitute for whale oil. The new well-drilling technology combined with an earlier advance to help spur the decline of whaling in the nineteenth century, prior to the industry's subsequent rise in the twentieth century. In 1849, a Canadian geologist named Abraham Gesner had invented a process whereby kerosene could be distilled from petroleum. Thus, whale oil was no longer needed for lamp fuel when petroleum became widely available.

But at the time *Flying Cloud* sailed, the ports of New Bedford, Nantucket, and New London bustled with whaling ships offloading casks of oil. New Bedford alone boasted a fleet of more than two hundred ships, the largest concentration of whalers in the world. At any given time, there were hundreds of whaling ships on the oceans, out of a total worldwide fleet of approximately one thousand. The whalers did not follow the routes of merchant vessels. Their captains were not making a passage. There was no destination other than home.

After the departure of the whales, the passengers settled back into their lethargy. The sound of *Flying Cloud*'s hull moving through the water, the occasional grunt or cackle from the animal pens, the creak of a block or the snap of a line—all these noises were familiar and conveyed a peaceful feeling. Later in the evening, the passengers gathered on deck and sang songs. They told stories, many of which were starting to sound old, as they were often repeated. The crew also relaxed, and all seemed well aboard, despite the undercurrent of discontent in the forecastle.

The wind favored the ship on the last of the run down to Cape Frio and beyond, farther down into the South Atlantic. It came in from the east-northeast at a perfect slant off the port quarter and filled every sail. It held for a day in that direction, then backed to the north-northeast and northeast, where it held through July 8, carrying the ship an additional 712 miles. Showers and hazy skies prevailed in the early days of winter in these latitudes, though the sun made its appearance conveniently enough for Ellen to take most of her daily sights.

As the days passed, *Flying Cloud*'s course, though it bore gradually to the southwest, put her farther and farther offshore. The coast of Brazil dropped away as she made her southing, sloping inward three hundred miles to the west, where it became the United Provinces of La Plata, or present-day Argentina. The balmy weather of the tropics faded perceptibly as the ship proceeded south to the high latitudes. In the predawn hours the damp, clammy air forced the officers and crew to don their wool sweaters, and soon they would wear their heavy pea jackets over them.

The fair wind hurried the ship into darkness as well as cold, with the sun sinking below the horizon earlier every day. It was odd seeing the daylight hours grow appreciably shorter in a single day, as it did when the ship sailed well. On July 6, the sun set at six o'clock. The next day it set at five-twenty. It played tricks on the mind to sail so palpably into a deepening winter when the senses were used to a gradual adjustment, the shortening of the days occurring without notice. It disoriented and depressed, made one feel as though the ship were headed for the edge of the earth, and, in fact, that was not very far from the reality of it.

The ship flew before fresh northerly winds through the early part of the morning of July 9, under full sail at the heels of violent squalls for much of the night. She covered three hundred miles in only twenty-four hours, an average sustained speed of more than twelve knots and the best run yet. She boomed along in perfect trim, her studdingsails set on both sides. The wind gradually shifted to the northwest to come in broadside off the right side of the ship, and by noon it fell off to a light westerly that ushered in a darker expanse of evil-looking clouds. A long, heavy swell set in from the southwest and kicked up a nasty cross sea.

Rain pattered on the glass panes of the skylight above the table in the great cabin and drummed on the deck in a regular pattern punctuated with the fall of larger drops from the rigging. Thunder, low and indistinct, rumbled far away in the distance, and slowly grew louder as the main part of the shower approached. The rain increased and the wind freshened, filling the sails, heavy and dark with fresh water. In warm climates, the passing of a thunder shower while snug in harbor, tucked under an awning or belowdecks, at times soothed and comforted, the rain a pleasant break from the tropical heat. But this latest in a series of thunderstorms did little to improve the mood of the passengers. They sat quietly at the table and nibbled their dinners. The large swell rolled the ship and made some of them feel queasy. The motion of the vessel and the chilly dampness that permeated their clothing added to the general discomfort.

Now more than a month out of port, the passengers longed for the simple pleasures of life, reading the latest newspaper, taking a walk under shade trees, or enjoying a night out at the theater. They missed their homes in the East, their families and friends. The usual doubts about the unknown, both immediately ahead as the ship neared Cape Horn and farther in the future, nagged at those among them who let their minds wander too far afield.

Concern about the future stained Sarah Bowman's days with anxiety, an anxiety that easily matured into fear the longer her mind lingered on what might happen, attracted and yet repelled by the emotion. The resulting fallout tainted the positive and brought out the more negative side of her nature. As the ship approached Cape Horn, she became less able to resist her anxiety. There was much talk of Cape Horn passages at the dinner table, and while she knew the tales were always embellished they still distressed her. The others failed to grasp the irony of telling stories of sinking with all hands aboard a storm-tossed vessel with a badly damaged main-mast.

One day, not long back in the voyage, Sarah had painted Ellen Creesy a beautiful rose, which was accepted with warm thanks and a smile. Ellen's sensitivity and kindness to passengers and crew impressed Sarah and led her to share her fears. Despite Ellen's effort to reassure her, however, Sarah remained worried.

While Ellen sought to comfort, Perkins did little to soothe Sarah's fears. If there was talk of storms and death at sea off Cape Horn, he delighted in it whenever Sarah was around, he and Mr. Coffin, who was much in his favor. Perhaps he was intuitively aware of her ill feelings toward him, knew that she thought him arrogant and a tyrant to the crew, which she did, or perhaps he was just indifferent.

Sarah retained a civil demeanor around the captain, but she wrote of him to her sister, Kate: "The captain speaks of the sailors as if they were dogs. I hate him cordially." In defiance of his orders, when he was not about she routinely slipped tidbits secreted from the table to the man at the helm.

Just as the moods were dark among the people aft, the day bred in the crew a somberness befitting the foul weather. Most of the men were experienced seamen who knew the ways of life aboard a hard-driving clipper ship and took great pride in a job well done. But there were greenhorns among them who viewed their presence aboard merely as an expedient way to get to the goldfields. They planned to desert as soon as they reached San Francisco, and because doing so would cost them all but the pay advanced prior to setting sail, they saw their duties as a bother. They considered the Old Man a devil, and two of the crew in the starboard watch hatched a plan against him.

Such men were called backslackers or soldiers, and in the worst of cases, marines. To call a sailor a marine meant he was lower than the lowest boy aboard, not fit even to slush the mast or clean the latrines. The sailor's disdain for marines was natural enough. Marines kept discipline aboard the men-of-war, as if they were seagoing police. The sailors' dislike of marines was passed from forecastle to forecastle in true keeping with tradition. All the merchant ships had a share of backslackers, as did all businesses with more than a handful of people working the enterprise. In 1851, with so many sailors intent upon trading their marlinespikes for picks, there were more of them than usual.

The storm gathered strength as the day progressed, building the seas and lashing their tops temporarily flat in the heaviest rains. The last of the daylight faded early, and the clouds hung low and heavy. The world became a varied mix of gray and black. The lightning flashes against the pale shadow of light to the west, over the pampas beyond Buenos Aires, streaked in bright threads across the sky. As the night deepened, the momentary bursts of light lit up the waves and exposed their frightful dimensions.

Fearing for the vessel's safety, Perkins ordered the men aloft to take in sail. The wind pressed them against the starboard ratlines as they ascended the wildly whipping masts more by feel in the dark than by sight. They inched across the yards, dazzled with the lightning and deafened with the thunder and wind. The topsails double-reefed, and all the square sails alow and aloft of them tightly furled, the men clambered back down to the deck, cold and soaked through under their oilskin jackets, pants, and seaboots. Under topsails and staysails alone, *Flying Cloud* stood up to the wind.

Below in her cabin, Ellen braced herself in one of the chairs, a book in her lap, and listened to the rain and the wind howl through the rigging. It was a lonely sound, like the wind in the eaves on a dark winter's night. The warm yellow glow of the lamp, the Oriental carpet, her husband's oak desk, their comfortable double berth, these somehow accentuated the feeling of bleakness, of being alone on a stormy sea.

The porthole suddenly shone white in a flash of lightning. Moments later a tremendous peal of thunder startled her, even though she knew it was coming. The short time between the flash and the thunder indicated the squall was close, very close. A sudden gust heeled the ship hard over to the left, and she accelerated with a rush as she shouldered aside the waves.

A knock on the stateroom door interrupted her thoughts. She opened the door to find Ching, clearly agitated.

"Mrs. Creesy! Mrs. Creesy, come quick," he said, his hands firmly gripping the narrow doorframe to keep from losing his footing. "It's Mrs. Gorham. She's bad. Very bad."

Just then the ship entered the worst of the squall. A blast of wind pushed the clipper over on her side and sent the papers and books on Perkins's desk falling to the floor, despite the fiddles built up on the edge to keep objects in place. Although the trunks were lashed to fittings to keep them secured, they shifted and pulled at the leather straps. The clipper slowly came back up on a more even keel and rushed forward, the topsails able to catch the full force of the wind above the large waves.

Ellen timed her steps to the roll of the ship and charted a course from one firm handhold to the next. She worked her way through the officers' quarters and the great cabin until she reached the narrow passage in the aft section where some of the passenger staterooms were located. In the passage she contented herself to weave, bouncing from one side to the other, with Ching in her wake.

She knocked lightly on Mrs. Gorham's door and Pearl let her in, tears streaming down her face.

"What's happened?" Ellen asked, as she went to Mrs. Gorham's berth. She lay very still and complained of severe pain about the abdomen. Ellen felt her forehead, found the skin cool and dry.

"She drank this," Pearl said, holding a bottle of what looked like medicine. "She thought it was her elixir."

Ellen examined the label. "This is poison!"

Judging by the amount of liquid in the bottle, a powerful household substance used to kill vermin, Mrs. Gorham must not have consumed much. It was a good sign. Just what Ellen could do she did not know, and she felt helpless for a moment. Deeply unsettled, Ellen leaned close to Mrs. Gorham and said, "All we can do is keep you warm, I'm afraid. I don't know what even a doctor could do." Ellen turned to Ching. "See she has some extra blankets."

"Yes, Mrs. Creesy," he said, and rushed off.

No one spoke. The storm outside sounded all the more menacing in the dim light of the stateroom. Ching returned with a blanket a few minutes later. He draped it tenderly over Mrs. Gorham.

"We should leave her to rest," Ellen said.

"I'll stay with her, Mrs. Creesy," Pearl said.

Ellen nodded and closed the stateroom door. She hesitated a moment, suddenly very tired. She picked her way back through the great cabin, holding on at every step and getting bruised just the same when the ship rolled and dashed her against a bulkhead, doorframe, or piece of furniture. Once back in her stateroom, she went straight to bed, hoping Perkins would not remain long on deck. Sleep did not come, however. As she lay alone beneath the blankets, the sounds of the ship laboring hard, the wind, and the waves kept her awake. Thoughts concerning Mrs. Gorham entered her mind and filled it with questions. To carry poison for killing vermin in a place like San Francisco, famous for its population of rats and fleas, was not unusual at all. But to mistake the bottle for another containing a remedy? To drink enough to cause illness?

Outwardly, Mrs. Gorham gave all impressions that she was happy. Yet she said things that led Ellen to believe she might not be as content as she let on, nor as sanguine of the prospects for her new life in the West. Mrs. Gorham freely admitted that she felt nothing more than cordial respect for her husband, whom she had married at the age of fourteen, nine years earlier. Mr. Gorham, a man twenty years her senior, had left her in New York for three of those nine years while he made his fortune in San Francisco, before sending for her. Might she not have a deep ambivalence about having to join him? She certainly had no choice in the matter, unless she took an irrational, drastic step.

Had Mrs. Gorham really consumed the poison by mistake, as she claimed? Or had she toyed with suicide and wisely kept silent about it? It was entirely possible the long voyage had instilled in her a dread of reuniting with a husband she might not know or like any better when they were together again. On so long a voyage, Mrs. Gorham had plenty of time to think about any matters that bothered her. Perhaps too much time.

Chapter 15

In the early gray of the next morning, the dim light was barely able to penetrate the thick layer of clouds. The seas rolling toward the ship looked almost abstract, a perfect image of chaos. They loomed out of the walls of rain and towered high above the deck with steep, overhanging crests that one could hear breaking above the howl of the wind. The shoulders of the waves extended a quarter mile and rose to heights of more than thirty feet, and when breaking, the force of the water carried away anything not lashed down.

The fury of the storm increased steadily and gathered strength as it blew across the barren grasslands of Patagonia and the broad, fertile expanse of the pampas. The gale held the chill of the Antarctic, though the temperature remained above freezing. There was a bite to the wind the experienced hands aboard knew well. It foretold of days, possibly weeks, of fighting the westerlies below the fortieth parallel through snow and ice storms. The foul weather soured the spirits of most of the men before the mast.

Below and up forward there would be no hot food or drink for breakfast, just a dying man's dinner, cold food served in times when the severe weather made it too dangerous to light the galley stove. There was the chance the fire might flare out of control, or more likely that water running down the stovepipe would douse it. If the cook was lucky enough to get the hell box lit, a violent lurch of the ship might throw him against the hot iron, or at the very least send his pots and pans flying as well as their contents. The want of hot food on such a foul, cold morning added to the discomfort of everyone aboard.

The steep and closely spaced seas battered *Flying Cloud*. They were not the big, alpine waves that marched unobstructed around the lower end of the earth, but close kin instead, making up in confusion and disorder what they lacked in majesty. The ship buried her bow deep as she careened down the face of one wave into the trough of the next. The larger groups of waves reached well above the lower yards and crashed down on the deck, sweeping her from stem to stern. The water flooded the forecastle and deckhouse. It soaked the belongings of the crew and drowned some of the livestock trapped in their coops and pens. It flowed down the stairs into the aft cabin, to the great distress of many of the passengers. Most particularly, the storm frightened Sarah Bowman. She retreated to her stateroom, feigning illness.

Perkins lashed himself to the rail within shouting distance of the men at the helm and the officer on deck. He gave orders when necessary, but otherwise set his jaw and held on. *Flying Cloud* began to lose her footing on the tops of the largest waves. As the clipper reached the summits, she hesitated. The helmsmen lost control and she slipped down the sides of the waves to hit the troughs. She shuddered under the impact from the tips of the masts to her keel. It was as if she had been picked up and dropped on rocks. She was moving too fast, out of harmony with the rhythm of the storm.

Knowing he could no longer drive her at such speeds, Perkins ordered the topsails close-reefed down to their smallest size. The crew soon had the fore, main, and mizzen topsails reduced to patches of white, tiny compared to their huge dimensions when fully set. There was, however, little difference in the clipper's speed and motion. She slowed just enough for the men to handle her.

The wind backed to the southwest late in the morning and came in with a ferocity to rival the storms off Cape Horn. The wind blew the tops off the waves and painted white streaks of foam down their backs. Spray filled the air. The rain felt like rough sand against the skin and blinded any man who faced the storm. In such serious heavy weather it took a minimum of two good men to steer *Flying Cloud* as she pitched and rolled in the monstrous seas. The helmsmen threw all their weight against the spokes of the wheel to keep the ship on course.

On her current heading, *Flying Cloud* ran the risk of going aback. Going aback meant the wind suddenly caught the sails from the front instead of the back side. If that happened, the wind pressing the sails backward against the masts toward the stern could rip the spars off their supports. The sailors at the helm were well aware of the potential danger, and they concentrated on their work. To keep on course required them to steer just about at the point of going aback, but not quite. It was dicey business. The regular two-hour tricks at the wheel were reduced to shifts of one hour. Once relieved, the sailors who had been steering staggered forward, their arms and shoulders sore from the exertion, their minds numb from the intense mental effort needed every second they manned the helm.

The ship sailed at the very edge of control and went beyond it. The main staysail suddenly split. The rending and loud bang as the canvas opened up reached the poop deck, and a moment later the fore staysail blew out. In the few minutes it took to get hands to douse them, the staysails tore into long streams of white against the darkness of the sky even as the men worked to secure them. With the wind now southwest, directly on their desired track, *Flying Cloud* could not keep her course. Perkins sent a man below to advise Ellen he needed a new heading.

Ellen settled in at the table in the officers' quarters, a shawl over her shoulders to ward off the dampness, her face drawn from lack of sleep. Mrs. Gorham, though still very ill, appeared somewhat better, for which Ellen was grateful. The incident cast a somberness over the passengers. With the storm pounding the ship, morale aboard had never been lower. The clipper had not yet even reached the west winds and gales of the roaring forties. If Cape Horn lived up to expectations, the voyage would no doubt get a lot worse before it got better.

Ellen concentrated on her duties, let them take her mind away from her less tangible responsibilities. The storm made it impossible to determine speed with any accuracy. Leeway as the ship moved sideways off her course because of the wind and waves remained difficult to figure as well. She estimated their noon position based more on her instincts than on her technical skills as a navigator. There were times when experience made all the difference. *Flying Cloud* sailed about 120 miles west of Cape Polonia and only twenty miles from the edge of the shoals of the Río de la Plata, a large funnel-shaped estuary that served both Montevideo and Buenos Aires. Two major rivers fed the estuary, the Paraná and Uruguay. Sediments from the rivers stained the sea brown and carried many miles east of La Plata, a natural sign for navigators that land was near.

In fair weather, sailing across the flats of the estuary to close with the shores of the United Provinces of La Plata to the south made good sense. The inshore route was shorter than staying well away from the land. However, even with a favorable wind direction, crossing the flats in heavy seas presented too many dangers. Waves in the shallow water of the tidal basin might soon grow too steep for the clipper to handle efficiently. There was also the possibility of running aground. Ellen plotted a southeasterly course to steer clear of the shoals.

The new course kept *Flying Cloud* sailing as much to the south as possible while still allowing for plenty of sea room. However, on the new heading, the wind blew broadside on the right side of the ship, hard off the starboard beam, and exposed the vessel to the full force of the breaking seas. As the seas broke over the rail, there was always the chance that a rogue wave of precipitous height might overwhelm the clipper. The danger was quite real. The waves still had not reached their maximum height. Over time Ellen expected them to grow much larger.

There was another factor to consider as well. The farther along *Flying Cloud* sailed on the new course, the farther she went into the Falkland Current, which flowed off the coast in a northerly direction at over a knot. In recent days, Ellen had set her courses steadily closer to shore to avoid the influence of the current. But the storm forced her to sail directly into its path. Under the combined influence of wind, waves, and current, *Flying Cloud* would make considerable leeway to the north, losing time and miles even as the vessel's bow pointed to the southeast. Despite these liabilities, however, Ellen had chosen the best option.

If there were no time constraint, running off with the wind astern made the most sense. Running in the same direction as the wind promised a much smoother ride than sailing with it blowing directly over the side of the ship. But doing so meant sailing back to the northeast toward Africa and adding days to the passage. Therefore, safe as it was, running off could not count as a viable tactic, unless the weather grew far worse. The ship could also heave to, essentially parking in place and drifting slowly downwind. That, too, was unacceptable.

Ellen weighed many factors in making her navigational decisions. She based her recommendations on safety, how the elements might impact on the ship when steered in a given direction, the need to make good time, and the likelihood of her husband's accepting her advice. The last consideration required her to take bolder navigational chances than she otherwise might. Why recommend a course she knew he would overrule, such as running off or heaving to? Her success in navigating the ship depended on her ability to keep balancing the variables, both human and natural, as she encountered each successive challenge.

But Perkins's influence went only so far. Ellen shared his desire to best *Surprise*'s ninety-six-day run to San Francisco. It was a challenge welcoming to the competitive side of her nature. She knew what setting a new record meant, financially and in terms of her husband's reputation. Fond of sailing since her girlhood, she thrilled at the ship's sailing characteristics when driving hard with all possible sails set. She was torn between a conservative approach to her duties and her tendency to get caught up in Perkins, the ship, the bigger picture. Part of her was very much willing to ride the edge with her husband.

Forbidden to come on deck because of the dangerous seas raking the ship, Ellen sent the steward up to the poop deck with the new course, south 43 degrees east. A few minutes later, she felt *Flying Cloud* turn and her motion change as the waves shifted aft until they hit the ship broadside on. The motion had been rough when sailing hard to windward against the storm with the violent plunge and lift as the bow rose and fell to the crests, shouldering them aside in tremendous sheets of spray that blew back and away into the air. But now with the waves abeam, the ship rolled frightfully. When a particularly large one struck, the vessel lay over on her side.

The sailors at their stations lashed themselves to the rigging to keep from being washed overboard. In working the ship, they moved about the decks using a network of lifelines strung fore and aft. These safety precautions were vital. There was no way to launch a boat to recover a man lost overboard at the height of a storm. The attempt might smash the boat into the side of the ship before the rescuers got clear.

If a sailor lost his grip on the lifelines, the seas swept him over the side and out of sight within seconds. His life expectancy in the water amounted to minutes. If he did not drown immediately, the cold water killed him in less than fifteen minutes from hypothermia. The struggle to stay afloat wore him out and he quickly died. Many of the sailors did not know how to swim. The old hands aboard thought it best to die fast rather than remain alive for a short time knowing death was near.

Most of the passengers kept to their staterooms or gathered together in small groups in the great cabin. While the storm howled, young Willie Hall passed some hours reading Herman Melville's *White Jacket* to Sarah Bowman and Edward. The two Bowmans sat close together in rapt attention and a good deal of alarm. Melville's tale recounted storms at sea in vivid detail.

Sarah Bowman later wrote of the storm: "We are off 'La Platte' and have encountered a severe gale. . . . I have been playing sick and kept to my stateroom the two last days ashamed to have them all know how frightened I was. Ah, with what a remorseless sound the immense waves strike our proud ship—making furious but vain efforts to overwhelm us."

But for these little gatherings there was nothing for the passengers to do. There were only cold meats and stale bread to eat, no hot coffee or tea, no steaming plates of chicken, pork, or lamb. The meals were very important to the passengers, because eating represented a break in the usually dull routine. They all depended on the camaraderie to help pass the time. Finding it difficult to move around without being thrown into a bulkhead, the majority of the passengers took to their berths and lay there listening to the chaos outside. They stared up at the beams over their heads, minds unfocused, drifting from one thought to another.

Up on the poop deck, Perkins caught sight of a ship to leeward, a small brig. The two-masted sailer labored hard on a course that kept her in company with *Flying Cloud*. The vessel disappeared up to her topsails while at the bottom of the troughs, then suddenly emerged at the top of the crests. He watched her struggle and felt sympathy for her people. *Flying Cloud,* a much larger and faster ship, was better able to handle the conditions, and even she found them a distinct challenge. The brig barely held her own.

A violent squall roared down on the two ships, hurling a wind that felt like an invisible wall. The fierce gust knocked *Flying Cloud* over on her side again. The deck canted beyond 45 degrees and kept going over until the weight of her cargo gradually righted her. She staggered under the tons of water washing over the lee rail and gathered momentum as the gust diminished. Perkins looked to leeward and saw the squall had torn off the brig's main and fore topmasts. The spars hung suspended over the side of the ship. She heeled hard over and the waves frequently buried her entire length, leaving only the stubs of her main and foremasts and the tattered sails flying from her lower yards visible above the crests.

Though the brig might well founder, there was nothing Perkins could do for her people. If the ship went down in such a storm, all hands would be lost. There was no question about that. The sea was indifferent to the value of human lives, and it forced a seeming indifference in men like Perkins. Crippled and dead in the water, drifting downwind fast, the brig fell astern, and in a short time she vanished into the murk.

"Godspeed," Perkins mumbled, squinting into the gloom at where the ship had been moments before.

Thomas Austin carefully made his way toward Perkins, advancing hand over hand along the length of the lifeline. His faced looked particularly grim.

"Captain Creesy," he shouted. "The main masthead. It's badly sprung, sir."

Perkins scowled, his face creased with deep lines. His beard was matted to his face, making him look almost wild or malevolent. He glared up at the rigging, resigned to what he had to do.

Chapter 16

T here comes a time at sea when the spirit of the most intrepid of individuals finds itself worn down, humbled, and ready to quit. The relentless power of wind and waves pitted against the creation of a man makes plain the insignificance of even a grand ship in the face of its fury. It is not easy to come to terms with powerlessness, the inability to control one's own destiny, and to give one's self over to nature in acceptance of its simple rules. It is more natural to resist and carry on, regardless of the obstacles and the hardships.

Yet, the wise mariner knows enough to recognize the moment when the sea has won, if only temporarily. As humbling as it may be, the last vestige of control often comes from giving up the larger, seemingly more noble struggle. There is a relief in such decisions, an uplifting of the spirit when the hour appears the darkest.

The news of the latest injury to the mainmast forced Perkins to face the reality of the situation, to try to subdue his obsession to drive *Flying Cloud* to her very limits until it was again safe to do so. The main masthead protruded up about fourteen feet from the crosstrees, the place where the topmast was fidded. It in fact provided the support for the topmast and the topgallant pole mast above. That it was twisted and sprung indicated instability in the entire rig. The mainmast, the most important and the heaviest spar aboard *Flying Cloud,* was slowly coming apart under the stress of the high loads.

As the waves broke over the side of the ship, the impacts hurled her against the waves on her downwind side. When she hit, she came to an abrupt momentary stop. Every time she did this the masts whipped and snapped back and forth, causing great strain on the rigging. The masts worked in the partners that supported the heel of the spars and jerked against the fids keeping them in place. High aloft at the main truck the slender spar bent and vibrated in the wind, which blew far stronger high above the deck.

The violent movement of the masts worked the hull's beams, frames, knees, and planks. Virtually every part of the ship came under intermittent loads, flexing and compressing and compacting the wood in a way that threatened to force the caulking from her hull and deck seams and to part structural components from their members. A new ship, *Flying Cloud* had yet to work herself into good season. There was a necessary settling for a vessel on her maiden voyage, and the storm was the first real test. There was some question as to how long she would hold herself together. Other untried vessels had broken apart or had the hull seams open and leak when facing adverse conditions for the first time. As stout as his ship was, Perkins knew no vessel had limitless capabilities.

He surveyed the scene, surreal in its confusion, thinking the storm might well intensify and increase the danger to the ship. The afternoon was already growing old, and in a few hours darkness would make any action to relieve the ship impossible until morning, which might be too late. There was little time to execute his decision. He turned his attention back to Thomas Austin and gave him his orders.

"Mr. Austin. Lay the men aloft to send down the main skysail, royal, and topgallant yards. Send down the booms of the topmast and lower yards," Perkins shouted, leaning close to the mate's ear to make himself heard.

"Aye, aye, sir." Thomas Austin looked nervously aloft, glad that as first officer his duties kept him on deck. The second officer,

Thomas Smith, would go up to supervise the men aloft, as it was his responsibility.

Seeing the hesitancy in his first officer's eyes and on his face, Perkins's temper flared. He had been aware that the first officer relaxed whenever he thought his captain was not about. He had been aware of the conversations with the passengers, the excessive fraternization he had expressly forbidden. Dinner conversation was fine, but on a well-disciplined ship the officers kept their distance from the passengers when on duty.

"Get moving, Austin," he roared. He deliberately omitted the mandatory respect owed to the man by addressing him without calling him Mr.

Austin nodded. "Yes, sir," he yelled and slowly worked his way forward, picking every step with care.

Water waist-deep rushed over the weather deck and often swept even the best of the able-bodied seamen off their feet. The men relied on the strength of their hands and arms as they clung to the lifelines to keep from being washed overboard. They carefully climbed the windward ratlines, taking care to hold on tight. They thought out and timed every move. The minutes dragged on as the strongest men climbed high up the mast, hanging on with both hands as the ship lurched and pitched. The force of the roll tried to heave their bodies toward the roaring wind away from the safety of the ratlines. But the wind pinned them to the rigging, opposing the force of gravity.

Several hands inched out on the skysail yard. One moment the deck, about 125 feet below, appeared visible through the rain and flying spray, the next it disappeared underwater. There was a sickening feel in their stomachs as the ship rolled and the yard pointed nearly straight down, gravity pulling them toward the waves. They cast off the sheets and clewlines, careful not to let the lines tangle and snag the yard. They made the ropes fast and moved off the yard, overhauled the tye, and made it fast, too.

Without its supporting lines, the yard began to bang and sway in the wind. It hit the masts and rigging, and the men frantically worked to keep it under control without it crushing their arms and hands. Austin, below at the foot of the mainmast, saw the men aloft hand-signal to haul away. He ordered the crew on deck to haul on the halyards to raise and cant the yard enough for the men to free the lower supporting lines, the lift and the brace. To do this required one of them to lean precariously out from the safety of his perch to get at the lines, all while the ship's motion tried to fling him off. The lines made fast, the men signaled Austin down on deck to lower away the yard. They removed the support lines on the other end and rigged guy lines to keep it from flailing as it was lowered to the deck.

As the yards and lower booms came down, dozens of hands grabbed hold of the spars to keep them from floating free. A loose spar could stove in the bulkheads, crash through the deckhouse or into the forecastle, and pulverize the bones of any man it hit. The sailors lashed the spars in place on the deck. They often worked at steep angles as the ship rolled and the deck tilted, adding gravity to the forces pitted against them.

It was dangerous work, but the men knew that the captain's orders meant they all would be safer with less weight aloft. The crew worked with a will until the light began to fade—cold, wet, and tired, and not without scrapes, bruises, and rope burns that smarted from the salt water. Their oilskins chafed raw the backs of their hands and necks, and their backs and shoulders ached. There was no relief in the deckhouse or the forecastle. Water soaked everything.

Perkins ordered the men back on regular watches, shifts of four hours on and four off. All hands had been on deck most of the day, without food or rest. The off watch stumbled into their berths and did not bother to search for dry clothing in their seabags. Most fell into a deep sleep, in spite of the cacophonous mix of storm and ship, the groan of wood and the shriek of the wind. Being able to sleep wet and hungry almost anywhere was a matter of pride among the sailors.

There were two among the crew, however, who took little pride in anything. In their view they had had a bit too much of the monkey, a sailor's expression meaning they had received more harsh treatment than they felt fit to stand. Small, petty-minded, and vindictive, the two sailors proceeded to put their plans against the captain into action. While the rest of the starboard watch rested or slept in the darkness of the forecastle, one of the men slipped unnoticed beneath his berth. With an auger, he silently drilled two holes through the deck, creating an opening to the 'tween decks and the cargo hold below. The man carefully hid the auger, which he intended to return to its proper place among the carpenter's tools on the next watch, and climbed back into his wet berth. But he found sleep long in coming and his next turn on deck too soon.

The starboard watch of the crew drew the hardest lot on the ship. They lived in the forecastle, a tiny, dark triangular space on the main deck at the tip of the bow with the forecastle deck as its roof. The bowsprit extended into the center of the room, and on each side of the bow were two tiers of berths. Up forward on either side of the bow were two holes, known as hawseholes, through which the anchor chain ran when the cable was rigged. At sea the hawseholes were stopped up with wooden plugs to prevent water from pouring in. In the aft section of the forecastle were two latrines, and a bulkhead to keep the weather out.

The clipper's sharp bow buried itself deep at sea and often sent a continuous welter of green water and spray cascading down from the forecastle deck. The water created a waterfall-like effect at the forecastle door and found its way into the crew's quarters, soaking anything left on the floor and encouraging the growth of mildew. The motion at the bow was also the most violent anywhere aboard the ship. The noise of the sea parting just feet away would keep a landsman awake for days.

The deckhouse was crowded and as equally prone to having a bit of sea come through the door as a crewman. The men of the larboard watch put up with the odor of the coops, sties, and pens just outside the deckhouse and the noise of the animals at all hours. Nevertheless, it was altogether more comfortable than the forecastle. The sailors could open a window to let fresh air in. The motion of the ship was less pronounced farther aft, nor did they have to hear the incessant wash of the sea against the bow.

The men in the larboard watch were more content than their peers up forward.

Perkins stayed on deck until he was certain the ship was riding well and he had done all he could to ensure her safety. Under close-reefed topsails, *Flying Cloud* boomed along, the crests not quite high enough to blanket them in the trough. The reduced weight aloft made a difference. The ship seemed steadier, less prone to the violent and acute rolling, and she pounded less severely against the seas, though the storm continued to intensify. However improved the ship's state, the towering mainmast shorn of its yards looked unnatural, like a finger in a web. The loss of the upper sails—how long would that last? And how many days would the slower speeds add to the voyage?

Perkins turned command over to Thomas Austin, who had the watch, with strict orders to call him if conditions merited. Down below in their cabin, Perkins told Ellen of the most recent events.

"We'll have a slower run to Cape Horn without the upper sails," he said glumly. "But it had to be done."

Ellen reached over and touched his hand and said, "You did right by the ship and her people, Perkins. You have to believe that."

They talked quietly together, their voices lost in the noise of the storm. Their cabin was a retreat, a place apart from the press of running the ship. Perkins asked after the passengers, how they were holding up.

"Mrs. Gorham has improved a little. The others have made the best of it. Except Mrs. Bowman won't come out of her stateroom."

Perkins chuckled. "She will eventually. When she feels ready for Cape Horn."

"I should think that might be quite a long time, then," Ellen said, half smiling at her husband. "Mrs. Bowman will never be ready for Cape Horn."

The night did not pass easily for the Creesys, nor for anyone else aboard. The ship labored on her course, but still she thrashed along making progress to the southeast. Perkins was not long asleep, stretched out in his clothes, his wet oilskins hung up in a futile attempt to dry them, when the steward called for him.

"You're wanted on deck, sir. Right away."

In the dim light of the lamp, Ellen watched him pull on his rain pants, seaboots, and jacket, his big frame partially obscured in shadows. He seemed tired, the weight of his duties heavy enough to slow his usually agile movements. The wide brim of his foul-weather hat darkened his forehead and eyes. The light illuminated the lower part of his face and shone on his beard, still damp and matted. The pitch of the wind in the rigging increased dramatically, and they both felt the ship accelerate as she dug in and raced ahead at the approach of the squall.

"Be careful out there, darling," she whispered.

"Try not to worry," he said gently. He closed the cabin door behind him and rushed up the companionway stairs. As he came on deck he saw the sky to the southwest, already as black as the inside of a hat, grow darker still.

Chapter 17

The southwesterly storm raged on through the night and did not show any signs of abating on July 11. As the hours dragged on, *Flying Cloud* drew closer to the axis of the Falkland Current, where its flow was the strongest. The wind, waves, and current moved in harmony, proceeding together in the same northerly direction. Though the seas would have been far more frightening and dangerous if the wind and current opposed, the nearly two-knot flow still created turbulent waves with steep, unnatural slopes. It could have been worse, but it was bad enough.

At noon, Ellen did not bother to venture outside. The danger was too great and there was no hope of taking a sight. She estimated their position based on dead reckoning alone. She put *Flying Cloud* about 240 miles east-southeast of Cape Polonia. Though they sailed southeast, their true track was more easterly, because the elements pushed the bow steadily away from the course the helmsman steered. There was no way to know exactly where they were. Her last fix was two days old, and the longer she went without an observation the more her dead reckoning deteriorated, until it was nothing but a blind guess.

The ship kept on through the early afternoon, her lee rail awash, the windward side tilted high. Unknown to all but two of the peo-

ple aboard, every plunge of the ship sent water cascading down
onto the cargo. One of the conspirators had removed the hawsehole stopper. With the hull leaned way over to the left from the
force of the wind, a steady rush of white water shot through the
port hawsehole and filled the forecastle with water. The flood
flowed down through the holes bored through the deck under the
crewman's berth. The sailors planned to enlarge the holes and at
every opportune time when the seas ran high to set the hawsehole
stopper adrift and flood the cargo, damaging much of it at a high
cost to the captain, who owned a share, and the ship's owners and
the merchants. The two men thought the hole might remain undiscovered indefinitely because it was out of sight. What better way to
get at the Old Man but to have him drive hard to San Francisco
only to arrive with a ruined cargo?

The sabotage was discovered when a member of the starboard
watch opened the forecastle door and a small wall of water rushed
up to his knees and out to mix with the seas washing over the rail.
He slammed the door shut and got Thomas Smith, who immediately alerted the captain that the forecastle was flooded. Conclud-
ing the obvious, Smith told Perkins that the hawsehole stopper
must have come adrift in the rough seas. With the ship heeled far
over on her left side, the hawsehole was constantly underwater. It
would be difficult, if not impossible, to secure the stopper without
coming over to the port tack, which would bring the opening to
the high side of the ship.

Perkins ordered all hands on deck to prepare for a complicated
maneuver known as wearing ship. Wearing ship meant turning the
vessel by bringing the wind across the stern instead of across the
bow, as happened when tacking. In such high winds and seas, tacking posed too much of a danger, because as the bow came straight
into the wind the sails would slam aback with great force and might
dismast the ship. The wind always blew from behind the sails when
wearing ship, eliminating the danger of going aback.

All the men stood ready at their stations. The helmsman pushed
the wheel and *Flying Cloud* began a slow turn to the left. The wind
moved from directly broadside on the right side of the ship to

Wearing a Square-Rigged Ship

Wearing: turning the stern through the wind

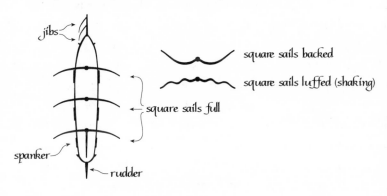

jibs

square sails backed

square sails luffed (shaking)

square sails full

spanker

rudder

wind

main and mizzen yards
pointed into the wind,
sails luff

wind

foresails blanketed,
easier to trim for
new heading

wind

spanker
taken down

Wear
Begins

reset
spanker

wind

Wear
Completed

wind

spanker pushes
stern through
the turn

ILLUSTRATION BY
MARGARET WESTERGAARD

points farther and farther toward the stern. The men moved the yards to keep the sails full during the turn, as Perkins shouted orders through his speaking trumpet, his voice hoarse from the strain of the last two days. Slowly, the clipper kept turning and the wind moved dead aft and then forward up the left side of the ship while the crew continued to position all the yards for the new course. *Flying Cloud* completed a wide U-turn that now faced the ship's bow to the northwest back toward the coast of Brazil.

Below in the cabin, Ellen knew the ship had changed course. It was obvious because the cabin now canted right instead of left as the vessel leaned over on her side from the force of the wind. The course change concerned and perplexed her. There was no possible explanation for it, unless it was done to avoid a collision with another ship. While it did not occur often there were times when she was trapped below not knowing what was happening. For a person of action and courage, remaining below caused great frustration. She considered rushing up on deck. Restraint and the clear understanding of how dangerous it was up there kept her from acting on the impulse. The passengers all wanted to know what was going on, and there was nothing to say to answer their questions.

Perkins waited impatiently for word from the carpenter that the hawsehole was again secure. Every minute he sailed to the northwest sacrificed miles he had driven hard to win, and he wanted desperately to wear ship back to the south as soon as possible. In a race against time, every hour counted. He watched Thomas Austin emerge from the forecastle and make his way aft, confident he would soon have his wish.

"Captain Creesy, sir," Austin said. "You are needed forward. There has been deliberate damage to the ship."

Austin quickly explained. After the ship had settled on the port tack, the carpenter had gone forward to plug the hawsehole. Busy at his work, he became aware of a sound coming from under one of the aft berths and upon investigation discovered a crewman hiding under a berth in the act of enlarging a gash cut into the deck.

"We're holding the man up in the forecastle, but he's not talking," Austin said.

"We'll see about that," Perkins said, his voice scarcely audible above the storm.

Up forward, Perkins examined the damage. Two holes has been drilled about four inches apart. The man had dug out the space between them with a marlinespike, a sharp metal tool with many legitimate uses onboard, but certainly not sabotage. A small amount of water still flowed over the jagged edges of the three-inch pine planks down below onto the cargo. Seething with anger, Perkins turned to the man and kicked him. He cuffed him with his open hand.

"I ought to have you flogged," he said, moving close to the crewman. "Why did you do this?"

The man remained silent.

"I'll have the starboard watch in here, Mr. Austin."

"Aye, aye, sir."

A few minutes later the starboard watch, more than two dozen hands, gathered in the cramped forecastle. Most looked surprised, bewildered. It did not take long for one of the men to implicate a second saboteur. The man who owned the berth above the holes had been seen coming out of the forecastle with an auger in his hand, quite damning given the nature of the damage. No one had thought anything of it at the time, but the witness thought better of it now, he said.

The second man was brought to the captain. Perkins glared at the two men for a long moment. The roar of the storm made the time stretch. "Put them both in irons," he said. "Starboard watch back on deck and pump her bilge dry!" he shouted, and worked his way back to the poop deck using the lifelines.

An hour later, at around four o'clock in the afternoon, the storm still in full fury and the light fading fast, the carpenter sent word that all was secure up forward. All hands save two brought *Flying Cloud* back around to steer toward the southeast, and the ship struggled to make up the miles she had lost. The two crewmen in irons sat shackled to a bulkhead in the darkness of the 'tween decks. They were hungry, cold, and wet. Below them the water in the bilge sloshed about, sending up a foul, nauseating stench. The ship's rats scrambled near and occasionally bit them.

Perkins recorded the incident in the ship's log on July 12. Here is the entry as Perkins wrote it, with no corrections of spelling, grammar, or punctuation:

> Heavy Gales & sea. 3 P.M. wore ship to NW after running off an hour in consequence of Laubourd hawse stopper getting adrift & filling fore castle full of water, after getting round Carpenter discovered two auger holes had been boared in the Deck close to the after sill of the fore Castle & to the side, under the after birth, which has been done by some one of the sailors, on Enquiry found the man under whose birth the hole was had been seen coming out of the fore Castle with an auger in his hand. put him in Irons—Also a man who was seen to work at the holes digging with a marling spike which led to its discovery—then holes are about three and a half or four inches apart and the interveening space Dug away to all appearances with a marling spike making one Large hole—say four inches long by one or one and a half wide;
>
> During the time of washing away the Hause stopper and getting the ship on Lauboard tack the water over this hole was from two to three feet Deep consequently must have admitted a large quantity of water into the between Decks on & among the Cargo, at four having secured Hawse Stopper & hole in the Deck wore ship again to Southward through the night hard gales & harder squalls.

The actions of these two men, though quickly discovered, achieved something of the intended objective. The water over the opening in the forecastle was deep, and a large amount of it must have entered the hold. The extent of the damage to the cargo would remain a mystery to Ellen and Perkins for the rest of the voyage, until the stevedores began the unloading and all the contents of the hold could be closely examined. It was impossible to tell by any other means.

The sabotage was very much on Ellen's mind as Perkins stirred her awake before dawn the morning after the incident. Counterbalanced against her dark mood was the cheery realization on awakening that the storm's power appeared spent at last. The ship still labored hard on the starboard tack. There was no discernible change in her motion. But the sound of the wind in the rigging had changed from a shriek to a steady, haunting moan. It was a harbinger of a change in the weather, and it helped lift her spirits.

"It looks like she's blown about as hard as she's going to blow," Perkins said quietly. "I saw some sky to the south, just a patch, but the stars were there."

"Is it safe enough to go on deck?" she asked, bracing herself up in bed against the roll of the ship.

"I think so. In several hours the seas will go down some."

"The passengers will be relieved."

They sat together for a few moments in silence, neither speaking about the incident of the previous day, having already discussed it. But the vindictiveness of the act lingered and weighed heavily on them. In Ellen, it bred a mix of emotions—anger at the men, and a sense of betrayal, since she always treated them kindly. She felt protective of her husband, his career, reputation, and financial well-being. But it also sparked a question that many advocates for the sailors were raising along the waterfront concerning how hard was too hard to drive the men. Had Perkins stepped over the line? Gone too far?

Experienced sailors knew clippers were the roughest of the merchant fleet, and a goodly number avoided them for that reason. But with so many men headed for the goldfields, the green crewmen who shipped often found themselves in a situation they lacked the skills to handle. Had these men broken? Or had they acted out of petty spite? And why, despite their ignorance, should they loathe Perkins? Perhaps ignorance was the answer after all.

Ellen turned the matter over in her mind as they dressed and went into the great cabin for yet another cold breakfast. The pale gray light of predawn illuminated the skylight and faded into the soft yellow light of the lamp. They were alone at the table, with some bread, cheese, apples, and cold tea Ching had brought for them. They nibbled together in silence, lending support to each other just from sitting close. After they finished eating, they shrugged on their foul-weather gear and went up on deck. Perkins followed close behind Ellen up the stairs to the poop deck, to catch her if she fell. They gripped the windward rail until they reached the mizzen shrouds. They hooked their arms around the thick rigging and braced themselves in place.

The wind and sea, as cold as it was, invigorated Ellen. The moist air filled her lungs, tingled her cheeks, tousled her hair. She looked up at Perkins and followed his gaze to the south. A jagged rent in the clouds exposed a swath of light blue. Shades of orange, purple, and red colored the tops of the clouds but could not penetrate the dark undersides. The waves marched and broke as far as the eye could see. The horizon was still obscured, making sea and sky appear as one indistinguishable void.

The wind had begun to shift to the south earlier in the morning. It gradually changed direction enough to allow for a course change that would take *Flying Cloud* parallel to the coast. Ellen brought the ship from a heading of south 43 degrees east back to south 41 degrees west, roughly the same course they had steered prior to the storm. The crew wore ship to the port tack. *Flying Cloud* sailed close-hauled. With the wind blowing hard over the left side of bow, it was a wet, slow pound to windward.

The Falkland Current now flowed directly against them, instead of pushing the ship from the side. Since the current flowed toward *Flying Cloud*'s bow, leeway to the north was eliminated. The ship plowed straight ahead, stemming the backward thrust of the current. Ellen easily accounted for its influence on the ship's speed by deducting two knots from the estimated rate made good through the water. There was no need to account for leeway on the present heading, which simplified her dead reckoning. Based on her best judgment, the ship had made far more easting than southing. The clipper had held station through the storm.

The sun broke through the clouds intermittently, but enough to make it possible to take a sight. Ellen retrieved her sextant from below and returned to the poop deck. Perkins stood ready to mark the time and note the readings. The wind still blew fresh and kept the waves from diminishing much in size. Rather than being potentially lethal, the seas hovered at the edge of tolerably dangerous. Sailing with the wind off the bow, *Flying Cloud* climbed and descended the waves, sending water and spray flying aft over the forecastle onto the weather deck. The up-and-down, seesaw effect as the ship charged through the water made it difficult for Ellen to keep the horizon steady when she lifted her sextant for the observation.

Braced in the mizzen shrouds, she watched the waves and waited for the few moments when the ship reached the summit of the larger seas. From that high vantage point she glimpsed the horizon. She raised the sextant, but before she could catch the sun the stern dropped into the trough. She had learned long ago to exercise patience under such conditions, to allow herself to move in the sea's rhythm and wait for her chance. At the right moment, on a particularly high wave, she arched her waist and back to compensate for the angle of heel. She held the sextant exactly perpendicular to the horizon, brought the lower edge of the sun down to it, and shouted, "Mark!" She quickly read the measurements from the sextant and Perkins jotted them down.

Throughout the morning, Ellen took sights at intervals, waiting for the waves and the clouds to cooperate. At noon, she worked out a rough position. She was disappointed in the results. The ship had sailed only forty miles in the last twenty-four hours. The day's run ranked as the worst of the voyage thus far. As if intent on adding to Ellen's disappointment, the clouds returned to cover the sky in the afternoon and the south wind shifted back to the south-southwest, making it impossible to hold the course again. Ellen brought the ship round to north 84 degrees west, or nearly due west on a direct slant for the coast south of the Río de la Plata. The new course put the blustery wind slightly forward of the port side. It was at last a good angle for sailing well, and that pleased Perkins.

Every mile *Flying Cloud* sailed left the Falkland Current farther astern. Ellen planned to duck inshore of the current and hug the coast to make as much westing as possible. This allowed her to line up the ship for the shortcut through the Strait of Le Maire. The famous strait was a narrow, treacherous stretch of water between Tierra del Fuego and the Isla de los Estados, or Staten Island, and it was a passage favored among the clipper ship captains. Once a ship was through the strait, Cape Horn stood less than a day's sail away.

The new route to California allowed a vessel to proceed as far west as possible in latitudes with more favorable winds and weather. On this path, ships passed through the Strait of Le Maire, or at the very least inside of the Falkland Islands. It was a riskier course, since it brought the vessel close to shore in one of the worst stretches of ocean in the world. However, the faster passage around the tip of South America justified the potential hazards.

In the past, mariners had favored another way to the Pacific Ocean. The captain of a ship picked up the southeast trade winds and sailed straight down the middle of the South Atlantic outside, or east of, the Falkland Islands. The course kept the vessel well off-shore and away from the swift tidal currents and rocks along the coast of Patagonia. At first glance, the tactic made sense. After all, a ship was safe at sea away from the complications of wind, water, and tide near land. Yet the captain paid a price for his caution, sometimes with the blood of his crew. In the environs of the Falk-land Islands the winds blew from the west most of the time. A ship on the old route around Cape Horn endured days and often weeks of hard sailing against the prevailing westerlies. The Southern Ocean Current also hindered progress to the west. The old way was rough at any time of year, and in winter it was worse.

The moderating weather brought the passengers out on deck for the first time in two days. They clung to the rails and stared at the seas rolling toward them with awe and fascination. Most had never seen the ocean in such an angry state. The sight instilled more fear in Sarah Bowman, as did the captain's comment that the storm was "but a taste of what we can expect off Cape Horn." That his words were true added to her anxiety. The decks were wet, the motion still rough, and most of the passengers returned below to the great cabin to pass the time playing cards or chess, or reading quietly on the leeward settee.

The crew worked until dusk checking and repairing the rigging, drawing it tight where it had stretched slack during the storm. This task alone required many hands and many hours. Other crewmen coiled the confusion of lines, put everything right in the galley and in their quarters. They cared for the surviving animals, which had not been fed since the storm began. They pumped the bilge regularly to check the amount of water in it. The sabotage accounted for most of the water in the hold, but a new ship often worked her seams in a bad storm. There was the possibility *Flying Cloud* had opened up a bit, and the bilge checks confirmed that she was making more water than usual, though to Perkins's relief, not enough to cause major concern.

A practical man, Perkins concluded that the two men in irons would best serve the ship if they were back on duty. It was a difficult decision to make. He took what they had done as a personal attack, and he looked forward to seeing them in court upon arrival in San Francisco. There were fifty-nine sailors aboard *Flying Cloud,* and yet the loss of even two hands reduced the ship's efficiency. He suppressed his personal feelings and offered to free the men on their promise they would make no more trouble during the voyage; if they did, they would spend the rest of the trip chained in the bowels of the ship.

"You will be taken care of in San Francisco," Perkins told them. "I can assure you of that. Until then I expect you to earn your pay."

The decision elated the two men. One night in irons at the height of a storm was enough to convince them that clinging for life on the main topgallant yard in a gale was far less punishment. They harbored the same ill will for the captain, the same ardent desire to escape from *Flying Cloud,* which they considered a hell ship. Perkins was aware of this, but he needed them at their stations. A captain ran many risks, and this was one he felt compelled to take.

At six o'clock in the middle of the dog watch, the Creesys, the officers off watch, and the passengers, including Mrs. Gorham, who was much better, were just sitting down for a hot supper. It was a simple meal, yet as welcome as if it had been much fancier. The stove in the great cabin, lit for the first time, exuded a comforting warmth that dissipated the winter chill.

A crewman burst into the room, out of breath.

"Captain Creesy, sir. Mr. Smith needs you on deck. The main topsail tye has carried away!"

Chapter 18

Perkins stepped from the portico onto the weather deck and peered aloft into the darkness at the main topsail. The large, billowing sail shook and flapped in the wind and was visible only as a dim splash of white nearly a hundred feet above the deck. The strain of all the hard sailing *Flying Cloud* had endured since leaving New York had caused yet another part of the rig to give way, with possibly dire consequences.

In this case, the damaged part of the rig was the main topsail tye, a heavy chain used to support the two-ton weight of the yard. When the sail was set, the press of the wind against the canvas added to the load on the chain. With the chain broken, all that kept the yard from falling to the deck was the hemp ropes still attached to it. The loose chain rattled and banged ominously against the main topmast. Perkins would have little time to assess the situation and respond before the rest of the rigging supporting the yard also broke.

Perkins shouted orders to the officers and crew, finishing with an obvious statement: "Get the strain off the gear now, boys, before she goes!"

The crew hauled up the lower edge of the sail to the yard, reducing the area of canvas exposed to the wind and lessening the stress on the rigging. The men carefully and slowly eased the yard to its position on the mast when no sail was set and pulled taut the braces to steady it. Once the yard was lowered, the best and most experienced men scurried up the ratlines and out onto the spar to furl the sail in darkness nearly complete except for patches of stars shining in breaks of the clouds. The men knew the yard could fall and kill them, but they kept working despite the danger. The sail furled tight, the men rigged a new chain to replace the tye. The twisted and stretched links of the broken chain revealed the magnitude of the forces at work on the masts and the ropes that kept them upright.

At this stage of the voyage, Perkins, like any good sailor under similar circumstances, began to wonder whether his ship was safe. The accident marked the second round of problems with the topsail yard alone. First the yard carried away completely, including the tye, and had to be repaired and sent back up again. Now a second tye had given way under the strain, not a very encouraging sign. In addition, the mainmast was sprung below the hounds, and the main masthead was also badly damaged. There was clearly too much strain on the mainmast and the rigging. Even after the weight of the upper yards and lower booms was removed, the mast appeared weak. How much more could it take? Perkins simply did not know, and yet he had to keep going. He could not give up and run to the nearest port. There was too much at stake.

The repairs completed, Perkins ordered the men to reset the topsail, but not all of it. He told the crew to put in a single reef to reduce the sail area, lessening the strain on the mainmast. The men climbed back up to the yard, released the gaskets to unfurl the sail, and returned to the deck to haul the yard up to its position when the sail was set. The yard weighed more than two tons with the weight of the sail, and hauling it up to its proper place on the main topmast required an effort similar to that of lifting a large automobile approximately forty feet in the air with only block and tackle and manpower to accomplish the feat.

"Topsail haul!" Perkins cried.

Ranged in a line along the halyards, the crew heaved in time as the chanteyman sang out a long drag chantey. His voice boomed out, "Around Cape Horn we've got to go!"

The crew responded, "To me, hay, o-hio!" and pulled hard on the halyards, raising the heavy yard several feet.

"Around Cape Horn to Callao!"

"A long time ago!" the crew sang out. The yard rose higher.

"Around Cape Horn where the stiff winds blow!"

"To me way, hay, o-hio!"

"Round Cape Horn where there's sleet and snow!"

"A long time ago!"

"I wish to God I'd never been born!" the chanteyman called.

"To me way, hay, o-hio!"

"To drag my carcass around Cape Horn!"

"A long time ago!"

With the main topsail yard raised and the sail set and trimmed, *Flying Cloud* charged on through the deepening night. The cloud cover lifted as the hours passed, exposing the sea to the cool blue light of the moon. The moonlight shone on the sails and made them ghostly wisps of dull white against the darkness. The stars spread out across the sky in dense patterns, swirls and eddies of cosmic light. The break in the weather was particularly welcome. It allowed the people aboard *Flying Cloud* to witness a rare event, an eclipse of the moon.

The cold, moist air sent shivers through the passengers as they gathered on deck, voluntarily risen from their first good night's rest since the storm to witness the eclipse. Few would see such a cosmic display again, and none would be likely to ever see it from the heaving deck of a clipper making her way through the darkness of the South Atlantic. Wrapped in her heavy wool overcoat and wearing gloves and a scarf to keep the cold away, Ellen stood close to Perkins and gazed at the moon. The workings of the heavens, no longer as mysterious as they were for earlier mariners, nevertheless fascinated her. They reminded anyone with a sensitivity to nature of its majesty. Its simple beauty captivated the mind.

The first indication of the lunar eclipse appeared at three-thirty on the morning of July 13. A tiny sliver of darkness slowly hid the edge of the moon, born of the earth's shadow as it blocked the reflective light of the sun. Ellen smiled as the moonlight gave way to darkness.

The waves, easily distinguished in the light, faded into oblivion. The sails, too, fell into shadow. That they still flew was apparent by the ship's motion and the swaths of blackness aloft that hid the stars. The moon disappeared, leaving only a rim of light. The passengers talked excitedly, necks craned, fingers pointed skyward.

Ellen whispered to Perkins, "Isn't it a wondrous sight?"

He smiled in the dim light and looked down at his wife, who was at the moment filled with a girlish excitement. The natural world was her haven, a haven she found endlessly full of new treasures. It had been that way since her childhood growing up on the rocky shores of Marblehead. She was steeped in the life and ways of the sea, with its beauty and harshness. Many women of the town resented the ocean that took their men from them for years at a time, and sometimes forever. But for Ellen the sea seemed part of her soul, the essence of her spirit. In her Perkins had found a companion as well as a lover, a woman to share moments such as these with an appreciation for them that he greatly valued.

"It is indeed," he said quietly. He reached out and took her hand in his.

The steady pace of the earth and moon in their orbits soon moved them out of alignment with the sun. The moon slipped away to continue its daily cycle, and the shadow receded and merged with the night sky. The soft moonlight again bathed the ship in its glow. It illuminated the backs of the seas, the faces of the sails.

"Quite a show, eh?" Laban Coffin said to Sarah Lyon, the two of them standing a little apart from the rest of the passengers, as they often did of late.

"It's a glorious sight," Sarah answered. "I never expected to see something like this."

Laban smiled. "Life is full of the unexpected, my dear. It's one of its great gifts."

Whether deep in the heart of a fertile mountain valley or on the broad ocean, the coldest time of the day came in the predawn hours. The sun's warmth drained away long before, the coldness of the earth took hold and grew more pronounced as the night wore on to finally reach the lowest temperature of the day. In a short time, the cold drove the passengers below, back under the blankets of their snug berths.

The wind held fair through the morning and came in at an efficient slant off the left side of the ship. The wind angle allowed Ellen to put more southing in the course, and she brought the ship around to south 67 degrees west. Perkins ordered all sails set full on the fore and mizzen masts, and he ordered the reef shaken out of the main topsail to increase the sail area to its maximum dimensions.

Late in the afternoon, the ship passed back over the edge of the continental shelf extending offshore 120 miles southeast of Cape Corrientes. The shallows stretched southwest to form a shadow continent beneath the seas similar in shape to the land to the west. The shelf protruded outward in a thumblike extension around the Falkland Islands, as if the tip of South America were a tail in motion, swinging to the west and leaving behind an impression of its passage on the ocean floor. The edge of the continental shelf was remarkably uniform, unlike the coastline, indented in funnel-shaped river basins and the wide gulfs of San Matías and San Jorge cut from the shores of desolate Patagonia.

Flying Cloud ran her southing down in fine, cold weather that held through the afternoon of July 14, making her way quickly back to the coast. She had covered over 350 miles since the storm abated. The long run offshore had cost time and miles, but the steady progress with a fair wind helped make up for the delay. At around four o'clock, under gathering clouds to the northwest, the barren coast of Patagonia appeared dead ahead some twenty-five miles distant. The light of the setting sun looked pale and diffuse and imparted an otherworldly feel to the people on deck, as if to reinforce their very real, though temporary, disconnection with the rest of the human race.

Patagonia. The name of this region of South America conveyed a sense of isolation. Stretching from the base of the Andes to the sea, the great plains of Patagonia formed a desert of wiry brown grass and low thorny bushes from horizon to horizon. Situated in the wind shadow of the Andes, the region received less than ten inches of rain every year, and its soil was infertile and rocky. Deep valleys cut through the plains provided shelter from the wind for the few Spanish settlers along the rivers Colorado and Negro. There was little in the way of game for the people to hunt. The prime source of meat was the guanaco, or wild llama, supplemented with deer and wild cattle.

Naturalist and explorer Charles Darwin described the guanaco in his *Journal of Researches*, in which he detailed his voyage aboard the HMS *Beagle* between 1831 and 1836. He wrote:

> The wild guanaco is an elegant animal in a state of nature, with a long slender neck and fine legs. . . . They have no idea of defence; even a single dog will secure one of these large animals, till the huntsman can come up. In many of their habits they are like sheep in a flock. Thus when they see men approaching in several directions on horseback, they soon become bewildered, and know not which way to run. This greatly facilitates the Indian method of hunting, for they are thus easily driven to a central point, and are encompassed.

Short cliffs three hundred to four hundred feet high fronted the shoreline of Patagonia. The number of harbors was quite limited. It was a part of South America no settler wanted, because it offered nothing but a hard, cold life. Only the Indians claimed the land as their own, and they fought the Spanish to keep them from pushing farther south. The inhospitable land and the hostile Indians discouraged southward expansion. Spanish settlements so numerous on the fertile pampas near Buenos Aires thinned to a line of tiny outposts that eventually ended altogether south of the Río Negro.

In contrast, the environs of the Río de la Plata estuary were highly prized. Fanning outward from the estuary to cover roughly a fifth of the United Provinces of La Plata, the broad pampas supported vast fields of grass ideal for raising cattle. The rich topsoil made the pampas the breadbasket of the country. The majority of the inhabitants of the provinces were settled in the region, most notably in Buenos Aires.

The Spanish founded Buenos Aires in 1580, and the city grew steadily. It became a major seaport, providing a solid economic base for the region with a steady flow of imported goods from Europe and exports of farm products such as beef, wool, and hides. The residents of the city called themselves *porteños*, "people of the port." In the early 1850s, the city and the surrounding provinces were embroiled in revolution. The dictator General Juan de Rosas had ruled violently since 1829, killing rebels and the Indians of the pampas, with ruthless abandon. Yet, despite the violence in most of the region, Buenos Aires thrived. It truly was a splendid city. Darwin described the town when he was there in 1833.

> The City of Buenos Ayres is large; and I should think one of the most regular in the world. Every street is at right angles to the one it crosses, and the parallel ones being equidistant, the houses are collected into solid squares of equal dimensions, which are called quadras. On the other hand, the houses themselves are hollow squares; all the rooms opening into a neat little courtyard. They are generally only one storey high, with flat roofs, which are fitted with seats, and are much frequented by the inhabitants in summer. In the centre of the town is the Plaza, where the public offices, fortress, cathedral, etc., stand. Here also, the old viceroys, before the revolution, had their palaces. The general assemblage of buildings possesses considerable architectural beauty, although none individually can boast of any.

In 1852, General Justo José de Urquiza overthrew General de Rosas in a bloody revolt, bringing an end to more than two decades of unrest in the provinces. The country adopted a constitution very similar to that of the United States and formed a confederation to bind the nation together as one entity. However, Buenos Aires, long the most prosperous locale in the region, refused to join. For a time it remained an independent state within the larger United Provinces of La Plata.

The world was very much in a state of flux in the early 1850s. Nations were striving to find their own sense of identity, their own places within the larger context of the global village. The pioneer

spirit thrived in both North and South America, for both continents remained virtually untapped in terms of true economic
potential. Settlement had occurred for centuries, but the pace had
been slow until the 1800s. As *Flying Cloud* raced southward
toward Cape Horn, she played a small part in the big picture of
world events. The clipper ships were symbolic of technological
developments underway in the 1850s that ultimately led to the
modern age and changed the way of life for people in nearly every
corner of the globe.

The break in the bad weather *Flying Cloud* encountered proved
short-lived. But as after most blows, a calm preceded the next
round of her fight to reach Cape Horn. The clouds thickened, light
rain fell, and the fair wind dropped off. The clipper slowed and
rolled in the swells, the sails limp and powerless. As a break in the
daily shipboard routine, Perkins allowed Whitney Lyon and several
other passengers to take one of the ship's small boats out for a try
at some fishing, with members of the crew at the oars. It seemed
odd, the graceful clipper temporarily stopped on a slick, oily sea the
color of gravel, and the little white boat stationed not far off full of
men fishing as if they were on holiday off Sandy Hook. Whitney
caught no fish and resorted to amusing himself in his customary
pursuit of the Cape pigeons. These were small, hardy seabirds that
nested on the rocky coast. The birds were unafraid of people. They
perched on the rail and presented ideal targets for Whitney, who
took pleasure from firing beans at them. The shrill cries of the Cape
pigeons filled the air as they took flight.

The wind freshened somewhat and brought with it thickening
clouds. The breeze did not come in steadily from any given direction
for long, however. It continued to shift and kept Perkins and the
crew busy working the ship to best advantage. With a weather eye to
the wind, Perkins squeezed every possible mile out of the ship, and
despite the brief calm and shifty winds, the latitude fell away rapidly
with each passing day. It seemed to many aboard that the voyage
had gone on for an eternity. But actually the ship was just forty-
three days out from New York and already within striking distance
of Cape Horn, about a week's sail away if the wind cooperated.

For several days now, Perkins had had a lookout posted at the bow at all times with strict orders to keep watch for any sign of icebergs. Calved from glaciers on the shores of Antarctica only six hundred miles off Cape Horn, the bergs rode the Southern Ocean Current from west to east through Drake Passage. A branch of that current flowed between Tierra del Fuego and the Falkland Islands to form the north-setting current that bore the islands' name. The bergs occasionally made it as far north as the Río de la Plata off Uruguay, though it was rare to see them at that latitude. The lookout saw nothing of interest until the afternoon of July 15.

"Sail, ho! Sail, ho! Fine on the port bow!" the lookout cried.

Word of the ship spread quickly among passengers and crew, and everyone came on deck to take a look. They had seen vessels loom on the horizon, skysails and royals just barely visible above the rim of the earth. Always *Flying Cloud* left them astern within an hour or so. Of all the ships they had seen, to only one thus far had they spoken. Perkins was hoping to speak a ship bound for the United States. He wanted to inform Grinnell, Minturn & Company of the vessel's swift progress, and the passengers wanted to send word to their families back home.

Flying Cloud quickly caught up with the other ship, a hulking, bluff-bowed craft of the old design. The vessel looked ravaged and had obviously suffered greatly in the recent storm. Large patches of her topside paint were peeled away. Rust from anchors streaked her bow. Green slime and weed clung to the hull just above the waterline, as did a long band of white barnacles. In keeping with the usual practice, the captain of the ship being overtaken maintained his course and the set of his sails to ensure a steady, predictable rate of speed. This allowed Perkins to come in close and match the speed of the slower vessel.

"Back the main topsail, Mr. Austin!" Perkins shouted through his speaking trumpet. "Keep the foresails drawing full."

"Aye, aye, sir!" Austin replied, and gave the crewmen their orders.

The men raced to the braces and the main topsail backed with a snap and boom as the wind slammed the canvas against the mast. *Flying Cloud* slowed down and was soon in position for the two captains to exchange greetings. The sailors stood at their sail stations ready to act fast if the two ships drew too close together and quick action was needed to sail clear. Perkins leaned against the windward rail of the poop deck, Ellen at his side. They were close enough to the other ship to hear her wash as she lifted and fell to the swells, kicking up foam at the bow as she moved through the sea.

"Ahoy, ship *Harriet Raymond!*" Perkins shouted.

"Ahoy, ship *Flying Cloud*," the captain replied. "How long have you been out?"

"We are forty-three days from New York bound for San Francisco."

Ellen smiled as she saw the captain turn to the other officers on deck, a look of disbelief clearly visible on his face.

"Say again!"

Perkins obliged. He, too, smiled.

"You have a fine ship there," the man called. "We are eighty-three days out of Boston bound for Valparaiso."

Now it was Ellen and Perkins whose faces showed surprise. *Harriet Raymond* would certainly set no records on this voyage. She had set sail from Boston on April 22, four days before Ellen and Perkins took *Flying Cloud* down to New York under tow. The passengers buzzed with excitement. The news drove home just how fast their swift sailer really was.

"Any news from home?" the captain asked.

"We've spoken only one ship, a Frenchman. We've had no news from home since leaving port."

"That's as I expected. A successful voyage to you, captain," he called to Perkins, and Perkins wished him the same.

The ships filled their sails and drew apart. *Flying Cloud* raced ahead with the southeasterly breeze. The hull of the other vessel grew less distinct and soon merged with the sea, leaving only the expanse of sail visible. Within an hour the skysails of the other ship sank below the horizon astern. *Flying Cloud*'s people found themselves alone again. The meeting was a bittersweet occurrence. It reminded them of their absolute isolation.

Chapter 19

B etween July 12 and July 18, *Flying Cloud* advanced south-west 1,131 miles on course for a direct run to the Strait of Le Maire. As she sailed close along the coast of Patagonia under a heavy, overcast sky that seemed low enough to engulf the skysails, each day brought her closer to Cape Horn.

In the waters surrounding *Flying Cloud*'s present position were some dangerous rocks, Las Rocas Santa Cruz, approximately sixty miles east of the Patagonian coast. The sun had not broken through the clouds in four days, making it impossible for Ellen to take a sight to tell just where the clipper sailed in relation to the hazard. Without an observation she could not know for certain whether she had strayed too far west and placed the ship in danger of running onto the rocks. With only seven hours of daylight each day, the bulk of the passage took place at night when it was much more difficult to spot the breakers; on a calm day with good visibility, the abundant kelp that grew on the shoals might be spotted too.

The only way to get an idea of the ship's proximity to the rocks was with the deep-sea lead line used for soundings. Using the lead, Ellen could gauge the water depth and the composition of the ocean floor and match the findings to the depths and type of material on the bottom marked on the chart. The charts were by no means completely accurate, but they served as a guide and might provide Ellen with a better understanding of where *Flying Cloud* was.

The cries of "Watch, ho! Watch!" rang out in the still air as the men hove the deep-sea lead and the line paid out. Down the lead sank, spinning the line from the tub on the deck at twenty fathoms, thirty, forty, until the lead struck at sixty-five fathoms, or 390 feet. The depth indicated the ship was over the deeper part of the continental shelf, far enough east of the rocks for Ellen to relax a little.

The weather grew more ominous as the day wore on. The clouds lowered and darkened, transforming the sea and sky into varying shades of gray and black. A light rain fell. The ship sailed slowly on with a fickle north wind off the stern. An easterly swell rolled in on the left side of the ship, an obvious clue that the ocean was in turmoil many miles away, the dog before the master, as the sailors called it. It was rare to encounter light winds in the high latitudes of the South Atlantic, where the west winds blew with fury more than half the time. Another storm was coming, of that Ellen was certain. The elements gathered strength, unfelt at the moment, except for the rising swell.

The next day, July 19, patches of blue appeared briefly in the sky, but not enough to make a pair of a Dutchman's pants, which the sailors believed foretold the imminent arrival of foul weather. The sun emerged briefly, and Ellen, on station ready with her sextant, obtained her latitude and longitude, her much-awaited fix. She placed *Flying Cloud* about four hundred miles north of the Strait of Le Maire, an easy two-day sail with a good wind. Ellen adjusted her course to aim for the narrow opening of the strait just to the east of the island of Tierra del Fuego.

Tierra del Fuego, located due south of the Strait of Magellan, was the largest of the many isles composing the long archipelago of the same name. These bits of land were the tops of submerged mountains, the last remains of the Andes. Extending approximately two hundred miles south of Tierra del Fuego, the archipelago occupied 26,872 square miles of the world's roughest ocean and ended at Cape Horn. Navigating in the vicinity of these rocky protrusions almost always shrouded in fog demanded great care because of the swift tidal currents, the uncharted reefs, and the gales that swept the region most of the time.

The region was unmatched in its inhospitable nature. Even Patagonia to the north seemed bountiful in comparison. Yet, despite the desolation, Tierra del Fuego was inhabited by a people known as the Fuegians. The Fuegians plied the maze of narrow channels and islands, carved into sharp relief by the immense power of the glaciers, in small canoes, from which they caught fish, seals, and seabirds. The coastline was bold, with high, steep cliffs that cut off access to the densely forested lands beyond. The Fuegians were a people left marooned by virtue of geography. But they were not a forgotten tribe.

Voyagers as far back as Ferdinand Magellan had known about the Fuegians. Magellan wrote of seeing fires burning in the night as his ship, *Victoria,* lay to her anchor between the mainland of South America and the mountainous island to the south that formed the strait he hoped might lead him to the Pacific Ocean. He called the island Tierra del Fuego, "Land of Fire," and as he sailed west and encountered the Indians, he and his men considered them as strange and primitive as any people they had ever seen. Other sailors shared Magellan's opinion for a long time to come.

Like the Spanish up the coast, mariners left the Fuegians to their sorry lot without much interference until the late 1800s, when most of the Fuegians died from diseases that were inadvertently introduced into the population. The only early effort to settle the environs of Tierra del Fuego failed in 1584, just four years after the founding of Buenos Aires. After that the Fuegians remained largely out of contact with the rest of the world for more than 250 years. There were several failed attempts among missionary societies from England and countries in South America to bring the word of God to the Fuegians and thereby civilize them. But the Fuegians remained impervious to the influences of the missionaries. In fact, they chased the ministers and priests away, and in some cases they massacred them.

As a result of the California gold rush, there was an increase in the number of merchant ships sailing through the Strait of Magellan as well as the Strait of Le Maire, which extended in a north-south direction along the coast of Tierra del Fuego. Coastal traders serving the ports of Rio de Janeiro, Buenos Aires, and Valparaiso added to the traffic. Sealing and whaling vessels frequented the area as well. As a consequence, the Fuegians had more contact with European and American sailors.

Coming upon a small band of Fuegians, the sailors sought to trade but found the Indians lacked anything of value and had no real talent for commerce. The Fuegians did, however, possess great talent for begging. Upon sighting a vessel, they paddled their canoes out to the ship and shouted, "Yammerschooner! Yammerschooner!" Translated into English, the word meant "Give me." If gifts were not handed over, the Fuegians made every attempt to steal whatever they could. They proved troublesome for any mariner forced to drop anchor anywhere in Tierra del Fuego.

During the voyage of HMS *Beagle*, Charles Darwin had ample opportunity to observe the Fuegians:

> While going one day on shore near Wollaston Island, we pulled alongside a canoe with six Fuegians. These were the most abject and miserable creatures I anywhere beheld. On the east coast the natives, as we have seen, have guanaco cloaks, and on the west, they possess seal-skins. Amongst these central tribes the men generally have an otter-skin, or some small scrap about as large as a pocket-handkerchief, which is barely sufficient to cover their backs as low down as their loins. It is laced across the breast by strings, and according as the wind blows, it is shifted from side to side.
>
> But these Fuegians in the canoe were quite naked, and even one full-grown woman was absolutely so. It was raining heavily, and the fresh water, together with the spray, trickled down her body. In another harbour not far distant, a woman, who was suckling a recently-born child, came one day alongside the vessel, and remained there out of mere curiosity, whilst the sleet fell and thawed on her naked bosom, and on the skin of her naked baby! These poor wretches were stunted in their growth, their hideous faces bedaubed with white paint, their skins filthy and greasy,

their hair entangled, their voices discordant, and their gestures violent. Viewing such men, one can hardly make oneself believe that they are fellow-creatures, and inhabitants of the same world.

The harsh conditions the Fuegians endured also made a significant impression on Darwin. During his time in Tierra del Fuego he explored the islands in small boats. He climbed mountains to observe the terrain. He found it utterly bleak, as somber as the inhabitants of the region.

There was a degree of mysterious grandeur in mountain behind mountain, with the deep intervening valleys, all covered by one thick, dusky mass of forest. The atmosphere, likewise, in this climate, where gale succeeds gale, with rain, hail and sleet, seems blacker than anywhere else. In the Strait of Magellan, looking due southward from Port Famine, the distant channels between the mountains appeared from their gloominess to lead beyond the confines of this world.

The passage through the Strait of Magellan proved harrowing for sailing vessels from the time of its discovery in 1520. At the eastern entrance of the strait, the tidal range ran up to forty feet and created tidal currents as swift as ten knots, enough to carry a ship onto the rocks even with sufficient wind to fill the sails. The prevailing west winds, which blew on an average of five days out of seven, often blocked the passage for vessels headed to the Pacific Ocean. Ships caught inside with a headwind found the anchorages foul with kelp beds and jagged rocks, and water depths too deep for the anchor to find bottom. The winds funneled in from the high mountains down through the narrow cuts between the islands in furious squalls known as williwaws that achieved velocities exceeding one hundred knots. A williwaw literally lifted the surface of the sea into the air in clouds of roiling spray. The airborne water clung to the black-and-gray cliffs and froze into blue ice, imparting a grave beauty to the seascape.

Magellan's discovery, at first appearing great, faded in luster as the reality of the potential danger for sailing vessels became clear. Shortly after the discovery, other ships tried to use the strait to get to the Pacific Ocean. Most of them sank or had to turn back. Magellan's *Victoria* and two of the accompanying vessels on the expedition were the only ones successful in transiting the strait in those early days of exploration and discovery. For more than three centuries the strait saw little use. However, with the advent of the ocean-going steamship, the Strait of Magellan presented a better route to the Pacific Ocean. In spite of its shortcomings, it was safer for steamers than braving the towering waves and furious winds of the Southern Ocean. At the time *Flying Cloud* sailed, a regular procession of mail and cargo steamers churned back and forth through the strait's twisting channels.

The clipper ships, though, avoided the 310-mile Strait of Magellan. It had taken Magellan a month to sail through the passage. Despite the improved seaworthiness and maneuverability of sailing vessels of the mid-1800s, it might still take weeks to get to the Pacific Ocean. In the open sea, a well-sailed clipper could cover 310 miles in one day. It was faster and safer for the clippers to head offshore into the Southern Ocean via the Strait of Le Maire. *Flying Cloud* would soon enter the treacherous waterway. At only fourteen miles wide and subject to fierce tidal currents, it was a fool indeed who tried sailing through in poor visibility. Maury's sailing directions warned mariners never to try it at night, or if the weather was likely to shut down and leave the navigator blind. The dark, cloudy weather *Flying Cloud* faced did not bode well for an easy passage.

Nevertheless, the wind seemed to promise a fair chance of at least getting down to the entrance of the strait. It gradually shifted to the east-northeast, which meant it blew off the left side of the ship and nicely filled the sails. Winds from an easterly direction were very rare in the region. Perkins was not about to waste the favorable breeze. He ordered the studdingsails set, and the men jumped to it. The sailors ran the studdingsail booms out to the mark on the yards, rigged the tackles, and set the sails as the last of the daylight faded.

The wind ushered in exceedingly cold air, so cold the passengers stayed below huddled around the stove in the great cabin wearing their overcoats. The officers and crew on deck wore heavy flannels under their pants and shirts, sweaters, and pea jackets. They pulled their wide-brimmed hats low around their ears and faces, haggard and drawn with fatigue. When not working the lines the sailors beat their arms against their bodies to keep warm, known as flogging the booby, and stamped their feet to keep them from going numb. Their fingers froze, despite the protection from heavy wool mittens.

Ellen went to the galley to see the cook. Busy making bread, his hands deep in a bowl of soft dough, flour dappling his hairy forearms, he looked up and greeted Ellen with a smile. Of all the crew, he had the most contact with the captain's pretty wife. With her gentle voice, sensitive eyes, and caring ways, she was always welcome in his galley. She smiled back at him.

"There will surely be a blow soon," she said. "Make certain the crew is fed a good hot supper with extra meat. They will be much in need of it, I think."

"Aye, Mrs. Creesy. I'll see they receive the best from the barrel. No old horse for them tonight, eh?" He laughed, a twinkle in his eyes.

"No old horse," Ellen laughed with him.

Freezing rain mixed with sleet made the decks slick. It coated the rigging in a thin layer of ice. The wind increased, pelting the sails in a patter of tiny crystals. The canvas froze and became board-stiff. Moderate squalls came in one by one. Each successive disturbance blew more violently than the last. Still, Perkins kept *Flying Cloud* driving under every stitch of canvas she could carry. The enormous courses bellied out from the lower yards, and the studdingsails strained, bending the booms in the frigid gusts as she cut through the water at an average speed of twelve knots, hitting fifteen knots in the squalls.

In the intense blackness of the night, the red and green running lights attracted the attention of those on deck. The whirling sleet and rain created a halo around the lanterns, like two unblinking eyes peering into the maw of the approaching storm. The waves built along with the wind and soon matched the direction of the swells. The water hissed and seethed as *Flying Cloud* sliced through the seas, heeled to starboard at an ever more acute angle. Perkins left the deck only to come below for supper and a mug of hot black coffee.

"It is a foul night out there," he said to his wife as he lifted his mug. The ice that had formed on his beard and hair melted in the relative warmth of the cabin. Droplets ran down his tanned cheeks, dripped down his oilskins onto the floor. "We are having our taste of the southern winter at last."

"It is not agreeing with Ellen Lyon, I'm afraid," she said. "She's down sick from the cold. She's feverish and suffering from spasms. I gave her an antispasmodic. She's resting easier. Her brother and sister are with her now."

Perkins nodded. "Winter or summer, Cape Horn is no place for passengers," he muttered. "No place for them at all."

He frowned, but his face lightened a little as he looked at Ellen, her eyes sparkling and bright despite her fatigue. "They are lucky to have you to look after them," he said. "They would receive little attention aboard most clipper ships."

"*Flying Cloud* is not like most clippers," Ellen said. She reached out and smoothed back his wet hair plastered against his broad forehead. "She's got you for her captain."

Chapter 20

Through the night the gale increased, forcing Perkins to take in first the studdingsails and next the topgallants. The skysails and royals on the fore and mizzen masts had long since been doused. Though the ship sailed under reduced canvas, she did not slow down much. An over-canvased vessel with the wind abeam did not sail to her maximum efficiency. Relieved of her lofty sails, *Flying Cloud* stood more upright against the force of the wind, and because she better kept her feet, she was able to battle the wind and waves and make good more miles, at least for a time. Yet, the gale developed still more, matured from adolescence to adulthood, until it approached storm proportions. The vessel labored hard and shipped much water over the rail.

Standing on deck amid the thick, cold weather, the skirts of his oilskins flapping in the wind, Perkins called for all hands to close-reef topsails and furl the courses before conditions grew even worse. He was particularly concerned about the mainmast. The strain on it had to be relieved at once. As the ice collected on the spars, rigging, and canvas, the weight aloft increased markedly, as did the danger that another part of the rig might carry away or the repairs already fashioned might come undone.

In absolute darkness, the crew ascended the ratlines to carry out their captain's commands. They picked their way carefully up the masts, clutched the icy ropes with bare hands, and crept out on the yards already coated thick. The sails snapped and tore at their hands and threatened to knock unwary sailors off their tenuous perches on the footropes. The crew beat their hands, bloodied and bruised, upon the yards to keep them from freezing. A sailor aloft in a Cape Horn gale would certainly die if his hands became useless from the cold. Unable to grip the lines, he would plummet to the deck or into the sea more than one hundred feet below. His duty demanded that he remain well able to tie and untie knots with dexterity, and to hand a line with a will.

The men worked for more than an hour to get the topsails reefed down and the courses furled. Like battle-weary soldiers they came down to the deck, only to find themselves waist-deep in the freezing water washing fore and aft as the ship rolled and pitched. Many of the more experienced sailors preferred work in the tops to that of the deck. It might be more dangerous aloft, but a man never found himself hip-deep in a wave. Not a single man had any dry clothes. The crew grumbled and cursed to themselves, at their captain, who was the easiest to blame for their misery, and at the weather, which they universally hated regardless of their opinion of the ship's master.

"Send the off watch below, Mr. Smith," Perkins said. "No doubt they will soon be needed again. They'll have no day of rest tomorrow, be it Sunday or no."

"Aye, aye, sir. I'll see to it," the second mate said.

At around nine o'clock on Sunday morning, July 20, the dark clouds to the east grew pale with the weak light of the sun shining unseen above the impenetrable layer. The towering waves became distinct. Their overhanging crests, the white threads of foam down their backs, and the flying spray made a hideous sight, one that bred terror in a landsman unfamiliar with the ways of the sea and ships. To add to the misery of those aboard, snow replaced the rain and sleet, and it came down hard. It cut the visibility to almost nothing, just a few hundred yards or so around the ship, lost in a whirling chaos of white and gray. The snow caked the lee sides of the deckhouse and the skylight coaming on the poop deck, and settled in and around the belaying pins and in the center of coils of line. The water on deck washed the snow clumps to leeward, and little by little the scuppers froze closed, cutting off some of the drainage for the weather deck.

Ellen struggled into her warmest clothes in their cabin and joined her husband on the poop deck. Deeply worried, she had to tell him of her concerns, despite the danger to herself in going topside. She slipped as the ship pitched and rolled, plunged and yawed. She was flung against the bulkheads, doorframes, and the furniture secured to the floors with iron bolts to keep it in place in heavy weather. She winced in pain at each impact. As she made her way to Perkins, she saw anger in his expression.

"Get below! This is no place for you now," he cried.

"We've run down our southing! We're closing rapidly with Tierra del Fuego."

"I know that. Whereaway do you estimate?"

"Cape San Diego bears south nine degrees west, about ten miles."

"Good. We'll get clear then."

"We can't be sure," she said, her voice tight and a little shrill.

Through the night the ship had made good an estimated 287 miles, based on Ellen's fix the previous day and the dead reckoning plots she had kept up as the storm built in strength. The ship was in a terribly vulnerable location, was in fact in danger of becoming embayed in the southeast-trending curve of Tierra del Fuego that ended at Cape San Diego. The east-northeast wind and the waves worked together to push *Flying Cloud* to the west toward a lee shore, among the worst situations for a sailing ship.

The sideways motion through the water was clear with just a glance at the wake. The band of white water astern did not run fine and straight. It angled off eastward, indicating that as *Flying Cloud* sailed she moved to the west. The log, too, confirmed Ellen's fears. When the log was streamed it carried off to the east, further indicating their motion toward the shore. Since a square-rigger could not sail well to windward, especially in bad conditions, *Flying Cloud* might not be able to claw her way off the rocks. She made considerable leeway as she surged forward toward the Strait of Le Maire. The dangerous coast drew closer by the minute.

In the blinding snow, in near whiteout conditions, the clipper could well go ashore on the rocks without the lookouts seeing the breakers. Icebergs carried through the strait might emerge from the curtain of white ahead and ram the ship. Propelled by both wind and waves, icebergs moved quickly, like islands set adrift in the tempest.

"I hate to give up our southing," he cried back to her. "We've fought so hard for it. I hate to give up this fair easterly!"

"Fair easterly? Perkins, we have the people to consider."

They looked hard at each other for a long moment. Perkins, of course, could risk taking the ship through the strait. That was his decision and his alone. If her estimate was right, they would clear Cape San Diego and roar through the narrow opening toward Cape Horn. It would be a victory over one of the worst stretches of ocean on earth. But if she was wrong and had not accounted for enough leeway, the ship at that moment could be steering straight for the rocks, and if Perkins kept on, the sea might claim them all. The risk was too great to continue on her present course, and she prayed he would admit it.

Similar thoughts raced through Perkins's mind. Reluctantly, he had to agree with his wife. It would be foolish to risk the Strait of Le Maire in the thick of a Cape Horn blizzard. The swift tides, the whirling eddies, the standing waves and off-lying shoals—it would be too easy to bring on a disaster. If *Flying Cloud* struck in these conditions, she would sink with all hands. Launching a small boat would be impossible. It had happened to many a ship; it could easily happen to them, too.

"All right. We will play it safe. Now get below before you freeze," he shouted over the wind.

A look of relief passed over Ellen's face. Perkins might be a hard driver, ready to gamble all on a toss, but his sense of the sea always won out in the end. He had lived upon it since he was a young boy and had gotten to know it even before he shipped off to serve aboard ships in the East India trade. From the earliest days of his boyhood, sailing dories to the outer islands off Marblehead and Salem and messing about aboard his father's schooners, he had learned, as she had, that to tempt the ocean was to court its worst retribution.

As Perkins grew into his teenage years, his time aboard the merchant ships reinforced all he had learned as a child. As a cabin boy, he gained experience of both men and the sea. He studied navigation and applied his knowledge deftly enough to earn quick promotions. He lived with and fought with the toughest hands before the mast, and gradually worked his way up the chain of command to find a place in the aft cabin with the officers. By the time he was twenty-three, Perkins had earned his first command. It had been fourteen years since that final jump to the top, and he had worked hard as a captain to better himself. When Ellen first met Perkins, he had still been honing his skills. Now, at the age of thirty-seven, gray hair heavy in his beard, deep wrinkles on his face, he was at the height of his powers as a mariner.

But even the most experienced captain still made mistakes. Failure to heed the lessons learned over decades invited disaster. Too many captains trying to round Cape Horn had forgotten that tempting the sea spelled trouble. The skeletal remains of their broken ships littered the rocks along the islands stretching south into the ocean off Tierra del Fuego, and the depths below. As Ellen made her way back to the cabin, she heard her husband's voice boom from the speaking trumpet. She glanced up at him. He leaned over the forward rail of the poop deck, the snow heavy on his beard. He looked wild, untamed, and a little dangerous.

"All hands, all hands, Mr. Austin," he shouted. "All hands to wear ship to the north!"

Ellen carefully descended the steps leading to the cabins below as the men jumped to their stations at the braces. When Austin signaled all was ready, Perkins ordered the two men at the helm to slowly turn the ship to starboard.

"Pay her off easy, easy," he screamed to the sailors struggling at the wheel, his voice barely audible over the wind.

He squinted into the blinding snow in an attempt to time the turn in a smooth, a patch of waves smaller than the average. The seas came in groups, with every seventh to ninth attaining the most prodigious heights. Sometimes these larger groups merged with a cross sea reared up from the swift tidal currents, or married together to form a rogue wave two or three times the size of the others. To get caught stern to during the turn and hit with one of the monsters could end up pooping the ship, an apt name for it. During a poop, the breaker towered high above the men on the poop deck, rushed forward at twenty to twenty-five knots, and broke over them. Tons of water smashed in skylights, carried the men overboard, and tore the ship's boat from its davits. The water roared forward across the main deck and smashed in the forecastle. This was the scenario Perkins wished to avoid.

Amid the swirling frenzy of the wind-driven snow it was difficult to find the smooths. Perkins conned the ship more by feel than by sight, from an intimate sense of the ship and the seas. *Flying Cloud* continued to come around. Several large waves broke over the windward rail and flooded the weather deck. Timing it right, though not perfectly, Perkins signaled Austin, who was forward, clinging to the lifelines and peering back at him through the snow, waiting for the order. The men worked the braces in time with the turn, and the wind and waves came around the ship to the starboard side.

Flying Cloud now headed due north, leaving the Strait of Le Maire astern, though very slowly. The wind backed from the east-northeast to the northeast, as if to block their escape. It came in hard off the starboard bow and intensified. With the wind howling from that quarter, waves thundered over the bow and cascaded over the forecastle deck to the weather deck below. As the clipper rose to meet the crests, her bow careened over the backside of the waves and remained airborne for a few seconds, until she dropped down hard and buried herself deep in the trough. The lack of buoyancy in the bow because of her sharp lines made it seem as though she might keep going straight to the bottom. Slowly, though, each time she shook off the tons of water and rose to meet the next crest, and the next.

Flying Cloud made little headway to the north. But it was enough to keep her off the rocks to leeward. Throughout Sunday she kept station, more or less hove to against the storm. The motion belowdecks was bad enough to keep most of the passengers snugged down in their berths. Sarah Bowman, Edward, the Lyon family, with Ellen still feverish, Mrs. Gorham and her maid, J. D. Townsend, Francesco Wadsworth, and Willie Hall were quite alarmed. Even the veteran traveler Laban Coffin, who knew the danger more than any of the others, found himself uneasy.

A Cape Horn blow offshore was one thing. But to encounter one with the wind blowing the ship toward the shore was another matter altogether. Too much could go wrong. The entire ship's company was in God's hands. That it was Sunday appeared a good omen to the more religious-minded aboard. Surely God would not send her down to Davy Jones's locker on His day. Surely the sailors with pure hearts did not have an imminent appointment to journey forth to Fiddler's Green, where all the good sailors went when their duty on earth was done, a kind of heaven filled with fair ladies and strong drink as opposed to the cold, dark, and eternally lonely Davy Jones's locker.

The stove had been cold for many hours, and the temperature inside the cabins dropped down close to freezing. The passengers saw their breath in the dim light from the portholes as they lay in their berths, listening to the hellish cacophony of the storm and wondering when it would end. They heard the larger waves coming in a deep growl, faint at first, until the waves bore down and hit the hull with a sickening bang. They heard the timbers of the ship working against their supports. It sounded as though at any minute the clipper might break apart. But each time she recovered, defiant and bold, and at that time more than any other she seemed actually to be alive, a living creature as real as they were, and as bent on surviving.

The short day ended and the long night began. It was unsafe to light any but the most essential lamps. The passengers and the crew off watch huddled in darkness and misery. The gales of the southern winter in these high latitudes could blow for weeks, and all aboard knew it. They wondered how much they could take, how the ship would fare. Sailors in these latitudes were known to go crazy with cold, hunger, and fatigue. The sea could reduce the most hardened seaman to a drone, weak, unable to think or respond quickly to orders.

The wind shifted abruptly to the southeast early on Monday morning, bringing with it rain mixed with snow. The ship rode much easier with the wind off her starboard quarter instead of hard on the bow, and hope that the ordeal would soon end began to eclipse the fear among the passengers. The southeasterly did not please Ellen, however. Based on her dead reckoning, she estimated the ship had made good approximately twenty-three miles in a northerly direction. She was convinced that the storm had pushed them too far west, and to make good the easting she had lost meant setting a course to the southeast. Again, it seemed the elements remained intent upon blocking their entrance into the Strait of Le Maire. The waterway was close, and yet it was far away. It required a struggle to reach unless conditions changed again, and this time in their favor. Together, Ellen and Perkins decided to turn south again and beat back toward Cape San Diego in hopes of getting through the strait in the limited daylight hours.

Exhausted, Perkins nevertheless kept to his station on the poop deck. He had slept little since the latest storm swept in. The pale light of early dawn broke through the clouds at around nine o'clock, and as the dull gray light eliminated the shadows he saw a large ship bearing northeast of their position. It appeared ghostlike out of a wall of thick, falling snow. The foresails streamed to leeward in tatters. He could see the crew trying to take the sails in, tiny black dots spaced on the yards, in a struggle they could not win. The ship heaved and plunged into the crests, and as quickly as it emerged from the gloom it disappeared again. Its presence added to Perkins's worry. The likelihood of a collision was small, but sighting the ship served as a reminder that it was not an impossibility.

The storm continued to rage. However, the clouds tore apart for a brief time, revealing patches of dark, deep blue sky, like the ancient ice of a glacier. He sent word for Ellen, and she was soon on deck ready to work. The wind whipped her long hair and dress and the scarf she wore around her neck.

"We'll have to work fast!" Perkins cried.

Ellen felt the pressure build as she waited, her husband standing close to steady her. The sun slipped in and out of the scud rushing across the sky. Above it thick layers of clouds opened and closed. She got one sight before the sky lowered again and banks of clouds obscured the heavens, making it seem almost as dark as night. Perkins walked her below, to ensure she was safe, and returned to his station.

Below, Ellen worked out the observation. Although her previous plots from her last fix were two days old, she advanced them to get a very rough idea of the ship's current location. If her estimates were correct, *Flying Cloud* was still in a good position to enter the Strait of Le Maire. The ship had stood up well against the elements forcing her toward the coast. Though the decision to turn south again involved risk, with luck they might still make it through the strait without another day lost to the storm.

However, contrary to Ellen's hopes, the wind and waves pushed *Flying Cloud* too far west again as the day progressed. As the last of the daylight faded on Monday afternoon, Cape San Diego emerged from the murk dead ahead. Ellen had no choice but to turn the clipper back to the north one more time.

Chapter 21

After two days of trying to reach the Strait of Le Maire, the weather relented early Tuesday morning and *Flying Cloud* sailed straight toward the entrance of the waterway. The waves diminished in size and the wind no longer screamed in the rigging. Best of all was the fact that the wind came from the east. In winter off Tierra del Fuego, mariners encountered east winds more frequently than in summer, but at all times the voyager headed west counted it as rare and rejoiced whenever an easterly blew.

Perkins stood near the helm, hands behind his back, and gazed at the sails and the sea. He beamed at Ellen as she joined him. A broad smile crossed Ellen's face, too. She was so excited she could have thrown herself into his arms and danced for joy. But she restrained herself in front of the second officer standing on the lee side of the poop, and the one man at the helm.

"The storm has brought us a gift, my dear," Perkins said, the happiness in his voice obvious. "An east wind!" He clapped his hands once, laughed, and pointed at the sails. The topsails were only single-reefed and the courses were set. *Flying Cloud* sailed due south through the boisterous seas. The dull light of dawn revealed the vast ocean out to the horizon. There was sufficient visibility to navigate by line of sight.

Rounding Cape Horn

Flying Cloud arrived off the Strait of Le Maire on July 20. But a gale with heavy snow forced Ellen Creesy to change course to the north. The bad weather continued until July 22. A rare east wind after the storm brought fine sailing for the run to Cape Horn.

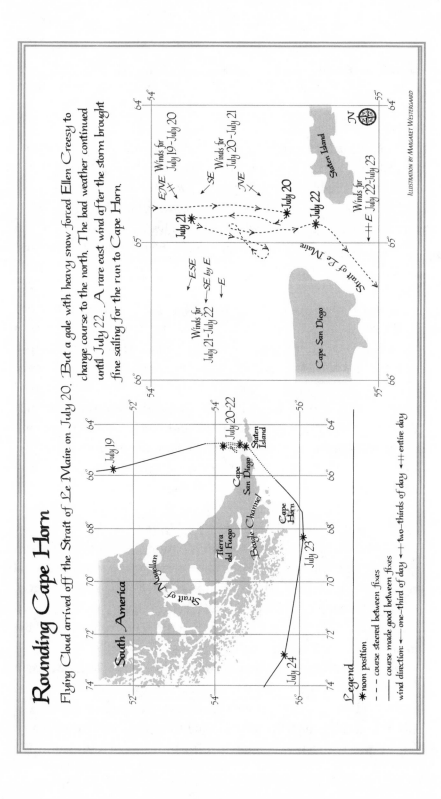

ILLUSTRATION BY MARGARET WESTERGAARD

"Don't whistle up more wind, Perkins," Ellen said, standing close to him, chiding him in a good-natured way.

"I wouldn't think of it. . . . Well, maybe a whistle or two to bring it on."

"Don't you dare!"

Perkins puckered up his lips, looked aloft, and let fly with a concert of his own to blend with the whistle of the wind through the rigging. A crewman aboard *Flying Cloud* said in an interview years later: "I have seen the Old Man sitting with his wife on the quarterdeck playing chess—he whistling for a little more wind, the boat then going at the rate of sixteen or seventeen knots." For Perkins, gales were welcome, as long as the wind blew from a favorable direction.

Ellen gazed at the sea and lifted her spyglass to scan the horizon to the south. At ten o'clock she sighted the dark purple heights of Cape San Diego dead ahead. Whiffs of smoke from the cabin stove and the bleats, cackles, and grunts of the animals reminded her of land, not the desolate reaches of Tierra del Fuego, but the cool springs and warm summers in New England. Here there was just the lonely sea, devoid of the sights and smells of the shore—no sweet-smelling flowers, no musky yet pleasant odor of horses, no tooting whistles of steam locomotives or the clink of silverware against fine china plates at the Astor House.

Dressed against the diminishing cold, the passengers gathered on deck and stared at the land as well. *Flying Cloud*'s rapid passage fueled their desire to reach their destination. It set up an expectation that their time at sea would be shortened beyond the typical run to San Francisco, which was often more than 120 days even aboard the clippers. The passengers leaned against the rail, talked quietly among themselves, and watched the waves roll toward them in an endless procession.

The east wind sped *Flying Cloud* into the Strait of Le Maire at around noon. As the ship entered the narrow confines between Tierra del Fuego and Staten Island, the sea state changed. The storm had left in its wake a large swell that refracted around Staten Island and rolled into the strait from both north and south. On either side of the ship, tall cliffs rose skyward. As *Flying Cloud* probed into the heart of the waterway, the waves became more tumultuous.

Long bands of disturbed water stretched out in every direction. A strong north-setting tide ripped through the strait against *Flying Cloud* and kicked up standing waves that smashed into her bow and reduced her forward progress through the water. The helmsman struggled to keep her on course, moving the wheel left and right as needed. The east wind blew over the left side of the ship and filled every sail. The easterly was a fine wind direction for making good progress, and it helped power *Flying Cloud* along at a good clip despite the fierce tide that sought to push the vessel back out of the strait.

Flying Cloud skirted close to the shores of Tierra del Fuego. Broad snow-covered cliffs rose up against the clouds in a forbidding display of natural beauty. The waves broke against the rocky shore, shot spray up the faces of the bluffs, and formed a light gray mist that partially hid their lower reaches. These waters were well known for their dangerous currents, the terrible weather, the inhospitable land. It had been thus since 1616, when Willem Schouten, a Dutch explorer intent upon finding a better way to the Pacific than via the Strait of Magellan or the long way around via the Cape of Good Hope, sailed through aboard his diminutive ship of 360 tons, *Unity*.

Schouten, too, encountered the eddies and whirls of a strong tide in the Strait of Le Maire, and the sharp standing waves that seemed never to move from their position. These waves rose and fell in one place, as though imprisoned in the strait for all eternity. Schouten sailed through against the tide and the waves. He named the large island to the left Staten Island, after the State's General, which governed Holland at the time. The strait he named for the main backer of the voyage, Isaac Le Maire, a man whose ill temper quite well matched the unpleasant nature of the waterway.

Unity sailed onward, east of the many islands below Tierra del Fuego. The islands grew smaller as they protruded into Drake Passage, until finally giving way to the sea at Cape Horn. Schouten stared at the last of the islands, a mere rock roughly five miles in length, topped with snow and fronted with immense bluffs, and understood he had at last reached the end of the South American continent. Schouten named the island Cape Hoorn, after his hometown of Hoorn, Holland. He did not name the island for the shape of the continent, which terminated in a shape very similar to that of a powder horn, or a funnel. It was a coincidence that the name he chose closely matched the actual form of the land.

Below Cape Horn the Southern Ocean constricted into a relatively narrow gap between South America and Antarctica known as Drake Passage. Here, the prevailing west winds that blew unobstructed around the entire length of the globe built enormous, majestic seas of thirty to sixty feet called graybeards. The wind and waves rushed through Drake Passage with such fury that sailing ships trying to make progress against them often remained trapped for weeks, even months, sailing back and forth until a break in the weather allowed them to pass into the Pacific Ocean.

The sailors aptly had dubbed the transit through Drake Passage from east to west "the wrong way round Cape Stiff." They called the ocean around Cape Horn "the devil's best mess." Sailing against the prevailing winds appeared to be the wrong thing to do, especially when the gales reached their maximum strength. The slow, bluff-bowed ships therefore took the much longer route to the Pacific, or the "right way round." The ships sailed down around the Cape of Good Hope and eastward across the Indian Ocean. They sailed with the prevailing westerlies and the monstrous waves instead of fighting against the elements. Many sailing ships attempting to go the wrong way around Cape Horn disappeared without a trace. They still did in *Flying Cloud*'s time and continued to do so for many years afterward.

The clippers, while much more maneuverable and responsive to the helm than their earlier cousins, nevertheless faced the formidable challenges inherent in any tangle with the Southern Ocean. The west winds could stop a ship in her tracks, clipper or not. To find an east wind was a blessing in these latitudes for the westbound mariner. A wise captain took full advantage of easterlies while they lasted.

Perkins ordered all possible sail set on the fore and mizzen masts. With a full spread of canvas, the ship picked up speed and was better able to stem the tide running hard against her. The coast of Staten Island gradually dropped astern and disappeared in the deepening twilight of midafternoon. The eastern edge of Tierra del Fuego, much closer at hand, remained in view until the last glimmers of daylight vanished over its craggy heights. A cold rain carried on the east wind pattered gently on the deck. All but the watch retired below, including Perkins, who was much in need of rest. While the wind blew fair and the weather held moderate, he satisfied himself that Thomas Austin could handle the ship.

But Perkins hesitated leaving the poop deck, anyway. He had been growing impatient with his first officer. Austin seemed more inclined to socialize with the passengers and to take for himself the easiest duty aboard than to work. He was too easy on the men. Sailors needed an unbending hand of discipline to keep the ship in good working order and sailing at peak efficiency. Austin was to Perkins a backslacker, a soldier, a marine.

It was not that Austin was an incompetent seaman. He could not fairly be called a lubber. The owners of the ship had placed him aboard because of his reputation as a fine first officer. However, the man lacked the soul of a driver, and as such he did not command much respect from Perkins. The fatigue of the last few days had caught up with Perkins, though. He told himself that for the moment, the ship was safely on course for Cape Horn without much to concern the officer on deck. It would not do to overtax himself, so he prepared to go below despite his misgivings with regard to the first mate.

"Mr. Austin. I am going below. See that not a stitch of canvas comes off her in my absence," he said, his voice stern.

"Aye, aye, sir."

"See that the lookouts keep a weather eye out for ice."

"Aye, aye, sir."

"Very well. Make it so," he said, and turned his back on the first officer and went below.

The east wind held fair through the night into Wednesday morning, wafting the ship along at roughly ten knots toward Cape Horn. In the first pale light of dawn, the sun ignited the horizon off the stern in fiery red. No clouds obscured the orb as it inched above the edge of the earth and colored the rolling swells a gray-blue tinged with pink and orange. The sky looked as if it reached all the way to infinity, a portal to something larger than life itself, and as grand as creation. The scene evoked the primeval as the ship's company gathered on deck and scanned the horizon to the west. The indistinct forms of the islands gradually became clearer. In the distance, the sun's rays illuminated the snow-covered mountains on the mainland, splashing them in shades of purple and blue. The peaks soared high above the sea, as though to touch the stars twinkling above and disappearing as the light increased. Hard off the starboard bow the rocky point of Cape Horn loomed out of a band of blue mist.

Ellen cut the corner close at hand, in keeping with Maury's instructions: "Hug the Cape as closely as the wind and rocks will allow." She doubled Cape Horn only five miles off. The island seemed much nearer than that, however. Blue ice streaked the cliffs, and the surf breaking at their feet shot upward to prodigious heights. The snow collected in the nooks and crannies of the rock walls contrasted against the basalt black of the bluffs. The sea and land swarmed with thousands of wild ducks and gulls. Albatrosses rode the updrafts over the swells, wings spread to more than ten feet. The cries of the birds mingled with the rush and whoosh of the bow wave and the hiss of the wake extending astern in an arrow-straight line. The temperature had risen to 52 degrees, very unusual for the Southern Ocean in the midst of winter.

The passengers chattered excitedly and pointed at the island. The crew climbed into the rigging for a better look at the scene.

The mist, the snow and ice, the rough faces of the cliffs, the sky thick with wheeling and winging birds—it was a picture few, if any, of the sailors had seen before. Fog often obscured Cape Horn. Most of the sailors passed it aboard ships sailing well offshore, the island remaining hidden from view.

Perkins stood close to Ellen on the poop deck. They held hands and gazed at Cape Horn, barely able to contain their delight. The east wind carried them quickly along, and as they rounded the island, it came in off the stern. Although seas rolled high, they did not break. The long, broad swells washed under the transom without making *Flying Cloud* pitch and yaw.

"We could not expect such luck once in five hundred times," Perkins whispered to Ellen, almost afraid to tempt the weather to change abruptly, as it well could. "It's remarkable."

"The ship has been blessed, darling. Look how she romps through the waves. It seems as though she is as happy as we are," Ellen said.

Sarah Bowman, Willie Hall, and J. D. Townsend, anxious to capture the moment, sketched the island and the panoramic background of utter desolation. The drawings would summon the memory of the day long after the voyage had merged with a thousand other recollections. Words scribbled in a diary lacked the ability to convey the beauty set before them.

Sarah Bowman, a talented painter, worked with zeal on her sketch. Relief flooded through her with every sweep of the pencil across the page. She wrote of passing Cape Horn: "In the distance the snowy mountains and frost covered rocks look like turreted castle forts and battlements, a soft blue haze descends and gives really a charm to the scene. Occasionally the stern dark rock rises abruptly from the ocean in strange contrast with the snowy background. I am glad to have seen all this—I shall sleep better tonight than usual."

Ellen and Perkins strolled over to the artists to view their works in progress. They complimented each of them. Standing behind Sarah Bowman, Perkins admired her work in particular.

"You draw very well, Mrs. Bowman," he said, his voice kind and gentle. He was aware of her prickly feelings toward him, but at such moments the pettiness of it seemed unimportant. The magnificent weather combined with the memorable scenery lifted the antipathy like a curtain. She looked up at him and smiled.

"Why, thank you, Captain Creesy. I think Willie has outdone me, though."

"I don't think so," he said.

Ellen leaned over to have a closer look. "You are too modest. It's beautiful."

"Might we have a copy when you are done?" Perkins asked.

Sarah Bowman felt pride well up with her other emotions. While she might not have liked Captain Creesy, he had to be commended for his good taste in art. She could draw him a copy of her original sketch with good conscience, especially out of consideration for his wife, whom she regarded fondly.

"Of course," she said. "It would be my pleasure."

"We can all be happy for this day," Ellen told the people on deck. "We have reached Cape Horn only fifty days, eighteen hours from New York. It has been an exceptional passage."

"May it continue," Laban said. He looked down at Sarah Lyon and returned her smile.

"We may well best the *Surprise*'s ninety-six day run. If any ship can do it, our *Flying Cloud* is the one," Perkins said, a little boastful, caught up in the moment as he was.

Perkins had good reason for optimism. Ellen had guided the ship over a course of more than 8,200 miles with an average daily run of 160 miles per day, far faster than most ships, even the clippers that had sailed before her. According to Maury, the average passage for a vessel from Cape São Roque to 50 degrees south on the Atlantic side of South America was only between 100 and 120 miles per day, depending on the time of year. *Flying Cloud* was well ahead of schedule.

The clippers owed their great capacity for speed to a number of factors. The most important was the design of the hull. The sharp bows and narrow width of the hull offered less resistance to the water as the ship moved forward than did a traditional vessel. However, that was not all that made them so fast. These ships boasted the tallest masts of any vessel afloat at the time. The clipper captain could set far more sail than the masters of other types of ships. In addition, the clippers were longer at the waterline, which also contributed to their swift sailing abilities. The maximum potential speed of a sailing vessel depended as much on the length of the hull as it did on the height of the masts.

The passengers remained on deck for hours, just watching the land sweep past. It was comfortable and pleasant, and a much-needed respite from the pounding they had all endured. The east wind left *Flying Cloud* late that afternoon, which surprised neither Ellen, Perkins, nor the saltiest of the crew. A moderate breeze from the east-northeast came in at a perfect slant off the right side of the stern and brought much colder weather more in keeping with the season. With all possible sails set, *Flying Cloud* surged into the South Pacific Ocean amid the whirl and bluster of snow squalls.

Chapter 22

Passing Cape Horn marked a milestone for every ship headed into the Pacific Ocean. For the coastal traders bound for ports on the west coast of South America, it meant the last leg of a long journey was at hand. The vessels rode the light winds and the north-flowing Humboldt Current to safe harbors with little danger of shipwreck once past Patagonia. For the clippers, leaving Cape Horn astern represented the midpoint of the voyage from New York. There were still many days remaining before those aboard could expect to make landfall at San Francisco. To find the best winds required the clippers to sail more than one thousand miles offshore through the southeast trades, the doldrums, and the northeast trades beyond.

Dozens of clippers at any given time followed the new route to California. The sea was a busy place. These vessels sometimes met and raced in company for days at a time, until the fastest ship pulled away. But more often than not the voyage from Cape Horn to San Francisco was completed without sighting more than a handful of ships, and speaking only a few. Far from land, the clippers remained alone, dependent upon the skills of the master and navigator to make port without delay.

The spirits of a ship's crew and passengers generally lifted after

Ocean Winds
North & South Pacific
July – September

Just as Flying Cloud failed to find the northeast trade winds in the Atlantic Ocean, she encountered unusual winds in the Pacific. The ship found favorable winds in the variables and a very narrow band of the doldrums.

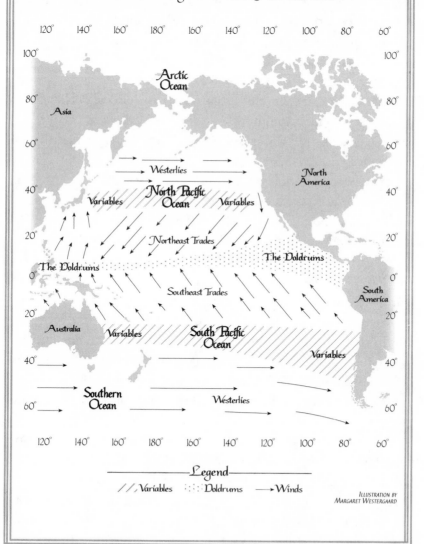

Legend
///, Variables   :::: Doldrums   → Winds

ILLUSTRATION BY
MARGARET WESTERGAARD

doubling Cape Horn, as did those of the people aboard *Flying Cloud*. Though the voyage was only half over, reaching their destination seemed all the closer, all the more real. The fear of the storms of the Southern Ocean abated as the days passed and the clippers put the tempestuous region farther and farther astern. The weather gradually grew warmer, the days longer. The sea turned to a tropical azure and puffy trade wind clouds filled the sky.

In the days of late July after passing Cape Horn, with the balmy trade winds still many miles away, the passengers and crew aboard *Flying Cloud* wore heavy coats against the chill of the south wind blowing up from the vast ice fields of Antarctica. The stove in the great cabin remained a focal point; the passengers gathered around it for warmth and conversation. The Cape pigeons winged around the ship and cried their shrill calls to the people on deck, as if to wish them all a pleasant goodbye. Soon the birds would vanish, left to their cold world of rock and ice as *Flying Cloud* roared toward the tropics.

Perkins ordered the crew to send up the main topgallant, royal, and skysail yards on the mainmast. The men rerigged the spars and set the sails, and went to work on the lower booms as well. The studdingsails extended outward from the hull to catch the wind, and *Flying Cloud* picked up speed. For the first time in almost three weeks the ship was whole, the profile of grace and beauty complete. The mainmast no longer protruded like a finger, unnatural, and evidencing weakness, but rose skyward in tier after tier of square sails bellied out from the force of the wind. *Flying Cloud* appeared in her full dress and seemed to exude an almost animate aura of glory and strength. That was an illusion, however. The mainmast was badly damaged, and no one aboard knew just when it might give way.

As the weather grew slightly warmer, the ship's company took advantage of light rains to wash their clothes. The crew plugged the drain holes for the deck and the rainwater collected in pools. Dirty clothes were soaked, soaped and rinsed in the water, and hung in the rigging to dry after the showers passed. It was a most unseamanlike look for a clipper. *Flying Cloud* resembled a laundry house. But the need to wash was dire. No one aboard had clean clothes, nor had anyone bathed since leaving New York. It was too cold for the passengers to sponge their bodies in the privacy of their staterooms, and anyway, the ship's fresh water was for drinking and cooking. The captain allowed no one to waste it on baths.

Ellen's plots on the chart showed steady progress. The latitude decreased degree by degree and longitude increased as the ship sailed on a northwesterly course deeper into the Pacific. Perkins kept to the deck as much as possible, suspecting his officers might fail to drive *Flying Cloud* as hard as he wanted. Studdingsails were set and taken in, and reset again. The yards were trimmed and adjusted dozens of times to accommodate every subtle change in the wind. The drill had long since become routine for the crew, and while they despised the extra work, they did not slack off in the least. The goldfields waited. Most of the men wanted to get there quickly.

Fine weather and fresh winds from the north-northeast hurried *Flying Cloud* onward. The sun sparkled on the faces of the waves and painted them with splashes of white light that stung the eyes with its glare. The wind wrinkled the surface of the water in dark patches as the gusts passed through. High banks of cirrus clouds rolled in and coated the sky in a transparent layer of pale white and blue. The clouds caught the light of the setting sun in strips of bright orange and red. As the last of the light faded and the cold of the evenings drove all but the watch below, the world around the ship appeared in deep hues of purple that gave way to the dark of night. The Southern Cross and millions of other stars peeped through the clouds, their pinpricks obscured in a dull expanse of icy vapor high above the earth.

During the early hours of July 30 the wind began to blow in earnest. The men on watch adjusted the sails accordingly. Midlevel clouds blew in under the high cirrus and scudded along to the northwest in mottled bands that gradually thickened. A large swell made itself felt as well. It rolled in from the southeast, indicating to Ellen that there was some heavy weather batting about somewhere far beyond their wake to the south.

Ocean Currents
North & South Pacific

In the Pacific Ocean, currents did not influence navigation as much as they did in the Atlantic Ocean. The only ones of concern were the Southern Ocean Current and those near the equator.

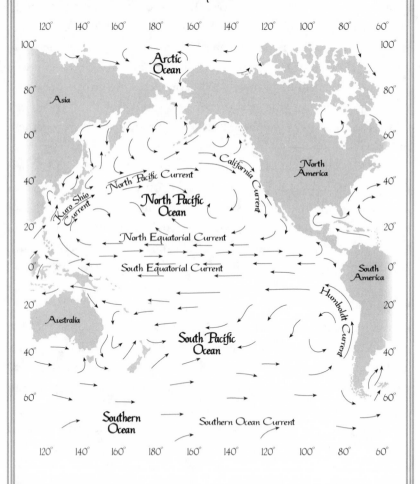

"We've got the dog before the master, I'm afraid," she said to her husband. "It looks like we're in for a blow from the southeast."

Perkins smiled. "Let it come. As long as it's not from the north or west."

Flying Cloud picked up speed as the wind and waves built. The ship sailed about eight hundred miles off the coast of Chile at nearly eleven knots, and much faster in the gusts. As the afternoon progressed, the clouds lowered and the wind increased further still, as did the ship's speed through the water. The sea and sky no longer appeared welcoming. Wind-driven waves formed atop the swells and began to break in long white crests dead aft under the stern. They rose up behind the poop deck, higher and higher, until they appeared certain to sweep over the ship. At the last moment, *Flying Cloud* outpaced the seas and the waves broke in roaring fury. The ocean boiled and foamed. Flying spray spanned each side of the hull forward to the mainmast. Night fell.

Standing with Perkins on the poop deck, Ellen gazed forward at the splashes of phosphorescence kicked up in showers of light green flecks in the water as the ship sailed into the night. Witch's oil, the sailors called it, the green of a firefly's tail. The odd spectacle resulted from the disturbance of millions of tiny creatures that illuminated themselves when pushed aside as the ship passed. Ellen gazed aft. The wake also left a trail of sparkles, as numerous as the stars now cloaked under a heavy layer of low clouds. The wake looked like a milky river.

"Perkins, look!" she said, and pointed astern.

"I see it," he said.

The approaching squall intensified the darkness behind *Flying Cloud*. The Creesys watched as it flowed over the heavens like a breaking wave washing up the sand of a beach, spreading a shadow as it proceeded to the high-water mark. The light of the binnacle dimly lit the compass. The warm glow from the skylight, deckhouse, and forecastle became all the more inviting, a symbol of the routine, of home and safety. The darkness passed overhead and plunged out in front of the ship. The demarcation between the first fringe of the squall and the ordinary cloud cover ahead disappeared.

Only the splash and play of the phosphorescence and the cabin lights illuminated the darkness, as Ellen went below for supper.

Below in the great cabin the passengers tried to eat their meal. The dishes slid from side to side and bumped into the fiddles on the table meant to keep them from ending up in the diners' laps. The glasses they wedged in place as best as they could, but the violent rolls spilled the wine if they were more than a quarter full. The lamps gyrated and sent a succession of ever-changing shadows to play across the room.

"I don't think I can stomach another storm," Sarah Bowman said. "I really don't."

Other passengers agreed with her.

"We're fast approaching the trades," Ellen said. "There will be no more gales there."

"This is just a goodbye from the Southern Ocean," Laban said.

They all fell silent for a moment and listened. They looked toward the stern, somewhat alarmed. They heard what sounded like a waterfall. The rumble and hiss grew louder and louder.

"Hang on!" Ellen said.

The passengers grabbed hold of the table with one hand and their plates with the other. They felt *Flying Cloud* sink stern first as she fell into a deep trough. The sound of the wave behind the ship intensified, and suddenly all was bedlam around them. The china in the sideboard banged and clinked. Wineglasses toppled. The gimbaled lamp swung in a wide arc and nearly hit the beam from which it was suspended. The wave hit hard with an explosive report. They heard it thunder over the skylight above their heads and rush past to cascade down over the portico into the waist of the ship.

Ellen said nothing, but she feared the clipper had been pooped. The men, if they had not been quick to grab hold of the rigging or rails, could have been swept away. She swallowed her fear for her husband and tried not to let the passengers know her true feelings. Just then Perkins came below, soaking wet. He braced himself in the door leading from the great cabin into the officers' quarters and surveyed the frightened faces of the passengers, and the deep concern on his wife's face as well.

"Don't worry," he said to them. "I'll not drive the ship under."

He sat down and Ching served him his supper. The dinner conversation was more subdued than it had been of late. The squall blew through and the ship settled down a little, as if to give credence to Perkins's assurances. Ellen looked at her husband, anxious about the safety of those aboard. However, excitement mixed with her unease. With the wind dead aft, *Flying Cloud* could run before the gale at full speed. There was nothing like it, nothing at all that could match the immense power that coursed through every timber, spar, and rope.

Little by little, Perkins stripped the canvas off *Flying Cloud,* and yet she did not slow down. The gale increased, and with less sail on she made her way more smoothly through the seas, keeping her speed to the maximum, exceeding even Perkins's expectations. The seas crashed all around them, chargers in the night, unseen as they rose and fell.

Chapter 23

The dim light of dawn slowly illuminated the empty world around *Flying Cloud*. The strong winds ripped the layers of low clouds into fragmented swaths of gray and black, and the sun began to shine through the gaps and paint their edges gold and orange. Radiant beams of sunlight streamed through the openings and struck the waves at sharp angles. Distant rain showers merged the sky and ocean into one continuous expanse of gray, causing the uniform procession of breaking waves to disappear in the gloom on the horizon.

There was a majesty to the scene that struck Ellen as beautiful and yet wild. The cold wind had less of a bite than in previous days, and she noted that there was more light at the hour of eight o'clock than she had seen in the weeks since *Flying Cloud* had sailed into the South Atlantic and the heart of the southern winter. Every mile brought the clipper closer to the warmth of summer and days of abundant sunlight in the Northern Hemisphere.

The last of the sand in the half-hour glass next to the helmsman ran out and he gave the ship's bell eight quick strikes, in sets of two. He capsized the glass again to mark the passage of the next half hour, a ritual repeated throughout the cycle of watches as the bells rang the men on and off duty. The man whose trick it was at the wheel for the forenoon watch came aft, respectfully wished Ellen and Perkins a good morning, and took his place at the wheel, relieving his mates from the larboard watch. He was soon joined by another man to help him steer.

Perkins stood near the taffrail with two members of the crew, ready to stream the log. Both he and Ellen were very curious about the ship's speed. The wind had intensified overnight, and it was possible that the clipper had sailed even faster than she had the day before. Throughout the preceding day, *Flying Cloud* had exceeded twelve knots, and during the squalls she literally lifted her bow as she surged forward at a remarkable rate. One man held the reel of the log line above his head to ensure that the line ran free. The end of the line was tied around a belaying pin at the rail. The other sailor held a twenty-eight-second sandglass and prepared to capsize it to start the sand running when Perkins gave the command.

Perkins took the chip, a wedge with a rounded bottom weighted with lead, and uncoiled some of the log line. He threw the chip overboard and the line paid out in the midst of the eddies and swirls of the wake that stretched far astern of the vessel. He called out, "Watch!"

The man holding the glass responded, "Watch!"

The line rolled off the reel at an incredible speed, spinning and pulling hard. The man holding the reel struggled to keep his balance against the motion of the vessel and the tug of the chip as it dug into the water and presented its face perpendicular to the surface. The drag of the chip was so strong it threatened to pull the man overboard. A third sailor quickly came to the aid of his mate. He grabbed him around the waist and held on tight. Within seconds, enough of the log line streamed behind the ship to begin timing her rate of speed.

"Turn!" Perkins cried.

The man with the glass capsized it and answered, "Done!"

The sand began to run from the top of the glass to the base, and as the seconds passed the log line spun off the reel faster than Perkins or Ellen had ever seen in all of their years at sea. The knots tied at intervals of forty-eight feet each represented one nautical mile traveled in an hour. Five, seven, ten, eleven knots flew past almost too fast to count. Twelve, thirteen, fourteen. A fierce gust hit the ship and the eighteenth knot, the last on the line, vanished over the taffrail before the last of the sand in the glass ran out.

Perkins turned to Ellen. "Did you see that?" he asked, the answer to his question obvious, but he needed to ask anyway. He could not believe what he saw.

"She's sailing at more than eighteen knots!" Ellen gasped, herself incredulous. "Eighteen knots or more!"

Perkins streamed the log again. Fifteen knots. Sixteen, seventeen.

"Remarkable," he nearly shouted, filled with surprise and wonder.

No sailing ship to his knowledge had ever traveled at those speeds. No smoke-belching steamer could match the sustained speeds *Flying Cloud* had reached and held, nor would they for another quarter century. No ship on the seas appeared faster. The largest clipper ship in the world, save for *Challenge, Flying Cloud* was a true queen. She was as graceful as a seabird and as fleet as a gazelle, totally within her element in the blustery conditions. Pride swelled within Perkins, and he said a silent thanks to builder Donald McKay. The Nova Scotia–born builder had woven magic into this ship, bewitched her with an uncanny bent for speed. The towering spars may have been too high, the forces too great for mere wood to withstand indefinitely, but by God, *Flying Cloud* held together despite her weaknesses. She was making good her course at the heels of a hard gale with as much canvas as he thought she could take. He craned his neck to look aloft at the topgallant sails still fully set on all three masts, aware he was pushing his ship to the very edge of her limits.

Ellen laughed, and if she had not needed to hang on against the violent rolls of the ship, she would have clapped her hands with joy. She had grown to love their ship, to appreciate the beauty and art of her lines and rig. She delighted in the thrill of the moment and was mindful that no other human beings on earth had ever before experienced such fantastic sailing. The wind howled above her head through the miles of rigging and seemed to speak directly to her soul, and she, like her husband, felt an intimacy with the vessel never more poignant or real.

Ellen could hardly control her excitement as she took her first sight of the day. Her hands trembled, and not altogether because of the cold. The enormous seas hid the horizon and revealed it in a steady rhythm. These were not the steep, nasty waves they had encountered off Tierra del Fuego, stirred up and made furious at the unseen influence of the tide and the relative shallows of the continental shelf. They were instead the long, rolling crests of deep ocean born from a wind that swept across thousands of miles of open water. Timing a clear spot at the height of the tallest waves proved relatively easy. More vexing, though, were the clouds scudding overhead. They hid the sun more often than they sped clear. Ellen waited patiently until both the sea and the sky cooperated.

At noon, Ellen had enough observations to work out an accurate fix. Perkins lingered close by as she went through her calculations at the table in the officers' quarters. She arrived at the day's run between noon of July 30 and their position on this day, the 31st. Not believing her figures, she went through them again.

"What has she run, Ellen? Tell me now!" Perkins said, pacing back and forth in the cabin.

A broad smile lit up Ellen's face. Her eyes sparkled and danced. She leaned back in her chair and smoothed her hair, making the moment last, teasing Perkins a bit.

"Ellen," he growled, with false anger.

"Three hundred seventy-four nautical miles!" she said.

Perkins raised his eyebrows and drew close to look at her complicated figures. "Are you sure?"

"I've double-checked the calculations. I'm sure."

They stared at each other for a long moment, and as she rose from her chair Perkins took her in his arms and kissed her. They seldom showed spontaneous bursts of affection like that, being restrained by social mores and their own sense of propriety. But in that private moment all the world faded away, all of its cares and worries and petty concerns. *Flying Cloud* had set a world record. No ship had ever sailed that many miles in one day before. It was a remarkable achievement, of the captain, the navigator, the crew, and the ship.

The news spread through the ship's company, and all aboard talked excitedly about their incredible run. "At this rate we'll make San Francisco in a matter of days!" said passengers and crew. Morale had never been better, not since leaving New York. The thrilling drive of the ship infected everyone in a universal sense of awe and wonder, and they all hoped it would last without the occurrence of another mishap with the rig.

When Perkins recorded that memorable day in the log his thin, flowing handwriting became bold and enlarged as he came to the description of *Flying Cloud*'s speed. He wrote:

Fresh breezes with fine weather all sails set At 2 P.M. wind South east at 6 squally [took] in lower and Top Gallant studding sails 7 [took] in Royals At 2 A.M. [took] in fore Top Mast Studding Sail Latter part strong Gales & high seas running Ship very wet fore & aft. Distance run this day by observation is 374 miles an average of 15 14/24th Knots. . . . During the squalls 18 Knots of line was not sufficient to measure her rate of speed. Top gallant sails set.

The gale continued to scud them northward before the south-easterly wind. Ellen adjusted their course, taking the westing out of it for the moment. She was content to sail northward and run down her latitude in favor of the direct route toward the southeast trades and the equator. She instructed the helmsman to steer north 8 degrees west, or just shy of due north, bringing the wind off the right side of the stern for a better, more efficient slant than from directly behind the clipper. *Flying Cloud* immediately rode with less of a roll. The waves washing under the stern tried to slew her broadside to them, but the ship's speed mitigated the power of the breaking seas. If anything, the clipper picked up the pace and went full out, putting a forward bend in the topgallant pole masts and the upper yards.

The gale grew to storm force late in the afternoon and the wind shifted to south-southeast to come in more or less dead aft once again. The crew clung to the lifelines rigged fore and aft down the waist of the ship. The tips of the lower main yards dug into the summits of the waves. White showers of spray blew off the yards toward the bow in a continuous torrent. Solid walls of water roared over the bulwarks and inundated the deck, flooding the deckhouse and forecastle and washing over the coaming of the doors that led below to the aft cabins.

The scene was now all too familiar to the passengers. They had been allowed on deck earlier to witness the spectacle of the clipper sailing at her top speed. It was a sight they deserved to see and would likely never see again. But conditions worsened to the point where even Ellen had to join them back in the damp, dark confines of the aft cabins. As luxuriously appointed as they were, in a storm the walls seemed to close in and depress the spirit.

At six o'clock, the last of daylight long gone, all hands were called to take in the topgallant sails. The ship could take no more abuse. She appeared more like a submerged log shooting through the rapids of a river during a spring timber drive than a proud ship sailing high above the sea. The press of sail threatened to send her skittering out of control, with an unexpected and potentially disastrous turn broadside to the waves. At such high speeds the turbulence around the rudder reduced the helmsman's control.

The crew fought hard to take in the sails, and several men high on the topgallant yards nearly fell to their deaths. The quick hands of their mates saved them, that and a significant amount of luck. Accidental death aboard a clipper was not unusual. All counted themselves as fortunate that no man had died on the voyage thus far. Many of the older sailors believed *Flying Cloud* was a lucky ship, that rare breed of vessel that came along only once in a while. They had served in the merchant marine long enough to know the good ships from the bad.

Flying Cloud was no plodder, nor did she seem intent on killing off her men, as some ships did. Many a sailor aboard the clippers lost his life in some brutal way. His arms and legs were crushed or torn from his body when he got them caught in the bight of a line.

His bones were smashed when he was pinned against the deck by a loose spar afloat in the roaring water. He was flung into space from the weather end of a skysail yard, and dropped to his death into the raging ocean over a hundred feet below. Nine men aboard *Challenge*, which sailed from New York on July 13 under command of Perkins's rival Robert H. Waterman, died before the vessel reached the Golden Gate, some by the hand of the ship's officers and others at the whim of the sea.

The topgallants taken in, the men double-reefed the topsails on the fore and mizzen masts. Perkins left the full main topsail set. This was the most efficient sail aboard, and one of the largest. He refused to shorten it. He was convinced the topmast could take the strain, despite the weakened main masthead and the damage to the mainmast below the hounds. It was a risk, but what kind of captain would he be if he cowered from it?

Through the night a succession of terrible squalls buffeted the ship and the waves raked her fore and aft. Lashed to the mizzen shrouds, Perkins kept to the deck. He still refused to shorten sail. He drove *Flying Cloud* as hard as he could, taking advantage of what he and his wife knew would be their last gale for many days. Soon they would find themselves in the balmy southeast trades, where storms seldom occurred. With a hard wind astern, it was the only course of action that made sense.

Toward the start of the morning watch, from four o'clock to eight, the wind began to drop. However, the seas ran just as high as they had at the height of the storm. Robbed of the wind's maximum strength, the waves toppled down on themselves in a frightening manner. There was always a time just after a gale began to blow itself out when the ocean fell into a state of chaos as it strove to return to some kind of order. At the climax of a storm, as horrifying as the conditions might be, there was still order. There was order in nearly every circumstance when far from the influence of a coast. But when the wind suddenly diminished, its fury spent, the waves lost the force that had kept them in a state of harmony. The ship rolled, pitched, and staggered through the troughs and crests.

"All hands to make sail!" Perkins told Thomas Austin, who had been standing watch with his captain. The Old Man's tendency to stay on deck as though he were as much a fixture as the binnacle or mizzen mast bothered Austin. It was insulting that the man seemed not to trust him, and even more so that he had of late dropped the courtesy of calling him Mr. He respectfully acknowledged the order through gritted teeth and stalked forward to see that it was carried out.

Tired from their work already, the sailors dragged themselves back up the masts to shake out the reefs of the fore and mizzen topsails. The canvas boomed as the wind filled it and the lines were hauled taut. The men moved still higher up the masts and set the topgallants, and soon the ship flew before a south wind with all the main working sails set except for the royals and skysails. The added canvas steadied the clipper and gave her the power to punch through the tumultuous seas.

Dawn on the first day of August came earlier than ever, its first light apparent well before eight o'clock. The ship had run down enough latitude to lengthen the hours of daylight significantly in one twenty-four-hour bash. It was a strange thing to sail from one region to another so quickly, making enough distance to perceive the passage of time that seldom received notice when ashore and locked into a life lived in one place. It had been thus for the passengers when sailing into the darkness of the South Atlantic. Now they experienced the reverse when sailing into the light of the South Pacific.

The ship pounded on, and as the morning light intensified it turned the sea to an azure expanse dappled with brilliant reflections of the sun shining bright in the clear sky. As usual, the log was streamed at the change of the watch. The ship still pranced ahead at a good clip, but the speed of the previous day eluded her. The precise conditions that had enabled her to attain eighteen knots or more through the water were rare. The wind had to reach a strength sufficient to drive her but not so high that she had to sail under well-shortened canvas. The waves had to help, not hinder, her, as they did when they swept in from the side or, worse, hard off the bow. No adverse tide or ocean current could further complicate matters.

Ellen worked out their position and was well pleased at *Flying Cloud*'s daily mileage. She had made good another 334 nautical miles. Together with her husband she looked over the numbers scribbled in the notebook she kept. The clipper had sailed 992 nautical miles during the last three days. Ellen multiplied 992 nautical miles, each of which was 6,080 feet, to get the total number of feet sailed. She then divided that figure by 5,280 feet, the equivalent of a statute mile well familiar to any landsman. Based on her totals, *Flying Cloud* had sailed 1,144 statute miles.

At that very moment, thousands of settlers were taking their wagons across the Great American Desert and over the Rocky Mountains toward the California coast. They battled against the elements and occasionally against hostile peoples whose lands they crossed. *Flying Cloud*'s 1,144 miles in three days equaled two and a half months of overland travel by wagon train. It was a fine example of why a ship sailing 16,000 miles might easily beat a ragtag band of wagons bound on a straight course across the hinterland.

Flying Cloud surged north of the thirty-fifth parallel into the area where Ellen expected to pick up the southeast trades. The time had come to sail in a more westerly direction to get the clipper farther offshore into the more favorable winds that lay ahead. Well satisfied with the voyage north into the Pacific, Ellen altered course to a northwesterly heading for the long run to the equator still fifteen hundred miles away.

Chapter 24

The hierarchy aboard a sailing vessel in the merchant marine was quite simple. The captain commanded with godlike authority. The master acted nearly as he pleased to demote or promote officers and sailors. He could make the lives of his men as easy as possible under the harsh conditions at sea or he could make them a hell worse than penal servitude.

The tamest among clipper ship captains made men who displeased them walk up and down the weather deck with an oar perched on their right shoulder. The sailor acted as if he were a mock sentry and was subjected to the scoffs and jeers of the other members of the crew. Posing as a soldier was a humiliation that cut deep for any sailor who took pride in his work. Taking a man's dignity, such as it was, served as ample punishment for some sailors, but for many others more drastic measures were required, and they were freely used on the clippers.

Although the U.S. Navy had outlawed flogging aboard its warships in September 1850, the practice was still widespread on merchant ships. The mate carried a rope with knots tied into it, known as a cat-o'-nine-tails, and whipped the man who was seen slacking off at his work. Formal flogging, when the sailor was tied to the shrouds, his shirt ripped from his back, also occurred, though less frequently than the occasional swipe with the cat-o'-nine-tails. Clubbing with a belaying pin was not unusual. Such treatment was common on both warships and the sailing ships in the merchant marine. There were even cases when the ship's officers shot members of the crew, wounding or killing them. Often, there was no penalty for aggravated assault or for murder. In court, judges tended to believe the captain's version of events.

However, the laws of the sea were in a state of transition in the days of the clipper ship. Advocates for better treatment of the sailors petitioned for sailors' rights in the courts and made progress in improving the conditions under which the crews served. One particularly aggressive advocate was Richard Henry Dana, Jr., a man well known among the captains along the Boston waterfront for his zealous defense of the lowly Jack. The issue of unjust treatment at the hands of a commander was very much at the fore in the early 1850s. To make a profit for the owners a captain had to drive his ship harder than ever before, and many a crewman found himself ill treated. Despite the bit of progress, a sailor with a grievance was still at a disadvantage. He had no recourse against a commander while at sea. He had to wait until he reached shore to petition for justice in court. While at sea the sailor endured whatever treatment he received from the captain. He could not question or show disrespect to his superior.

Perkins's displeasure with Thomas Austin had grown during the voyage. He complained bitterly about the first officer to Ellen in the privacy of their cabin. He called Austin a soldier, and many a term worse than that, names that would have made the female passengers think him crude and base. Ellen listened to his complaints and tried to subdue his temper. His smoldering anger concerned her. Maltreatment of Thomas Austin, who had been put aboard by Grinnell, Minturn & Company, as was the custom, boded ill for Perkins's future with the firm if the bosses considered his handling of the first mate unjust.

Richard Henry Dana described the special standing of the first mate aboard merchant vessels of the day in his book *The Seaman's*

Friend, which he wrote in the spring of 1841 after publication of *Two Years Before the Mast*.

> The law looks upon the chief mate as standing in a different relation to the master from that of the second mate or the men. He is considered a confidential person, to whom the owners, shippers and insurers look, in some measure, for special duties and qualifications. The master, therefore, cannot remove him from office, except under very peculiar circumstances, and then must be able to prove a justifiable cause . . .
>
> The master, from the power of his office, can at all times make the situation of a mate who has displeased him extremely disagreeable, and from this cause has great indirect influence over him; the law and the custom should therefore be strictly adhered to which rightly make the chief officer, in this respect, in a manner the umpire between the master and the crew, as well as between all on board and the parties interested on shore. The law also makes the chief mate the successor to the master, in case the latter should die, or be unable to perform the duties of his office; and this without any action on the part of the crew.

There had been other mates who displeased Perkins, who Ellen had long known was a perfectionist. It was both his strength and his weakness. His desire to see that all was shipshape, that every man did his duty well and quickly, made him a great captain. The tendency also alienated the officers under his command. Though many clipper captains filled out the log themselves, that duty really belonged to the first officer. The captain was, by custom, not to rebuke the first officer in front of the men, nor was he to take charge of a task if he found the first officer wanting. Rather, the fair and just procedure entailed calling the man back to the poop deck or down below to the captain's cabin for a private chat. Perkins ignored these customs. He filled out the log himself and felt no compunction about stepping in to take personal command of a situation whenever he felt his subordinates failed to carry it out to his standards.

Sarah Bowman was particularly critical of Captain Creesy. She wrote of his treatment of the officers and crew to her sister, Kate. "The Captain is an able seaman, no doubt, but I will not wrong my conscience by calling him a gentleman. He is overbearing and jealous of every attention bestowed by the passengers upon the Mate . . . Every man [of the crew] will leave at San Francisco . . . even the Second and Third mates will not make the entire voyage they consider the Captain so mean. However matters may be exaggerated. I'll hope so at all events."

Ellen was aware of the talk among some of the passengers about her husband's treatment of the crew as well as the officers. A ship was a small world, a mini-society with all of a society's good and evil. Not much escaped her perceptive eyes and keen ears. Based on rumor, the second and third officers intended to desert the ship at San Francisco. That many of the crew had the same idea in mind did not surprise her, but she had expected more from Thomas Smith and Henry Moore. She found it disconcerting that there were no rumors about Thomas Austin, that he among the mates appeared the most loyal and yet was subjected to what could easily be construed as ill treatment at the hands of her husband. She had seen very little that proved Austin was incompetent, just as she had seen little wrong with the way the first officer of *Oneida* had carried out his duties on the previous voyage.

Yet, Perkins found fault with *Oneida*'s first mate, fault enough to stay aboard the ship while the cargo of tea was unloaded in New York. The first officer was the man customarily responsible for offloading, issuing receipts to the shippers, tracking the inventory, and keeping the records. He was the man to whom command fell in port when the captain was not engaged in much else except his business dealings with the shippers and agents ashore. There was talk along the waterfront that Perkins was indeed a fine captain. There was also talk that some people in the industry regarded him as a notorious pencil sharpener, a term used to describe a man who did not know when his point was as fine as it could be. She did not share these sentiments, but she did understand why not everyone regarded her husband as the good man she knew he was.

"Austin has long neglected his duty aboard this ship," Perkins fumed on the afternoon of August 2. "He is content to backslack when he thinks I'm not looking."

"We'll soon arrive in San Francisco. Perhaps you can replace him there."

"We'll lose most of our crew to the goldfields. You know that. There will be no replacing him. But I can't abide him all the way to China, and then on to New York."

Ellen sighed and leaned back in the chair near his oak desk. She glanced at the door, shut tight against prying ears. "What do you intend to do then?"

"I'm putting the man off duty. I've had enough of his neglect and insubordination. He likes to socialize with the passengers. Well, let him become one."

"That could mean trouble. Mr. Austin is smart. He may well hire a sea lawyer," she said quietly. "I don't think he will get lost in the hills with the rest of the men."

"Let him do as he pleases. There will be no accounting until we return to New York."

Perkins opened the door of the cabin and sent the steward for Thomas Austin. When the first officer arrived, Perkins turned to Ellen and said, "Leave us."

She frowned, but said nothing. She left the cabin and went up on the poop deck, steering clear of all the passengers and Thomas Smith, who had the watch. The second mate looked at her, seeking answers from her disturbed expression. She turned away and looked out at the sea. A few minutes later, Thomas Austin walked slowly out from the portico onto the weather deck. She watched him stalk to the very tip of the bow atop the forecastle deck, where he sat down and looked straight ahead, shoulders hunched, his back to all the people aboard.

Perkins strode hotly across the poop deck and spoke a few words to the second mate. Thomas Smith's face showed no emotion. He was smart enough not to reveal his true feelings. He left the captain and went forward to tell Henry Moore, the third mate, that he now served as the second officer. Smith was now the first officer, at least until they reached San Francisco and he jumped ship.

The news burned through the vessel while Thomas Austin kept his station at the bow, humiliated and as angry as he ever had been during his time at sea. How could he face the men now that he was broken? A mere passenger? It was almost too much to bear. There was little more a man had than his pride and dignity, and to have it taken away was a sorry turn of events. The Old Man at least possessed the decency not to force him forward before the mast. However, he had been told to move out of his private cabin and move in with Henry Moore, itself a severe blow to his pride.

Ellen felt compassion for Austin, but she did not express it to anyone, especially her husband. Her place was to support Perkins. Nevertheless, she had misgivings about his actions on this day.

"It is done," Perkins said, standing close to her. His expression was wild, the anger still flaming brightly in his eyes. "Austin says he will sue me. He intends to file a formal protest as soon as we reach San Francisco."

"Oh, Perkins," she said. She fought back her emotions and turned to face the sea again. Oddly, the endless waves so blue and beautiful made her feel quite alone and empty, even though her husband stood nearby. The actions of a loved one were often beyond the scope of influence of another. It reminded her that in life one might find a partner, but never fully understand or know the innermost workings of the other person's heart. Human beings were complicated, unlike the sea, wind, and tide. The secrets of nature were more easily uncovered, analyzed, and comprehended.

"The matter will work itself out," he said, his anger subsiding a little. "I am right and he is wrong, and there will be just his word against mine. How far do you think he will get in court?"

"We shall see, I suppose," she said.

"A lot can happen between now and New York."

Perkins wrote in the ship's log: "Light breezes fine weather 3 P.M. suspended First Officer from duty on consequence of his arrogating to himself the privilege of cutting up rigging contrary to my orders & long neglect of Duty Middle light squalls & cloudy weather Latter fine."

Late that night a series of light squalls came in on an east-south-easterly wind, warm and moist with the first real hints of tropical air. The cold, white flash of lightning illuminated the sky, and thunder growled and murmured. The ship sailed easily through the regular, long swells, and by Sunday morning, August 3, she had entered the southeast trades. Again the ship seemed uncannily lucky. The southerly winds, relatively rare in the variables, had favored her for an exceptional run offshore of the South American coast with only one short stretch of calms and virtually no winds from an unfavorable quarter. Yet with the luck of the natural world, a whim of the winds and the sea, came the awkward tensions associated with humankind, the discord that seemed to go wherever there were people.

From July 30 through August 12, *Flying Cloud*'s daily progress to the west-northwest exceeded runs of two hundred nautical miles per day, save for the 10th, when she dropped one mile below the mark. The ship made her way in very pleasant weather typical of the trades with clear blue skies peppered white as clumps and balls of clouds passed overhead, and with gentle breezes off the starboard quarter, every sail drawing to maximum efficiency. The weather grew hot and the days long. The passengers and crew shed their winter clothes for their summer apparel. Flying fish and porpoises made routine appearances. They cavorted around the ship in performances that proved endlessly distracting for the passengers.

Games of chess and cards on deck, reading, and sketching helped break the monotony. Francesco Wadsworth, who spoke fluent French as well as Italian, spent time every day teaching Edward Bowman to speak French. The crew, with Thomas Smith now in charge, kept busy at their daily chores. The men holystoned the decks to a fine white. They hove taut and tarred the rigging, and repaired the sails. They scraped, sanded, and painted.

Flying Cloud crossed the equator and passed into the Northern Hemisphere roughly 2,400 miles off the coast of Ecuador and 1,100 miles northeast of the Marquesas Islands. There was a general sense of festivity aboard, as all the ship's company counted the days to San Francisco. They had crossed latitude 50 degrees south on July 26 and had reached the line just seventeen days later. They were only seventy-one days, two hours from New York.

Ellen consulted the tables in Maury's sailing directions. The monthly mean of the best passages from latitude 50 degrees south to the line in July was twenty-three days. The ship was six days ahead. The best mean passage from the equator to San Francisco in August was thirty-one days, meaning those aboard still faced another month at sea. There nevertheless was a great deal of optimism that *Flying Cloud* might better the time and arrive sooner rather than later.

Perkins was happy about the rapid progress of the ship. Yet, despite the fine sailing, he thought it possible that the good times were over. The doldrums awaited, and the northeast trades beyond might not cooperate for a fast passage. If any trouble arose or the ship encountered calms and bad winds, he would lose his crack at *Surprise*'s record and the bonus the company had promised to pay him were he to make the voyage in under a hundred days.

Maury warned that in August when a ship crossed the equator bound for San Francisco, "the navigator finds his position, quite as much as his skill, brought into requisition. The influence of the American plains and deserts begins now to make itself felt upon the northeast trade winds, paralyzing them, or turning them back, and converting them into breezes that baffle and perplex."

Perkins could only count on Ellen's skills and talent as a navigator and her command of Maury's new theories to see them quickly across the calm belts into the northeast trades. He had to trust her. While he did have confidence in Ellen, he also felt anxiety about the unknown that lay ahead. It bored into his mind and lingered just below the surface, like an uncharted reef capable of causing great harm.

Chapter 25

Fair southerly winds continued to favor *Flying Cloud* as she sailed deeper into the Pacific Ocean, each day passing without much to set it apart from the others. But true to expectations, the wind gradually died out and came in fitful puffs from the northwest. The clipper ghosted along and rolled in the swells at the edge of the doldrums about twelve hundred miles southwest of Baja California and seventeen hundred miles east-southeast of Hawaii. The clipper fast approached San Francisco, but there were still many miles to go.

The near-calm conditions tried the patience of all aboard, most particularly Perkins. However, he was not alone in his unpleasant moods. Thomas Austin tried his best to avoid the captain. Every time they passed a civil word or two, each knowing the true feelings of the other, the anger boiled again. The heat below made staying in the cabin unbearable, and as a consequence the deck remained crowded with people most of the time. There was no place for Austin to be alone with his humiliation. Conversation with the passengers remained awkward, and it was even more so with the crew. Austin took his meals after all the others had eaten, just to avoid the contact at the dinner table. The two men who had sabotaged the ship grew increasingly uneasy as they neared San Francisco. They wondered what penalty awaited. They made plans to escape overboard as soon as the ship's anchor was set in the bottom of the bay.

There was friction among some of the passengers as well. Ellen had been aware of the growing bond between Sarah Lyon and Laban Coffin, and of a conflict that stemmed from it. One of the unattached men among the passengers had made advances toward the young lady from Roxbury. There was a rumor one of them had challenged Laban to a duel, a situation that greatly disturbed Ellen and added to her worries. Duels had been outlawed in the United States since the early 1840s. A person who killed another in a duel could be tried for manslaughter or murder. If the secret rivalry between the two men exploded into violence, Perkins would be forced to stop it. Fortunately, the conflict did not result in gunfire, but it did manifest itself in a peculiar way.

As Ellen watched from the poop deck, the ship rolling lazily in the hot sun, Laban took to the deck with a shiny black pistol in what had become a new habit, a sort of odd daily ritual. In fair weather, the chicken coops were run out on poles over the rails, where the boys of the crew sluiced the filth from them without soiling the decks. Weather permitting, the coops were left suspended over the sea. As the ship rolled, the chickens cackled and squawked, and stuck their heads out between the wooden frames confining them. After consulting with the cook to see how many chickens he required for dinner, Laban would aim the pistol at the unsuspecting chickens and one by one blow their heads off. He seldom missed.

The shooting was done under the guise of sport. However, Laban's ulterior motive was to show he was an expert marksman well able to defend himself against anyone who cared to challenge him. It was a rather messy business, since the chickens' blood splattered the other birds and ran red and thick off the floor of the coop into the sea. But no one interfered with it, least of all Ellen, as distasteful as the display was. The man who had thought to challenge Laban never carried out his threat or made his identity generally known.

Traveling with passengers had proved a bit taxing for Ellen. She had eleven personalities to cope with. She acted as a buffer between them and her husband, who often said a merchant vessel was not a liner. Passengers did not belong on a clipper, whose sole purpose in his mind was to carry freight at the best possible speed from one port to another. The law demanded that he treat them with respect, and he did so, though at times it was a struggle for him to keep his sharp comments to himself. The run to China would be different. Most of the people would disembark at San Francisco, and the ship would be less prone to the volatility that arose when so many people were packed together for a long time. For the present all she could hope for was a continued veneer of civility, and that nothing further would occur to pierce it.

Flying Cloud wallowed in the swells of the doldrums, making only ninety-three miles to noon on August 17. Torrents of rain fell in the depths of the calm. The crew cursed the weather. Squalls passed through, adding a bit of excitement to the day. As each squall came and went, Perkins rushed the crew about trimming the sails and tacking to take every advantage of the temporary wind. By August 19, *Flying Cloud* had sailed clear of the doldrums, quite an accomplishment once again. It was very unusual to pass through the calm belt so quickly.

The northeast trade winds came in light at first, but gradually increased. Ellen kept the ship steady on course well off the coast of California, riding the northeasterly winds to ever higher latitudes and far out to sea until the clipper reached a point about thirteen hundred miles west of Santa Barbara. On August 24, Ellen brought the ship round to north 26 degrees east on an easterly course for the direct run to the Golden Gate. They were on their final leg of the sixteen-thousand-mile voyage. All of them looked forward to planting their feet firmly on land, where dinner plates did not slide away while the passengers tried to eat, where the very effort of walking sometimes required concentration on every step.

The happiness of the passengers was short-lived. The winds came in light and finally dropped off altogether. So close to port, *Flying Cloud* remained trapped in an unexpected calm. Ellen had carefully followed Maury's sailing directions and seldom deviated from them even when the temptation was great and the pressure from her husband was almost unbearable. She had held firm and prevailed. To have the winds die in an area of ocean where they should have blown fair frustrated and disappointed her.

Flying Cloud ghosted along, trying to make her way eastward. The dark, oily swells glistened like quicksilver in the sun. The passing clouds painted shadows on the sea and offered momentary respites of cool air as they blocked the sun and threw shade on the deck. A puff of darkness on the sea revealed the presence of some wind. It blew across the port bow and came in light, though with enough power to move the ship.

"Stand by for the starboard tack!" Perkins yelled.

As he bellowed orders and slowly, painstakingly brought the ship around, the crew rushed about covered in sweat with every muscle aching. It took an hour to tack the ship in such light winds. Sometimes her bow refused to turn and she simply stopped dead in the water. Furious cursing emanated from the poop deck, thick and sharp enough to make the ladies blush. Like a stubborn mule, *Flying Cloud* would not move, caught in irons, as the sailors referred to it. The sails blew aback and hung limp, blew aback and hung limp some more, until finally the ship gained enough sternway to back herself out of her inertia. Then Perkins proceeded to try again, and again, until he got her around to the new tack.

As if the wind sensed the rising fury of the ship's master, it backed around to another quarter. The sails went limp and aback, aback and limp.

"God blasted hell!" Perkins roared. "Stand by to come about!"

The crew again manned their stations, silently cursing the madman on the poop deck. With their calloused hands wrapped round the thick braces, the men hove to bring the yards around. Sweat poured off them. Salt from their bodies blinded and stung their eyes.

Ellen paced on the poop deck, keeping a weather eye on her husband. She knew at times like this it was best to leave him alone. She did not relish the company of the passengers, or anyone else at the moment. The tension was such that all she could do to contain it was take deep breaths and try to think about cool spring days in Marblehead, the pleasure of dancing with Perkins at the Astor House, and the thrill of a fine day's sail in a small boat when she had no responsibilities whatsoever. They were only eighty-four days from New York and only about a thousand miles from San Francisco. It seemed they had won, that they would indeed beat *Surprise*'s record. How could they not? Well, she thought, the weather always has to have its way with us, and if it so chooses we could be out here for many days.

"Helm down!" Perkins cried.

"Helm down, sir!" the helmsman replied.

The bow slowly turned for the next tack. The sails shivered and shook with a sickeningly weak flutter, like the wings of an injured bird. As the ship started to come through the eye of the wind, the foresails backed.

"Come on, come on, you damned wind!" Perkins muttered, his jaw set tight. "Bring her round. Don't fade on me!"

Flying Cloud stopped dead again and refused to move. The wind first came in off the bow, then off the right side of the ship, then from astern, and then back up the other side to blow from the tack opposite the one Perkins was trying for.

"This is worse than the doldrums," Perkins said, and sent a fusillade of curses forward for Thomas Smith to digest.

Thomas Austin, for once, found his position rather enjoyable, as he watched the Old Man sweat and fume. Perhaps there was some justice after all. If he were not so anxious to get to San Francisco, Austin would have wished for more calms and baffling winds to extend the entertainment.

"Sail, ho!" called the lookout. "Broad off the port quarter!"

All eyes turned aft for a moment. In all the commotion in tacking the ship, the vessel had crept up on them unnoticed. It was a bark, a three-masted ship, with square sails on the fore and mainmasts and a large spanker and topsail on the mizzen. With so little wind, it took a long time for the ships to draw near enough to speak each other. The bark looked old, weather-beaten. Heavy green slime covered the entire length of the waterline, and above the paint on her hull appeared dull and peeled in spots. Dozens of passengers lined the rails and waved to the people aboard *Flying Cloud*. A British ensign fluttered from her mizzen mast.

"Ahoy, ship *Flying Cloud*," the master called through his speaking trumpet. "Where are you bound?"

"Good day, ship *America Paquet*," Perkins shouted back, trying to mask the frustration in his voice. He assumed a false air of civility. "We are bound for San Francisco, eighty-four days out of New York."

"Eighty-four days? Well done, captain! We are bound for the same port, one hundred eighty days out of London."

God pity the passengers on that ship was a thought shared by many of the passengers aboard *Flying Cloud*. It had taken the other ship six months to sail about the same distance the clipper had covered in less than three. As with *Harriet Raymond*, speaking *America Paquet* drove home once again just how fast *Flying Cloud* was. The passengers counted their blessings and prayed for a fresh wind.

The captains exchanged a few more words and the ships slowly drew apart. The sails of the bark remained in sight for a good long while, but gradually, even in the baffling, unsteady winds, *Flying Cloud* left her astern. Perkins tacked the ship six times on that sour day, and for all the efforts expended they made good only an additional fifty-two miles.

Chapter 26

Little by little, *Flying Cloud* made her way east toward San Francisco. The calms ended at last, and fresh squalls and heavy rain from the north-northeast replaced them. The ship labored hard against the unfavorable wind and tacked several times to make good her easting. They were eighty-seven days out from New York and just six hundred miles off the coast. *Surprise*'s record would soon be theirs, if all went well. Fog, calms, or damage to the ship could still snatch away their victory. Neither Ellen nor Perkins tempted fate by mentioning what might go wrong. They preferred to believe in their ship and the good fortune she seemed to attract.

The winds held to the north-northeast into the morning of August 29. Before dawn the stars shone brightly in the sky, the constellations familiar reminders of home. But banks of dark, evil-looking clouds appeared as the sun rose over the empty sea. A large swell rolled in from the northwest, a harbinger of a spell of heavy weather to come. The dog was once again present, heralding the imminent arrival of the master.

Despite sure signs of approaching bad weather, Perkins kept all sail set. The wind increased and shifted to the northwest, and a series of hard squalls swept in. The wind painted the backs of the breaking crests a dark black and lifted spray into the air. *Flying*

Cloud took to the waves as if she could soar above them. The ship drove fast toward the coast, to the delight of everyone aboard, but most of all Ellen and Perkins. As they stood together on the poop deck enjoying the spectacular sailing, the tension of the preceding days faded away.

Suddenly, a loud snap came from up forward, then another followed by a tremendous crack. The fore topgallant pole mast ripped free from its supports nearly one hundred feet above the deck and fell forward. The ropes that still kept it upright, though at an acute forward angle, began breaking one by one. The parting lines sounded like bullwhips cutting through the air. The canvas tore free from the yards and thundered in the wind. When the last of the ropes broke, the twenty-five-foot mast crashed to the deck. The mishap occurred in under one minute.

"All hands, all hands, Mr. Smith!" Perkins cried. He turned to the helmsman and ordered him to bring the wind dead astern to blanket the remaining sails flying from the foremast. *Flying Cloud* careened off a crest and dug her bow deep. The water cascaded over the bow and carried some of the wreckage aft onto the weather deck and over the rails, partly into the sea. The helmsman fought to keep the ship headed downwind. But the drag of the debris robbed control from the rudder and tried to slew her around broadside to the wind. He held on and pushed the spokes of the wheel right and left as needed, and managed to keep the ship on course. The squall intensified as the men scrambled up the fore topmast and released the web of broken lines. Sailors on deck rigged emergency ropes and hauled the fore topgallant pole mast back aboard.

Ellen's heart sank as she watched the men work. To have come so far and so close only to have the sea turn against them in what should have been one of their happiest hours—it was almost too much for her. She tightened her grip on the rail and braced herself against the violent motion of the ship.

The crew worked with a will and in several hours cleared the wreckage enough to allow the ship to come back on course for San

Francisco. Without the upper sails on the foremast, *Flying Cloud* slowed considerably. But she drove on in spite of the damage.

"I'll have all hands at work through the night, Mr. Smith. I want that mast back in its fid by first light," Perkins said, after listening to the status report from the former second mate.

"We'll try," he said, his face drawn from the exertions up forward.

"You'll not try," Perkins growled. "You will do it."

"Aye, sir." Smith made his way quickly forward, away from the master.

Knowing full well that they were close to freedom and their dreams of gold, the men needed little encouraging from Thomas Smith and Henry Moore. They dragged the fore topgallant pole mast into position for sending up, as they did the yards. They salvaged what rigging they could, and they cut and measured new rigging as needed. They connected and ran what lines they could before night fell. In the darkness, they dragged spare sails up on deck and prepared to reattach them to the yards. They rigged tackles at the fore topmast, and completed a hundred other tasks to the best of their ability.

As the first light of dawn stained the dark, low clouds with tinges of deep red, the crew mustered on deck to continue making repairs. A bad sea was running. Occasionally a large wave broke on deck and knocked the men off their feet. They did not waver. They fought on, and as Ellen watched them hoist the topgallant pole mast up, slowly, slowly, their hoarse voices carrying aft to her as they chanted, she felt a deep sense of kinship with them and a deep sense of pride. True, many of them would leave the ship at their first chance, but they gave of their hearts and bodies freely at the moment as they struggled to make *Flying Cloud* whole once again. For that she was as grateful as she could be.

"Look at them, Perkins!" she whispered. "They are truly brave men."

A strange look passed over his face. He nodded, oddly quiet. "Most of them are every inch a sailor," he said.

Thomas Smith directed the men and cursed at any who lagged behind the rest. The topgallant pole mast banged against the lower masts, splintering them in places. But it was finally heaved back into position and the fid driven in place. The crew secured the stays and shrouds in an endeavor that consumed hours. *Flying Cloud* surged on through the waves, keeping her course for the Golden Gate.

The sailors sent the yards up next, fitted them to their tyes and lifts, secured the parrels, and ran the halyards, braces, and dozens of other lines. The yards hauled taut, the best men ascended the ratlines and inched out on the spars. Other crewmen on deck hove up the heavy sails, using the capstan on the forecastle deck. They worked for hours. They did not stop to eat. Perkins would not have allowed it had Thomas Smith asked. No crewman could rest until *Flying Cloud* was restored to her fullest potential for speed.

When the last of the repairs were completed, Perkins ordered all possible sails set. The canvas billowed out as the wind caught it, and one by one the fore topgallant, royal, and skysail began to draw. *Flying Cloud* picked up speed, cut through the water, and left a wake of whirling eddies and foam far astern, arrow-straight behind them.

Below in the officers' quarters, Ellen worked out their position and estimated they were less than two hundred miles from the Farallon Islands. At the last watch, the log had indicated the clipper sailed at ten knots. She expected to make landfall in the early hours of August 31, well before daybreak. There were some dangerous shoals off San Francisco. If a mariner put the ship in the wrong place, it meant trouble. Ellen stayed up all night tracking the ship's progress. To close with a coast was one of the most hazardous undertakings for a navigator. More ships sank coming into or out of port than they did far out at sea. At two o'clock on the morning of August 31, Ellen estimated they were only thirty miles off the Farallon Islands.

"We must heave to, Perkins," she said. "I dare not take us in any closer until daylight."

"We have made it," he said, shaking his head. "We shall make port tomorrow, a week better than *Surprise*. Eighty-nine days from New York to San Francisco!"

Ellen took his hand and squeezed it. "You have done well, my love."

"As have you."

They stood together in the roaring wind, the spray flying, the ship heeled way over on her side. The voyage had taken them to new heights in their respect for the sea, ships, and the men who sailed across the barren wastes to far-off ports. They had found in *Flying Cloud* a grand ship that went beyond their wildest hopes for speed, and as the clipper turned her bow toward the wind, backed her main topsail, and came to rest in the swells, they remained silent, lost in the glory of the moment and the joy in their hearts. At six o'clock that morning, the sun illuminated the silhouette of South Farallon Island, stark and desolate, a sentinel of the Golden Gate. A pilot schooner soon made her way toward *Flying Cloud* and embarked a pilot to guide her in to a snug berth off the hills of San Francisco.

Earlier that Sunday morning, an observer in the employ of Sweeny & Baugh, a communications company, ascended the stairs to the top of the firm's semaphore tower on Point Lobos, ready to start his day, a bit fuzzy from his Saturday night reveling at the saloons. From his vantage point he had a fine view of the schooners, barks, brigs, steamers, and clippers as they rode a fair tide through the Golden Gate en route to an anchorage off the city. The day dawned bright and clear. After the passage of the northwesterly blow the atmosphere held a pristine quality to it, as if the air were cleansed and revitalized. The sun bathed the reddish hills and bluffs in a late-summer warmth that pleased the observer. It would not be long before the Pacific storms of winter tore through and the duty at the station became far less appealing.

With the morning tide flowing into the harbor, the day's steady stream of ships had already begun to come into the bay. Pilots were engaged as quickly as they became available. He raised his spyglass to scan the approaches to the city and caught sight of a very large clipper, with sharp lines and masts that seemed to scrape the sky.

She sailed fast. He saw white foam against her black hull at the bow. He signaled the next semaphore station farther up the line to report the arrival of a clipper, and settled back to his duty. He took a few minutes to admire the vessel. She cut quite a profile with the bluffs in the background, the brilliant blue waters of the bay all around her.

The observer at the next station in turn repeated the signal to the semaphore tower perched on top of Telegraph Hill, the last of the company's lookout points. It was a boxlike two-story house with a platform on top. An enormous American flag flew from a pole, bearing thirty-one stars. Although California had earned its statehood in 1850, the flags, as custom dictated, were not changed until the first Fourth of July after a state joined the Union. The flag fluttered and snapped in the wind atop the most prominent hill overlooking the bay nearly three hundred feet above sea level. It, and the semaphore signals, were clearly visible from the city sprawled out below. Businessmen kept a weather eye on the hill for news of new arrivals with valuable cargoes in the holds. The arrival of a clipper ship always attracted the merchants and small boat operators with offers to ferry passengers to shore at a hefty price.

The observer signaled the arrival of the clipper. He waited and watched, until the ship appeared off the North Beach, a cove crowded with anchored vessels. More than eight hundred ships filled the harbor, many of them abandoned and rotting into hulks. The clipper backed her main topsail. The anchor splashed into the bay and the bow of the ship pointed into the wind. Many of the residents of the city, most of them men, gathered on the beach below Telegraph Hill to admire the vessel. She was the largest sailing ship any of them had ever seen.

"What ship is that?" asked one of the onlookers.

A man with a spyglass squinted and peered at the golden letters on the ship's bow. *"Flying Cloud,"* he mumbled. "The clipper ship *Flying Cloud."*

Afterword

News of *Flying Cloud*'s record-breaking passage spread through the bustling city of San Francisco in the early part of September 1851. The swift voyage was a victory for the merchants and shippers with a direct interest in her cargo, and in particular for S. Griffitts Morgan. He was the man responsible to Grinnell, Minturn & Company for obtaining the highest profits possible from the sale of the commodities in her hold.

Flying Cloud's passage of just eighty-nine days, twenty-one hours from New York captured the imagination of most everyone who heard of it. After all, the ship had soundly beaten *Surprise*'s run of ninety-six days, fifteen hours. When *Surprise* dropped anchor in the bay on March 18 earlier that year it had seemed a near impossibility that another ship might strip her of the record. Now that *Flying Cloud* had shown the run could be accomplished at an even faster rate, all wondered what new ship might topple her from the top of her class.

The buzz of excitement resounded through the garish dance halls, the grand hotels, the stores selling everything from fine imported wines to carpet tacks. *Flying Cloud* was talked of on the rickety plank sidewalks, in the ramshackle shanty towns expanding outward from the city center, on the piers, and in the warehouses.

The citizens felt less isolated from the rest of the nation. It seemed right to expect that commerce to and from the East would only take three months, when not two years earlier it had taken twice as long. The euphoria found its way into virtually every corner of the town, and soon it reached the East as well as Europe.

Flying Cloud dropped anchor at eleven-thirty on the morning of August 31, and the day after she was moved to Cunningham's Wharf for off-loading. Most of the crew promptly deserted. As the sailors drank away what little money they had in the saloons, their story of the voyage fueled the general enthusiasm the fast passage had fostered. The Creesys watched with great suspense as the hatches were removed and the stevedores hauled the cargo from the hold. To the immense relief of the Creesys, most of the cargo was undamaged from the flooding caused by the sabotage, or as Francis Hathaway, part owner of the ship, put it, the "rascality," of the sailors. The record does not indicate what happened to the two disaffected crewmen. But it is safe to assume they were, as Perkins wrote in his log, "taken care of" in the courts.

Thomas Austin filed a protest against Perkins for what he felt was an unfair dismissal, and he fully intended to sue him for damages. An odd occurrence recorded in the documents of the S. Griffitts Morgan collection in the Baker Library at Harvard University offers a glimpse at the shrewd nature of Captain Creesy. Evidently, though it is not explained how, word reached New York shortly after *Flying Cloud* put to sea bound for China that the captain had died aboard ship.

On *Flying Cloud*'s return voyage to New York, Perkins spoke a ship. After some old newspapers were passed over to him from the other vessel, he had the unusual experience of reading his own obituary. The supposed death of the captain discouraged Thomas Austin from pursuing his lawsuit. He dropped the matter and must have been chagrined when he learned Creesy was alive, well, and prosperous. It has never been proved, but it appears likely that Perkins started the rumor of his death deliberately to put the first mate's case well into the doldrums.

The passengers disembarked, and most went on their way, ready to start their lives in a new country. It is not known what happened to Willie Hall or Francesco Wadsworth, though it is safe to assume they saw many more adventures. Sarah Bowman and Edward were reunited with Charlie Bowman, who had done quite well for himself in the retail businesses he had started in San Francisco. Mrs. Gorham presumably was reunited with her husband. Ellen Lyon was married aboard *Flying Cloud* on September 17 to Reuben Boise in a quiet though very festive ceremony. Ellen Creesy participated in the wedding preparations. She went shopping with Ellen and Sarah Lyon, helped sew the wedding dress, and made sure all went well on the wedding day. The Lyon sisters wrote that she behaved like a sister, or a mother, to them, and that they loved her dearly.

The romance between Sarah Lyon and Laban Coffin that began on *Flying Cloud* developed into a deep abiding love during the passage. Laban proposed to Sarah and offered to take her sailing around the world. She accepted, and they, too, were married aboard *Flying Cloud*. Again, Ellen Creesy took a great interest in the wedding. She even baked the wedding cake, which Sarah Lyon Coffin wrote was very good. The wedding was an even smaller affair than her sister's. Ellen Lyon Boise and her husband had already sailed for the Oregon Territory, and Ellen's father had departed for the Sandwich Islands. Whitney Lyon was in attendance. He had decided to stay in San Francisco and make his way there. The rest of the family learned of the marriage by mail. The wedding took place on October 4, shortly before *Flying Cloud* put to sea again bound for Canton, short-handed, and with Laban Coffin signed on as first mate. Of course, Sarah went with him. J. D. Townsend also continued on aboard *Flying Cloud*.

News of *Flying Cloud*'s passage reached New York about the same time Sarah and Laban were married. The New York papers trumpeted the voyage as evidence of Yankee superiority in shipbuilding and ship handling, and some writers even suggested that the clipper ships would remain supreme over the steamers. *The Times* of London and other newspapers across the Atlantic reported on the passage as well, though with somewhat less emphasis on the wonders of American ingenuity.

Upon hearing of *Flying Cloud*'s achievement, Francis Hathaway wrote the following to his nephew S. Griffitts Morgan:

> The arrival of Captain Creesy at San Francisco was cause for great excitement and much conversation. I greatly rejoiced in this great and unprecedented passage. Captain Creesy has won the great purse. It will probably be a long time before this passage is made in as short a time, and from what I know of Captain Creesy, the man that does it must have a smart ship and work hard to do it. The sailing of this ship 992 miles in three days and 374 miles in one day is incredible to many. It's a greater speed than any other boat ever made.

Ellen and Perkins Creesy were again at sea on October 20, 1851, on the second leg of their maiden voyage aboard *Flying Cloud*. The passage lacked the drama of the run to San Francisco, with light, baffling winds that must have sorely irked Perkins. The ship reached the approaches to Canton on December 3 and sailed for New York on January 5, 1852. On the passage home, the troubles with the mainmast continued. The crew had to repair the mainmast below the hounds, where it had sprung on the outbound passage, and the main masthead was further twisted and splintered in heavy weather, rendering it "almost useless" in Perkins's words.

Flying Cloud reached New York on April 9, 1852, and the Creesys were instant stars upon their return. There were grand celebrations at the Astor House in honor of the Creesys and their ship. The excitement in New York proved so intense that the couple left New York for the relative quiet of Marblehead, much in need of a brief rest prior to sailing again for California and China after the spars were replaced and the ship was fitted out for another passage.

On November 11, 1851, while *Flying Cloud* was stuck in light winds bound for Canton, *Sword Fish* sailed from New York. She came very close to beating *Flying Cloud*'s record. She arrived in San Francisco on February 10, 1852, after a passage of just ninety days, eighteen hours. *Surprise*, *Flying Cloud*, and now *Sword Fish* seemed to prove that the East and West Coasts of the United States were much closer in time than they had ever been before. Other clippers came close to surpassing *Flying Cloud*'s record, but none ever succeeded in doing so.

The American extreme clippers achieved their zenith in late 1852 and 1853. Hundreds of these graceful sailers roared on their way, putting into port and departing after easily selling their cargoes for incredible profits. Grinnell, Minturn & Company dispatched *Flying Cloud* to California less than one month after her return to New York. She sailed for San Francisco on May 14, 1852. Perkins had every intention of beating his own record, but he found there was fierce competition. These were the times when clippers often raced in company for days while making their passages. The rivalry between ships and captains was as keen as any among businessmen ashore, and the exploits of the fastest sailers were watched with great interest on both coasts.

All the clippers were one of a kind, and each had its best point of sail. *Flying Cloud* favored a big wind blowing at an angle off the stern, as did many. Others sailed better in lighter winds, and still others did better when the wind blew from dead aft. Depending on the wind and sea conditions, a given ship might do well against another on one day and suffer the next.

On July 1, 1852, Captain Charles Low aboard the fleet little clipper *N. B. Palmer*, off the shores of Río de la Plata, saw the skysails of a clipper coming up fast from astern. He climbed to the mizzen top with his spyglass and surveyed the vessel, determining it was Captain Creesy aboard *Flying Cloud*. Sighting *Flying Cloud* sent a thrill through Low. According to his writings of the encounter, he had sailed ten days after his rival. By all appearances he had overtaken the most famous clipper in the world and left her in his wake. Thinking he might race Creesy and show that *N. B. Palmer* was the better vessel, he hove to and waited for *Flying Cloud* to come up on him.

Charles Low wrote of the encounter: "*Flying Cloud* . . . ran alongside of me and Captain Creesy hailed me and wanted to know when I left New York. I replied: Ten days after you. He was so mad he would have nothing more to say." *N. B. Palmer* was hove to, while *Flying Cloud* was not. She drove ahead and left *N. B. Palmer* astern. Captain Low never did catch *Flying Cloud* after that.

Press accounts published in the *Boston Semi-Weekly Atlas* reported that "*Flying Cloud* overhauled the clipper *N. B. Palmer* and ran her out of sight in less than twenty hours, and beat her from the latitude of Rio de la Plata to San Francisco. . . ."

The newspaper did not mention that during *N. B. Palmer*'s passage one of the crew shot the first mate in the leg. Armed with muskets and pistols, the remaining officers subdued the crew. Low put into Valparaiso to send the guilty men back home to stand trial and to pick up additional crew to replace them. The delay cost him ten days. He arrived at San Francisco on September 30, 1852, after a passage of 130 days. *Flying Cloud* reached port on September 6. The reputation of *Flying Cloud* and her captain, though well deserved, was in part reinforced by somewhat slanted coverage in the media in some cases, as this example illustrates. By all accounts *N. B. Palmer* could have given *Flying Cloud* a good, solid race to the Golden Gate had she not suffered delay because of mutiny and attempted murder.

In addition, the clipper ship *Gazelle* sailed from New York on May 18, and she caught up to *Flying Cloud* shortly after crossing the equator. *Flying Cloud* left her astern, however. Off Cape Horn, *Gazelle* suffered a collision, lost her bowsprit, and was otherwise damaged. Despite this she arrived in San Francisco on October 1, after a passage of 135 days.

Flying Cloud proceeded on to China, and her second voyage ended upon her return to New York on March 3, 1853. A little over a month later, the Creesys sailed again for San Francisco. On this voyage she raced in company with the clipper ship *Hornet* in some spectacular close-quarter sailing. During a storm, the first officer and a crewman aboard *Flying Cloud* were killed when a wave swept them off the forecastle deck. Such accidents were common, but the deaths had a profound affect on Ellen and Perkins. The first mate was well liked and a capable officer. *Flying Cloud* returned to New York after off-loading her cargo in San Francisco, and on the homeward voyage just off California she twisted her rudder in a bad squall. Creesy did not beat back to safe harbor. Instead he sailed eighty days with a jury-rigged rudder, and returned to New York in a very respectable run of ninety-two days, arriving December 6, 1853.

Again, just about one month after arriving in New York, the Creesys were back at sea on their fourth voyage aboard *Flying Cloud*. The first leg to San Francisco was to become the most famous ever recorded in the history of the clipper ship, not so much for its drama but for its incredible speed. *Flying Cloud* sailed on January 21 and arrived in San Francisco on April 20, beating her own record by thirteen hours. Her passage of eighty-nine days, eight hours from anchor to anchor was never broken in the days of square-rigged ships. However, since 1989, modern, high-performance racing yachts have broken *Flying Cloud*'s record. But these yachts sailed much shorter distances and did much better when the wind blew against them.

On *Flying Cloud*'s homeward bound voyage of 1854, the Creesys almost lost the ship. In stormy, foggy weather in the China Sea, on August 27, *Flying Cloud* ran up on a coral reef. She hit hard enough to dislodge the protective wooden covering on the keel, called a shoe, and to cut through the keel to the bottom of the planking. The impact raised the bow three or four feet out of the sea and caused her to leak an average of eleven inches of water per hour. Her cargo was valued at over one million dollars.

Creesy managed to refloat the ship. But he had an important decision to make in concert with Ellen. There were ports Creesy could have put into for repairs. However, these were disease-ridden hotbeds of corruption. The cargo would have to be completely off-loaded before repairs could be made, and the expense involved would have been an enormous liability to Grinnell, Minturn & Company, to the insurance underwriters, and to all others with a direct interest in the ship and her cargo, including Perkins, who owned a share of the vessel. He decided to keep going, and despite the leak, which required the crew to man the pumps all the way to New York, he sailed on and arrived back home on November 24, 1854.

Creesy's resourceful actions earned him a special citation on February 3, 1855, from Walter R. Jones, president of the Board of Underwriters of New York. He was presented with an elegant silver plate service and was again the talk of New York. He and his wife did not linger long, though.

The Creesys set off on their fifth voyage twelve days later, February 15, 1855, bound for San Francisco. They arrived on June 6. Homeward bound from China, Ellen glanced out the porthole of their cabin and saw a man desperately trying to stay afloat in the wash of the ship. No one but her had seen the crewman. She raced on deck and had the ship hove to and a boat put out to rescue him. The boat returned without him. Perkins sent two boats out to search, despite the loss of precious time, with orders not to return to the ship until nightfall, or until they found him. They succeeded on this second rescue attempt, and as the story goes, Ellen nursed the crewman back to health in the comfort of the aft cabin. This incident was one of many that revealed Ellen's sensitivity and concern for the crew under her husband's command. *Flying Cloud* arrived back in New York on December 14, 1855.

The hard driving of the past four years had reduced *Flying Cloud*'s seaworthiness to the point where Perkins recommended a thorough overhaul, a very expensive endeavor Grinnell, Minturn & Company declined to undertake. Freight charges were dropping rapidly and insurance rates were soaring. The large number of clippers competing for cargoes left many companies in increasingly bad financial trim, and quite a few American firms sold their clippers to companies in Great Britain.

The American economy had begun to slip as early as 1853. With the worsening economic times, the once proud Yankee clippers were facing their twilight years. It was not altogether unusual in 1855 for a clipper to be engaged in hauling Chinese workers to South America to work in the guano pits, and to set sail with the holds brimming with the repulsive stuff. The Creesys, both exhausted from the years of nonstop work aboard *Flying Cloud,* retired from the business and went back to Massachusetts to lead a quiet life together.

Under a new commander, *Flying Cloud* cleared New York on March 13, 1856, and suffered greatly during heavy weather, which partially dismasted her, an eventuality Perkins had predicted if she was not fully reconditioned. The captain put into Rio de Janeiro for repairs. Her masts were shortened to make her easier to handle with a smaller crew. During this ill-fated voyage, *Flying Cloud* broke yet another of her own records. She sailed 402 nautical miles in twenty-four hours, sustaining an average speed of almost seventeen knots, a speed few clippers ever exceeded. Nevertheless, she made her worst run ever to San Francisco, arriving on September 14 after a passage of 185 days.

Evidently, the new commander had had enough. Grinnell, Minturn & Company hired the Creesys to take the wounded ship home to New York. The Creesys made their way to California by way of the isthmus, now easily crossed on the new railroad that had opened in 1855. The railroad across Panama contributed to the decline of the clippers, as did the soaring costs for repairs and the large crews needed to sail them. On January 4, 1857, Ellen and Perkins sailed for the last time on *Flying Cloud*, outbound from San Francisco. They arrived back in New York ninety-two days later, and Grinnell, Minturn & Company temporarily took their famous clipper out of commission.

The stormy economic times reached their lowest point in the United States in the panic of '57. Financial markets collapsed in Europe as well, and the world slumped into depression. The days of the California gold rush and fabulous profits for shipping companies appeared gone forever. Steamships had become increasingly efficient, though they were still much slower than a well-sailed clipper. The development of the compound steam engine enabled a steamer to use coal twice as efficiently as before. The sailing vessels that were coming down the ways in the shipyards that managed to keep in operation were medium clippers. These ships were built with wider hulls that made them capable of carrying far more cargo than their fleet cousins of just a few years past. Many shipyards turned to building steamers because it was more profitable.

After a layup of two and a half years or so, Grinnell, Minturn &

Company shortened *Flying Cloud*'s masts again. The once graceful vessel looked squat, old, and neglected. She was a victim of the decline that had scattered the clipper fleet. Still, her fate could have been worse. By 1859, many clippers had been converted into barges. They were shorn of their masts and miles of rigging and transformed into nothing more than floating hulks. At least *Flying Cloud* kept sailing. She served in the British tea trade, making the run between London, Melbourne, and Hong Kong.

On Christmas Day 1859, under command of Jack Williams, a svelte medium clipper called *Andrew Jackson* weighed anchor in New York at six in the morning. The voyage of this clipper was the closest any square-rigged vessel ever came to beating *Flying Cloud*'s best time on the run from New York to San Francisco. Williams discharged his New York pilot at noon and picked up a pilot off San Francisco at eight o'clock on the morning of March 24, 1860. He dropped anchor at six that evening, earning him a passage anchor to anchor of ninety days, twelve hours and from pilot to pilot a passage of 89 days, 20 hours. There was some debate as to whether *Andrew Jackson* deserved to claim *Flying Cloud*'s record. According to Williams's log, he arrived on the pilot grounds off the Farallon Islands eighty-nine days, four hours out of New York, but was becalmed and had no pilot available to guide the ship into port until the following morning, March 24.

Clearly if *Andrew Jackson* had had better winds on March 23 and there had been a pilot available, *Flying Cloud* might have been displaced from the record books. But such is life at sea. There is no accounting for its whims, its ability to favor one ship and not another. *Flying Cloud*'s place in history remained secure, though there was much talk of *Andrew Jackson*'s remarkable voyage.

Flying Cloud was put up for sale in 1861, at a time when many of her sisters were falling victim to the ravages of the American Civil War, which also contributed to the demise of the clipper. Under charter, she carried troops from Hong Kong to London, and she ended up serving in the immigrant trade from England to Australia. She spent her final days as a timber ship sailing on the North Atlantic between England and Canada.

While *Flying Cloud* was living out her last, Perkins came out of retirement to take command of the clipper ship *Ino* during the American Civil War. Always an independent man, he was accused of disobeying orders and dismissed from the Navy in 1862. He went on to command the clipper ship *Archer* for two years, but ultimately retired to Massachusetts, where he and Ellen lived in comfort on a farm near Salem. The couple never had any children. Whether they could and chose not to because of their busy lives and devotion to the sea, or whether they wished to but could not remains unknown. Perkins had done very well financially. In addition to his handsome earnings as a captain, five thousands dollars per voyage at the height of his career, he had considerable investments. Life still held promise, a chance to indulge in shoreside comforts and the social discourse Ellen loved.

However, not very long after leaving the sea for the last time, Perkins suffered a stroke in 1868 at the age of fifty-four. A long, debilitating illness followed. Ellen nursed him and cared for him in every way, until he died on June 5, 1871. His death devastated her. They had been inseparable, scarcely spending a week apart since their marriage in 1841. Two days after their thirtieth wedding anniversary, he left her a widow. Ellen lived alone for nearly three decades in the home they had bought in Salem after Perkins's stroke. She died of heart failure on August 25, 1900, at the age of eighty-five and was buried in the Creesy plot at Harmony Grove Cemetery in Salem.

Ellen far outlasted *Flying Cloud* as well. Not long after Perkins died, the ship they loved so dearly also ended her days. While she was riding at anchor in St. John in the Bay of Fundy on the night of June 17, 1874, a strong summer gale drove her aground and damaged her to such an extent that she was deemed a total loss. A year later, a team of workers from the harbor, under orders from the insurance underwriters, made their way out to *Flying Cloud* with barrels of kerosene. They doused her decks and the insides of her hold with the liquid and set fire to her. The flames roared high and filled the air with dense black smoke. The fire curled and licked at the masts, traveled out along the yards, and shot from gaping holes in the hull. The inferno engulfed the ship and she burned to the waterline. The embers hissed in the cold, clear North Atlantic.

It was a pitiful end for such a fine ship. Burned for her copper fittings, she was cannibalized for the last bit of profit she could offer. Yet she left the world a lasting legacy of glory that remains as bright today as it was when she first made South Farallon Island that brilliant sunny morning of August 31, 1851, and set the world to thinking that nothing hovered beyond the range of possibility, that the struggle of man and his inventions seemed destined to change the very shape of life and erect an enduring framework of modernity that might last for all time.

Appendix A

Master Shipbuilder Donald McKay

Along the East Boston waterfront among the buildings and piers a picturesque park with a wide promenade serves as an inviting place to sit and gaze across Boston Harbor at the city. A pavilion set at the end of the promenade acts as the centerpiece of the park. Etched in the pavilion's stone is the name of Donald McKay, a man whose fame in Boston lives on a century and a half after he presided over the construction of some thirty clipper ships in his shipyard at the foot of Border Street. McKay's clipper ships were among the fastest ever built, though their lines were not all that different from those of other builders from Maine to Maryland.

Some say he bred magic into his ships, that his poetic and artistic spirit became part of the unique character of each clipper to slide down the ways at his shipyard. A ship, unlike any other creation for pleasure or commerce, does indeed seem alive, as if the hull had some cosmic connection to the greater world of the sea, winds, clouds, and stars. Perhaps what the old-timers along the waterfront say about McKay is true, but regardless of the legends, the records of his ships stand as part of maritime history beyond any dispute.

McKay's most famous ship was *Flying Cloud*. Her record-breaking passages from New York to San Francisco have captured the imaginations of millions. Children studying American history in school learn about the ship within the context of the gold rush. When sailors gather to talk about the golden age of sail in the United States, *Flying Cloud* inevitably comes up. She is something of a mystery. From a purely technical standpoint, she really was not unusual, and yet she proved herself against the entire American clipper fleet. If ships are blessed with a spirit of their own, imparted to them from their builders and brought to full potential from the efforts of their captains, *Flying Cloud* was such a vessel.

Flying Cloud, however, was just one among many of McKay's ships. In September 1851, McKay launched *Flying Fish*. She set sail from Boston in November and made a passage to San Francisco in 101 days. The following year she set sail from New York on October 31 and arrived in San Francisco on January 31 after a passage of ninety-two days, four hours. Her log indicates that she was 156 miles closer to the Golden Gate on day eighty-eight than *Flying Cloud* on day eighty-eight of her 1851 voyage. Light airs and calms delayed *Flying Fish* off the harbor for three days. *Flying Fish*, like *Andrew Jackson*, came close to matching or beating *Flying Cloud*'s record.

Westward Ho!, Lightning, Champion of the Seas, and other McKay clippers also enhanced McKay's reputation for having an uncanny knack at building fast ships. McKay's *Great Republic*, truly a labor of love and a tribute to his own rather large ego, stands as his grandest undertaking. In 1853, he set to work on *Great Republic* with $300,000 of his own money on the line. *Great Republic* was 335 feet in length. She carried 15,653 square yards of canvas on four masts, and as such she was technically a clipper-bark. A fire nearly destroyed the ship, but McKay repaired her, and she went on to serve in the California trade. In 1856, she set a record from Sandy Hook to the equator on her way from New York to San Francisco. She made the line fifteen days, eighteen hours out of New York, and she reached the Golden Gate in just ninety-two days.

McKay's story is similar to many in America. He was an immigrant from a poor family. He worked hard and by virtue of his own talent and vision achieved his version of the American dream. Born in 1810 in Shelburne, Nova Scotia, McKay emigrated to the

United States at the age of sixteen. He became an apprentice to a major shipbuilder on the East River, Isaac Webb. Webb was hard on McKay, suffering him to work long hours and to steer clear of frivolous pursuits, such as drinking at taverns, dancing, or going to the theater. McKay learned the basics of shipbuilding and observed the details that went into operating an efficient shipyard. His early education served him well.

In 1833, McKay married his first wife, Albenia Boole. She was in some ways very similar to Ellen Creesy in that she was keen of mind and learned skills usually confined to the world of men. Her father was a shipbuilder and had taught her how to lay out the lines of ships at the drafting board. She knew the complexities of algebra and trigonometry. She taught McKay what she knew, and in doing so set the stage for his promising future as a shipbuilder. He was at the time employed at the shipyard of Jacob Bell.

McKay went on to pursue his work in New England and ultimately found the backing of Enoch Train and Company in establishing his own shipyard in East Boston. He was only in his mid-thirties, but he had proved himself a talented and hardworking man. Between 1850 and 1853, at the height of the clipper ship boom, McKay built twelve extreme clippers. From 1854 to 1858 he built nineteen medium clippers and clipper-barks. He persisted in building clippers long after many of his competitors had turned their focus on the steamships. That he ignored the changing times, until forced out of a practical sense of business to conform, speaks much to his spirit and true love of sailing vessels. Of all ships the clippers found a place in his heart that no other class of ship matched. He was a romantic figure in the age of the clipper, one well deserving of lasting memory.

Appendix B

Master Navigator
Matthew Fontaine Maury

In 1850, Matthew Fontaine Maury, lieutenant in the United States Navy and superintendent of the National Observatory, joined a group of celebrated scientists gathered in Charleston, South Carolina, for a conference organized by the American Association for the Advancement of Science. Maury was not well known in scientific circles at the time. He had published only two papers, one related to Cape Horn, based on his earlier experiences aboard a ship of the United States Navy, and one related to his research on the workings of the Gulf Stream. At the meeting, however, he was to read three papers.

Later in his career, two of these documents found their way in expanded form into one of the most popular books of science in the mid-nineteenth century, Maury's *Physical Geography of the Sea*. It was first published in 1855 and remained in print both in the United States and in Europe for approximately two decades. It was a text dedicated to revealing the workings of the atmosphere, rains and rivers, fogs and sea breezes, ocean currents and winds, and other natural features related to the sea.

As he stood before the men gathered to hear him speak, Maury delved deeply into such topics as the Gulf Stream and its influence on commerce at the port of Charleston. The cotton ships traveling the coast from Southern ports followed the Gulf Stream as it flowed northward. Its current added to the speed of the packet ships on their way to New York, the key commercial port for transatlantic commerce in the United States. But it hindered the packets on their return to the South. Long fascinated with the mysteries of the sea as evidenced in currents, tides, wind patterns, seasonal storms, and other natural manifestations, Maury also found in his research practical applications. He rightly concluded that an understanding of the ocean and atmosphere might greatly benefit the captains of the packet ships and the new clippers coming on the scene in 1850 as they sailed down the South Atlantic Ocean around Cape Horn on their way to the Golden Gate. If the captain knew where and when to expect fair winds or foul, and favorable or adverse currents, he could determine the best routes between ports.

By the time of the conference in 1850, Maury had already spent several years at work on a system that changed the way captains sailed the oceans. He and his staff at the National Observatory dusted off the hundreds of logs stored there and culled them for the data they contained. Virtually every log from the Navy was available, and in these Maury recognized a mine of valuable information. With the logs, he compiled averages for wind directions and velocities in a specific location during any given month of the year.

In addition, Maury acquired more general data concerning ocean currents and their strength in given locations, if currents were an influence. As he studied the data, he confirmed his conclusions that the trade winds shifted according to the season in a northerly or southerly direction, and that the doldrums, an area of calm between the trade wind belts, were wider in some locations and thinner in others. All of this impressed upon him that were navigators to plan their voyages with these factors in mind, sailing passages between ports could be shortened in both miles and duration.

Maury's work also led him to other conclusions, which he later wrote about in *Physical Geography of the Sea*. He realized that the incidence of storms in the North Atlantic was far higher than it was in the Pacific, that the winds in the South Pacific were steadier than in the South Atlantic, that the Southern Hemisphere was cooler than the Northern Hemisphere because there was less land in the former than in the latter, and that ocean winds had little influence on the direction of the major ocean currents. Today these conclusions are not terribly striking, but in Maury's time they were revolutionary.

Other scientists of Maury's day studied the oceans, and some of them were far ahead of him in technical theory. But none made the logical leap in applying that knowledge to the day-to-day press of business. Since the world's economy rested on the merchant fleets sailing the high seas, Maury's work became extremely valuable on both sides of the Atlantic Ocean.

In 1847, Maury published his first version of *Wind and Current Charts*. Essentially, these were printed charts that he marked up with symbols to denote prevailing wind directions, areas of storms and calms, and the paths of major ocean currents. He made these charts available to captains free of charge, but in return he requested that the captains keep abstract logs containing data on wind direction and velocity and other factors, which he could use to further refine the charts. By the time Ellen Creesy came to rely on his data it was becoming very accurate indeed.

Many captains scoffed at Maury's work and dismissed it out of hand because it often went against the prevailing wisdom of navigators during that time. In 1851, Maury added to his growing body of work with the publication of his *Explanations and Sailing Directions to Accompany the Wind and Current Charts*. This work was not recognized among the bulk of the merchant captains when it first became available. But over time no competent navigator sailed without it.

Maury was born in Fredericksburg, Virginia, in 1806. He spent his boyhood in the hills of Tennessee far from the salty winds of the coast, but nevertheless when he was nineteen years old he entered the Navy as a midshipman. His early experiences aboard the ships instilled in him a deep love of the sea and fueled his curiosity about its most intimate workings. His duties took him all over the world between 1825 and 1834.

In 1839, Maury injured his right leg in a stagecoach accident, and he never fully recovered. He was put into service working for the Navy's Depot of Charts and Instruments, which was later called the National Observatory. From this rather obscure position Maury pioneered advances in navigation that greatly facilitated the passage of vessels between ports. He earned the nickname "Pathfinder of the Sea." It was well deserved.

Glossary of Nautical Terms

The following definitions are meant to convey in simple terms the general meaning of the term in question. They are not meant as highly technical explanations.

Aback: A square sail is aback when the wind pushes it back against the mast.

Abaft: Toward the stern; behind some specific point or object on a vessel.

Abaft the beam: Behind the middle of the vessel.

Abeam: 90 degrees from the centerline of a vessel. Also, broad on the beam or off the beam.

Aft: Behind the midpoint of a vessel.

Aloft: Overhead, above.

Alow: On deck, or below an object that is higher.

Amidships: The center of a vessel relative to either length or breadth.

Awash: Just covered by the sea. A barely submerged rock is awash. When a deck is awash, the sea runs freely over it as if it were a beach.

Back: When the wind shifts counterclockwise, it is said to back. When a sail is backed, it is positioned so that the wind pushes against its front and slows the vessel.

Ballast: Weight placed in the bottom of a vessel to add stability. When a ship was fully loaded with cargo the weight kept it stable. When it discharged its cargo, stone or lead was placed in the hold to keep the vessel stable.

Beam: The greatest width of a vessel.

Beam ends: A ship is on its beam ends when it is pushed over on its side, with the masts parallel to the surface of the sea.

Beam reach: A sailing direction relative to the wind when the wind blows toward the side of the vessel perpendicular to the hull.

Beam sea: Waves that strike a vessel broadside.

Bearing: The direction from a ship to an object, such as another ship or a land feature, or to a compass point.

Berth: A bed aboard ship. Also, the place where a vessel is moored or docked.

Bilge: The bottom of a vessel's hold nearest the keel.

Binnacle: A structure near the wheel of a ship that houses the compass.

Bitt: A perpendicular timber on deck used to secure lines.

Blanket: One sail blankets another when it blocks the wind from the other.

Bluff-bowed: Having broad, wide bows. Bluff-bowed vessels are typically slow.

Bow: The front end of a vessel.

Bower: A type of anchor.

Bowsprit: A long spar jutting from the bow. A jibboom is attached to a bowsprit, adding to the overall length of the spar.

Brace: Lines used to pivot the yards on a square-rigged ship.

Broach: To come broadside, or sideways, to the wind and seas. This is very dangerous in a heavy sea.

Bulkhead: A vertical partition inside a cabin, similar to an interior wall in a house.

Bulwarks: The part of the sides of the ship that rises above the deck to create a wall-like structure.

Buntlines: Lines run under the lower edge of a square sail used to pull it up to the yard.

Capstan: A winch with a drum around which a line is wrapped. It turns on a vertical axis. It is the opposite of a windlass, which turns on a horizontal axis.

Catheads: Large, heavy timbers projecting from each side of the bow to which the anchor is secured while a vessel is inshore. When the vessel is offshore the anchors are secured on deck.

Chronometer: A clock used in calculating a ship's longitude. It provides Greenwich Mean Time—that is, the time at the prime meridian, or zero degrees longitude, which runs through Greenwich, England.

Claw off: To work a ship away from a lee shore.

Clew: The lower edge of a sail.

Clewlines: Lines used to raise the lower ends of a square sail to the yard in preparation for furling.

Close-hauled: With sails set to drive the vessel as close as possible to the direction the wind is coming from. A ship sailing close-hauled is also said to be sailing to windward, or beating.

Coaming: A low barrier built up from the deck at doorways and around hatches, skylights, and other openings to prevent water on deck from flowing below.

Course: A determined direction of travel from one point to another.

Courses: The lowest square sails on a full-rigged ship. The bottom edge is loose, not fitted to a yard. They are set on the main and foremasts.

Cutwater: The forward edge of the stem, or front piece of the bow, especially at the waterline.

Davits: Arms suspended over the side used to raise and lower a ship's boat, such as a lifeboat.

Davy Jones: The devil.

Davy Jones's locker: The opposite of Fiddler's Green; a kind of hell for sailors, cold and devoid of all pleasures.

Deadeye: A circular block of wood with three holes in it. It is part of the system used to tighten standing rigging.

Dead reckoning: Deduction of a ship's position based on course, speed, leeway, and time, without recourse to celestial observations.

Deckhouse: A houselike structure built on deck, usually to house the crew and galley.

Draft: The depth of the keel below the surface of the water.

Ebb tide: A tide flowing away from shore out to sea.

Embayed: A ship is embayed when it is blown into a position where it is nearly surrounded by land, usually with a wind forcing it toward shore.

Faked: A faked line or chain is one laid down in loose, looping figure eights. Faking a line allows it to run free without much chance of it tangling.

Fall off: To change course away from the direction from which the wind blows.

Fathom: A depth of six feet.

Fid: An iron bar used to snug a topmast or topgallant pole mast tight into its supports.

Fiddles: Wooden barriers around the edge of a table or counter to help prevent objects from sliding off in heavy weather.

Fiddler's Green: A sailor's version of heaven, where fair ladies and strong drink are plentiful.

Flood tide: A tide flowing toward shore.

Footropes: Ropes suspended under the yards. Sailors stand on these as they work the sails.

Forecastle:The cabin in the bow of a vessel, typically used for crew's quarters. Pronounced fo'c's'l.

Forecastle deck: The deck closest to the bow, above the forecastle cabin.

Foremast: The mast closest to the bow on a full-rigged ship.

Forward: The direction from the midpoint of a vessel toward the bow.

Furl: To gather in a sail.

Gaff-rigged sail: A spanker is gaff-rigged. It is a four-sided fore-and-aft sail with a boom at the lower edge of the sail and a spar, called a gaff, at the top.

Galley: The kitchen aboard a vessel.

Gaskets: Ropes wrapped around furled sails to secure them to their yards.

Greenhorn: An inexperienced sailor.

Green water: Solid water that washes over a deck, as opposed to spray.

Halyard: A rope used to raise or lower a sail or a spar.

Hatch: An opening in the deck that can be closed or opened.

Hawsehole: An opening in the hull at the bow through which the anchor chain or line passes.

Head: The wind is said to head when it shifts too far forward for a sailing vessel to sail into the wind's direction without adjusting course. Also, a latrine aboard a vessel is called the head.

Headway: A vessel's motion forward through the water.

Keel: The major longitudinal part of the hull, the backbone of a ship.

Heave to: To adjust a sailing vessel's sails so as to greatly reduce forward motion. A ship might heave to in rough weather, or to speak another ship.

Heel: To tilt to one side under a press of sail.

Hell box: Stove.

Holystone: To sand down the deck with a square piece of sandstone or other abrasive stone. The stones are called holystones or prayer books.

Hounds: A wide portion of a mast close to the top or masthead. It is meant to add extra strength and to support the structures above.

Jib: A triangular fore-and-aft sail set from the foremast of a square-rigged ship. There are a number of different jibs. They are attached to the bowsprit and jibbooms at the bow.

Jibboom: A spar fixed to the bowsprit to extend its length.

Keelson: A longitudinal structure attached above a keel to strengthen it.

Knee: An L-shaped piece of wood used to link structural components together.

Knot: A unit of measurement used to describe a vessel's speed through the water. It is equal to one nautical mile, or 6,080 feet, traveled in an hour.

Larboard: The left side of a vessel; same as port.

Latitudes: Lines drawn on a globe to measure distance north or south of the equator. The equator is marked as zero, and latitude measurements are designated in degrees north or south of the poles.

Lazaret: A space between decks used for storage.

Lead line: A device used to measure the depth of the water and to take samples of the bottom.

Lee: The side sheltered from the wind. A vessel can be in the lee of something, such as a landmass, that blocks the wind and waves.

Leechlines: Lines attached to the leeches, or vertical edges, of a sail and used to pull it up to its yard.

Lee rail: The rail that is away from the direction from which the wind blows. When a ship heels, the lower side is the lee rail. The high side is the windward rail.

Lee shore: A shore to leeward of a vessel. Very dangerous for a sailing vessel.

Leeward: Away from the direction the wind blows from.

Leeway: The sideways motion of a vessel when the wind, waves, or current pushes it off course.

Log: A device used to measure a vessel's speed. Also a logbook.

Logbook: A document used to record daily course, wind direction, weather, and other details.

Longitudes: Lines of measurement on the globe from pole to pole used to denote position east or west of the prime meridian at zero degrees, Greenwich, England.

Lubber: A landsman, or a sailor who is sloppy in his work.

Lubber hole: The opening in the platform at the joining of a mainmast and topmast, for example.

Main deck: The midsection of a ship. Also called the weather deck.

Mainmast: The mast in the middle on a three-masted ship.

Marlinespike: A sharp iron tool used in working on the rigging.

Masthead: The top portion of a mast.

Mizzen mast: The mast closest to the stern on a three-masted ship.

Monkey rail: A rail on top of the bulwarks.

On the beach: A sailor ashore between voyages is said to be on the beach.

Parrel: A rope loop that holds a yard to the back of a mast.

Plot: A mark on a chart to denote position. To plot is to mark the chart.

Poop deck: The aft deck on a merchant vessel.

Port: The left side of a vessel when facing the bow.

Quarter: The sides of a vessel closest to the stern. There is a port quarter and a starboard quarter.

Ratline: A rope tied between shrouds. Ratlines form a ladder the sailors climb to get up to the yards.

Reef: A shoal. Also, a reduction in sail area. Sails are reefed to reduce strain on a vessel in heavy weather.

Rhumbline: The desired course between two points.

Roadstead or road: An anchorage offshore, usually not very sheltered.

Roll: Sideways rotational movement of a vessel in rough seas.

Run: To sail before the wind, that is, with the wind coming from the stern.

Running rigging: Lines used to work the sails. Halyards, braces, and sheets are part of the running rigging.

Scud: To run before the wind in heavy weather.

Scuppers: Holes on deck through which water drains overboard.

Sextant: An optical device used to measure a celestial body's angle of elevation above the horizon, known as its altitude. It was one of the tools used to find a ship's latitude and longitude.

Shroud: A part of a sailing vessel's standing rigging. It is a rope run from the mast down to the side of a ship to help support the mast.

Slack water: The time between tides when tidal currents are at their weakest.

Soldier: Slang for a sailor who is neglectful of his duties or lazy.

Spanker: The fore-and-aft sail set on the mizzen mast. A spanker is gaff-rigged and looks like the sails on a schooner.

Spars: A catch-all term used to describe masts, booms, gaffs, and the like.

Speak: One ship speaks another when the two vessels stop so that the captains can converse.

Standing rigging: Ropes used to support the masts.

Starboard: The right side of a vessel when facing the bow.

Stay: A part of a sailing vessel's standing rigging. It is a rope run from the masthead behind or in front of the mast.

Staysail: A triangular fore-and-aft sail set between masts.

Stern: The aft end of a vessel.

Sternway: A vessel's motion backward through the water.

Studdingsail: A sail set on a boom that extends outward from the yards. Studdingsails add extra sail area to a ship, and on the clippers they imparted a triangular look to the sail plan when a vessel was viewed from fore or aft.

Tack: To turn a sailing vessel's bow through the wind to bring the wind from one side to the other.

Taffrail: The rail at the stern of a vessel.

Topgallant pole mast: The uppermost mast on a clipper ship. It is mounted on the topmast, with the mizzen, main, or foremast at the bottom.

Topmast: The mast above a mizzen, main, or foremast.

Topsides: The hull between the waterline and the deck.

Transom: Planking across the stern.

Treenails: Long wooden pins used to fasten planks to structural members. Pronounced trunnels.

Tye: A rope or chain that supports the weight of a yard.

Veer: When the wind shifts in a clockwise direction it is said to veer.

Warp: To move a vessel from one point to another using lines instead of sail power.

Watch: A period of time when a sailor is on duty, usually four hours. Also, the part of the crew that is on duty during a particular watch.

Waterline: The meeting point of the hull and the surface of the water.

Ways: The structure supporting a vessel while it is built or launched.

Wear: To turn a sailing vessel's stern through the wind to bring the wind from one side to the other.

Weather deck: The main deck.

Windlass: A winch with a drum around which a line is wrapped. It turns on a horizontal axis. It is the opposite of a capstan, which turns on a drum with a vertical axis.

Windward: Toward the direction from which the wind blows. The wind blows over the windward, or weather, rail of a ship. If a ship sails to windward, it must be close-hauled.

Yard: The spar perpendicular to a mast upon which a square sail is set.

Bibliography

Albion, Robert G. *Square-Riggers on Schedule*. Princeton, N.J.: Princeton University Press, 1938.

Allen, Oliver E. *The Windjammers*. Alexandria, Va.: Time-Life Books, 1978.

Balano, James W. *The Log of the Skipper's Wife*. Camden, Me.: Down East Books, 1979.

Banner, Lois W. *Elizabeth Cady Stanton: A Radical for Woman's Rights*. Boston: Little, Brown, 1980.

Batterberry, Michael and Ariane. *On the Town in New York from 1776 to the Present*. New York: Charles Scribner's Sons, 1973.

Blunt, Edmund M. *The American Coast Pilot*. New York: Edmund and George W. Blunt, 1863.

Bodin, Jeanne, and Beth Millstein. *We, the American Women*. Chicago: Science Research Associates, 1977.

Braynard, Frank O. *Famous American Ships*. New York: Hastings House, 1956.

Bunting, W. H. *Portrait of a Port: Boston, 1852–1914*. Cambridge, Mass.: Harvard University Press, 1971.

Carse, Robert. *The Twilight of Sailing Ships*. New York: Galahad Books, 1965.

Chapman, Charles F. *Piloting, Seamanship and Small Boat Handling*. New York: Hearst Corporation, 1972.

Chatwin, Bruce, and Paul Theroux. *Nowhere Is a Place: Travels in Patagonia.* San Francisco: Sierra Club Books, 1986.

Chidsey, Donald Barr. *The California Gold Rush: An Informal History.* New York: Crown, 1968.

Coles, Adlard K. *Heavy Weather Sailing.* New York: John de Graff, 1989.

Constable, George, ed. *Offshore.* New York: Time-Life Books, 1976.

Cornell, Jimmy. *World Cruising Routes.* Camden, Me.: International Marine, 1995.

Cressey, Ernest W. *Story of Your Ancestors: Cressey, 286 Years in America.* Westbrook, Me.: Henry S. Cobb, 1935.

Crothers, William L. *The American-Built Clipper Ship.* Camden, Me.: International Marine, 1997.

Cutler, Carl C. *Greyhounds of the Sea.* New York: Halcyon House, 1930.

Dana, Richard Henry, Jr. *The Seaman's Friend.* Boston: Thomas Groom & Co., 1851. Reprint. Delmar, N.Y.: Scholars' Facsimiles & Reprints, 1979.

Dana, Richard Henry, Jr. *Two Years Before the Mast: A Personal Narrative of Life at Sea.* Garden City, N.Y.: Doubleday, 1949. First published 1840.

Darwin, Charles. *Journal of Researches into the Natural History and Geology of the Countries Visited During the Voyage of the H.M.S. Beagle Under the Command of Captain Fitz Roy, R. N.* New York: Heritage Press, 1957.

Derks, Scott, ed. *The Value of a Dollar: Prices and Incomes in the United States 1860–1999.* Lakeville, Conn.: GreyHouse Publishing, 1999.

DeVoto, Bernard. *The Year of Decision: 1846.* Boston: Little, Brown, 1943.

Dobbs, David, and Richard Ober. *The Northern Forest.* White River Junction, Vt.: Chelsea Green, 1995.

Eagle Seamanship: A Manual for Square-Rigger Sailing. Revised by Lt. Edwin H. Daniels, Jr. Annapolis, Md.: Naval Institute Press, 1990.

Egan, Ferol. *The El Dorado Trail.* New York: McGraw-Hill, 1970.

Florent, Jerry G., ed. *With All Possible Sails Set: The Story of America's Fastest Clipper Ship, the Flying Cloud.* Kansas City, Mo.: Hallmark Cards, 1979.

Frothingham, Robert, arranger. *Songs of the Sea and Sailors' Chanteys: An Anthology.* Freeport, N.Y.: Books for Libraries Press, 1924.

Gamage, Virginia Clegg, and Priscilla Sawyer Lord. *Marblehead: The Spirit of '76 Lives Here.* Radnor, Pa.: Chilton, 1972.

Griffith, Elisabeth. *In Her Own Right: The Life of Elizabeth Cady Stanton.* New York: Oxford University Press, 1984.

Hiscock, Eric C. *Voyaging Under Sail.* New York: Oxford University Press, 1971.

Howe, Octavius T., and Frederick C. Matthews. *American Clipper Ships, 1833–1858.* New York: Argosy Antiquarian, 1967.

Karr, Ronald Dale. *The Rail Lines of Southern New England.* Pepperell, Mass.: Branch Lane Press, 1995.

Kemble, John Haskell. *Francisco Bay: A Pictorial Maritime History.* Cambridge, Md.: Cornell Maritime Press, 1957.

Lindsey, Benjamin J. *Old Marblehead Sea Captains and the Ships in Which They Sailed.* Marblehead, Mass.: Marblehead Historical Society, 1915.

Loomis, Harvey B., ed. *Navigation.* New York: Time-Life Books, 1975.

Lyon, Margaret, and Flora Elizabeth Reynolds. *The Flying Cloud and Her First Passengers.* Oakland, Calif.: Center for the Book, Mills College, 1992.

McClellan, Elisabeth. *Historic Dress in America 1800–1870.* Philadelphia: George W. Jacobs, 1910.

McKay, Richard C. *Some Famous Sailing Ships and Their Builder Donald McKay.* New York: G. P. Putnam's Sons, 1928.

Mammick, Anne. *The Atlantic Crossing Guide.* Camden, Me.: International Marine, 1992.

Maury, Matthew Fontaine. *Explanations and Sailing Directions to Accompany the Wind and Current Charts.* Philadelphia: E. C. and J. Biddle, 1855.

Maury, Matthew Fontaine. *The Physical Geography of the Sea and Its Meteorology.* Ed. John Leighly. Reprint. Cambridge, Mass.: Belknap Press/Harvard University Press, 1963.

May, W. E. *A History of Marine Navigation.* New York: W. W. Norton, 1973.

Norville, Warren. *Celestial Navigation Step by Step.* Camden, Me.: International Marine Publishing Company, 1973.

Novotny, Ann, and Carter Smith, eds. *Images of Healing: A Portfolio of American Medical and Pharmaceutical Practice in the 18th, 19th, and Early 20th Centuries.* New York: Macmillan, 1980.

Nurse, Charlie. *Argentina Handbook*. Chicago: Passport Books, 1998.

Pike, Robert E. *Tall Trees, Tough Men*. New York: W. W. Norton, 1967.

Shay, Frank. *An American Sailor's Treasury*. New York: Smithmark Publishers, 1991.

Shay, Frank, ed. *Iron Men and Wooden Ships: Deep Sea Chanties*. Garden City, N.Y.: Doubleday, Page, 1924.

Snow, Elliot. *Adventures at Sea in the Great Age of Sail*. New York: Dover, 1986.

Sobel, Dava. *Longitude: The True Story of a Lone Genius Who Solved the Greatest Scientific Problem of His Time*. New York: Walker, 1995.

Villiers, Alan J. *Falmouth for Orders*. New York: Scribner's, 1952.

Villiers, Alan J. *Men, Ships, and the Sea*. Washington, D.C.: National Geographic Society, 1973.

Whipple, A. B. C. *The Clipper Ships*. Alexandria, Va.: Time-Life Books, 1980.

Wilbur, Keith C. *Picture Book of the Revolution's Privateers*. Harrisburg, Pa.: Stackpole, 1973.

Williams, John Hoyt. *A Great and Shining Road: The Epic Story of the Transcontinental Railroad*. New York: Times Books, 1988.

Worrell, Estelle Ansley. *Early American Costume*. Harrisburg, Pa.: Stackpole, 1975.

Index

Page numbers in *italics* refer to illustrations.